Terrorism
and
Business

The Impact of September II, 2001

Dean C. Alexander

and

Yonah Alexander

 Transnational Publishers, Inc.

Published and distributed by Transnational Publishers, Inc.
410 Saw Mill River Road
Ardsley, NY 10502, USA

Phone: 914-693-5100
Fax: 914-693-4430
E-mail: info@transnationalpubs.com
Web: www.transnationalpubs.com

Library of Congress Cataloging-in-Publication Data

Alexander, Dean C., 1965—
    Terrorism and business : the impact of September 11, 2001 / Dean C. Alexander
and Yonah Alexander..
        p. cm.
    Includes bibliographical references and index.
    ISBN 1-57105-246-1
    1. Terrorism—Economic aspects—United States. 2. September 11 Terrorist
    Attacks, 2001. 3. Terrorism—United States—Prevention. I. Alexander, Yonah.
    II. Title.

HV6432 .A435 2002
330.973'0931—dc21   2002017997

Manufactured in the United States of America

Contents

CHAPTER I • TERRORISM AND BUSINESS: HISTORICAL AND CONTEMPORARY PERSPECTIVES

CHAPTER 2 • THE ECONOMIC COSTS TO THE UNITED STATES: AN OVERVIEW

CHAPTER 3 • TERRORISM AND CORPORATE AMERICA: IMPACT ON SELECTED SECTORS

CHAPTER 4 • WAR ON TERRORISM: THE ROLE OF INDUSTRY

CHAPTER 5 • TERRORISM AND THE IMPACT ON U.S. LABOR

CHAPTER 6 • TERRORISM AND U.S. GOVERNMENT RESPONSES

Disclaimer

The authors expended extensive time and energy in preparing this book. They relied upon information, derived content, and incorporated materials that were perceived to be correct at the time. Nevertheless, the authors cannot guarantee the completeness and accuracy of all the contents of this publication.

It is critical to underscore that the inclusion or omission of any companies or industries herein neither implies any endorsement nor judgment whatsoever as to the products, services, capabilities, and financial attributes of any firm; or in the case of an industry, the sector's viability or importance in the economy.

Moreover, the authors do not intend the reader to undertake (or refrain from undertaking) any business, security, safety, health, nor any other decisions, actions, or activities based on any information contained in this book. Any matter discussed in this book should not be relied upon in substitution for the exercise of independent judgment by the reader or in consultation with an adviser.

Against this backdrop, the authors cannot accept liability for any decisions, actions, or activities that may be taken by any person or entity based on anything contained in this publication.

Introduction

Over 2,000 years ago, the Chinese strategist Sun Tzu wrote in *The Art of War* about the significance of a surprise attack: "The enemy must not know where I intend to give battle. For if he does not know where I intend to give battle, he must prepare in a great many places . . . If he prepares to the front, his rear will be weak, and if to the rear, his front will be fragile. If he prepares to the left, his right will be vulnerable and if to the right, there will be few on his left. And when he prepares everywhere he will be weak everywhere."

If terrorism is a form of "warfare in the shadows," then the most spectacular and heinous manifestation of Sun Tzu's warning occurred on September 11, 2001, the "Day of Infamy." The United States, the only power with unmatched conventional and unconventional capabilities, was surprised when 19 terrorists mounted an unexpected and unprecedented kamikaze operation considered to be the deadliest in recorded history.

The perpetrators, wielding knives and box-cutters, hijacked 4 U.S. aircraft, which they used to crash into the Twin Towers of the World Trade Center in New York, the Pentagon, and a third location, not the intended target, a field in Shanksville, Pennsylvania. The surreal tale of terror of this tragedy unfolded with chilling and horrifying speed: At 8:45 a.m. American Airlines Flight 11, en route from Boston, Massachusetts, to Los Angeles, California, with 81 passengers and 11 crew members, crashed into the North Tower; United Airlines Flight 175, also headed from Boston to Los Angeles but carrying 56 passengers and 9 crew members, slammed into the South Tower at 9:03 a.m. Twenty-five minutes later, American Airlines Flight 77, scheduled to fly from Washington, D.C. (Dulles International Airport), to Los Angeles with 58 passengers and 6 crew members, smashed into the northwest side of the Pentagon. At 10:00 a.m., United Airlines Flight 93, headed from Newark, New Jersey, to San Francisco, California, and carrying 38 passengers and 7 crew members, crashed in Pennsylvania during a struggle between the hijackers and passengers.

The human, economic, political, social, and strategic costs of these simultaneous and massive attacks became tragically clear during the apocalyptic-type day. U.S. government officials have estimated that over 3,300 people died, or were missing and presumed dead, and thousands of others were injured. The 110-floor World Trade Center twin buildings, the symbol of American financial prowess, collapsed. All seven buildings in the World Trade Center complex fell or partially collapsed. Sixteen neighboring buildings sustained damage. It will take years to repair the damage done to the Pentagon.

New York City closed all bridges and tunnels in the area. The Federal Aviation Administration grounded domestic flights, and international flights to the United States were diverted to Canada. Evacuation was ordered from part of lower Manhattan and from the White House, Justice Department, State Department, Treasury Department, Congress, and the Supreme Court in Washington, D.C. Thousands of private and public offices in the Washington, D.C., area closed early on the day of the attacks.

In light of these developments, the Securities and Exchange Commission ordered the closure of U.S. stock markets. The principal U.S. stock markets reopened on September 17, 2001.

In the nation's capital a state of emergency was declared. President George W. Bush immediately placed the U.S. military on "high alert status" worldwide. He pledged to "do whatever is necessary to protect America and Americans," and promised to make no distinction between terrorists who committed the September 11 "acts of mass murder" and those nations that harbor them. President Bush also asserted that although the terrorists intended to frighten America into chaos and retreat, they failed because of the "nation's strength." Congress condemned the horrific attacks, vowed retribution against the terrorists and their supporters, and pledged their full support to the Bush administration during this time of crisis.

Almost immediately, the September 11 catastrophic attacks were connected to Usama bin Laden's al-Qaida (the Base). Al-Qaida (also known as the International Front for Jihad Against Jews and Crusaders, the Group for the Preservation of the Holy Sites, and the Islamic Army for the Liberation of the Holy Places) is a global network that operates in some 60 countries. Al-Qaida seeks to "unite all Muslims and establish a government which follows the rule of the Caliphs."

To achieve al-Qaida's goal, Muslim regimes, viewed as corrupted by Western influence, must be overthrown by force. Since in bin Laden's viewpoint the United States supports "corrupt" governments such as Saudi Arabia and Egypt, he declared "jihad" (Holy War) against the "Great Satan" (the United States). Bin Laden's disdain for the United States also stems from the presence of U.S. troops in Saudi Arabia—home to the 2 holiest sites of Islam. In several fatwas (religious rulings) issued by bin Laden and his associates in the 1990s, Muslims were instructed to kill Americans, including civilians, anywhere in the world where they can be found. Muslims are, then, duty-bound to prepare as much force as possible to attack the "enemies of God."

It is not surprising, therefore, that as early as 1992, al-Qaida declared that the U.S. military presence in Saudi Arabia, Yemen, and the Horn of Africa should be attacked. Major al-Qaida operations against the United States include: the October 3-4, 1993, killing of 18 U.S. servicemen on an anti-terrorism mission in Somalia; the November 13, 1995, car bomb explosion outside the American-operated Saudi National Guard training center in Riyadh, Saudi Arabia, killing 5 Americans and 2 Indians; the June 25, 1996, car bombing attack at Khobar Towers, a U.S. Air Force housing complex in Dhahran, Saudi Arabia, killing 19 soldiers and wounding hundreds more; the August 7, 1998, two truck bombings outside the U.S. embassies in Nairobi, Kenya, and Dar es Salaam, Tanzania, killing 234 people, 12 of them American, and wounding over 5,000 others; and the October 12, 2000, suicide bombing of the USS *Cole*, killing 17 and wounding 39 American sailors in Aden harbor, Yemen.

Other attacks by bin Laden's network have reached the United States itself. On February 23, 1993, a bomb was detonated in a garage at the World Trade Center in New York, killing 6 people and injuring over 1,000. On June 25, 1993, a Pakistani terrorist opened fire outside the headquarters of the Central Intelligence Agency (CIA) in Virginia, killing 2 and wounding 3 CIA employees.

To carry out these operations, particularly the most daring and devastating September 11, 2001 attack, al-Qaida established an effective organizational structure comprised of several key command and control components: the majlis al shura (consultation council) that considers and approves major policy and actions, including the issuance of fatwas and general terrorist strategies; the military committee that focuses on specific operations against its enemies; the business committee that oversees economic and financial matters; the religious committee that deals with theological matters; the media committee that works on printing information; and a travel office.

This organizational structure was developed to facilitate the activities of al-Qaida and its affiliate groups around the world. It is increasingly becoming evident that in the United States there exists an elaborate network of different militant Islamic-oriented cells linked with several well-known movements such as Hizballah (Lebanon), Hamas (Palestinian Authority), Islamic Jihad (Egypt), and the Armed Islamic Group (Algeria). These and other terrorist groups have representatives and "sleeper agents" in neighboring Canada and in every region of the world.

The co-founders of al-Qaida in the early 1990s were the "Emir" bin Laden (Saudi Arabian), Ayman al-Zawahiri (Egyptian), and Muhammed Atef (Egyptian). A special effort was made by the movement to recruit American members such as Ali Abdelsoud Mohamed. Born in Egypt and becoming a naturalized American citizen, Mohamed pleaded guilty on October 20, 2000, to 5 counts of conspiracy to attack American targets. Currently, he is cooperating with U.S. authorities.

To be sure, the activities of al-Qaida and its affiliate organizations have long been financed with bin Laden's personal fortune estimated at $300 million. The network and other militant Islamic-oriented bodies have also been funded by external sources, using charitable structures as fronts, such as the Holy Land Foundation for Relief and Development in Richardson, Texas. In addition, al-Qaida is financed through personal savings, businesses, financial institutions, and criminal activities such as narco-trafficking and robberies.

It is against this background that President Bush, speaking before the Congress on September 20, 2001, declared a global war against al-Qaida and terrorism in general. On October 6, 2001, the United States initiated massive air strikes against bin Laden's bases in Afghanistan and against the Taliban regime that supports his network. The Bush administration has also provided small groups of American commandos and on-the-ground help to anti-Taliban militias like the Northern Alliance (a loose coalition of disparate groups, such as Jamiat-I-Islami, Hisb-I-Wahadat, Junbish, and Harakat-i-Islami).

U.S. air and land support enabled the Northern Alliance forces to drive the Taliban fighters from most of Afghanistan, including the country's major cities—Mazar-i-Sharif, Kunduz, and Kabul, the country's capital. The sudden collapse of the Taliban front-line defenses was a remarkable military achievement for the United States and its allies. Although Mullah Muhammad Omar, the defiant Taliban leader, promised the "destruction of America," his surviving forces surrendered their last stronghold, the city of Kandahar. As of December 2001, Mullar Omar, bin Laden, and his closest associates—aside from Atef, who was killed during U.S. air strikes in Afghanistan—have eluded American and other military units.

It is noteworthy that following the September 11 incidents, bin Laden's operatives attempted to attack several U.S. and allied targets abroad. For instance, plots to bomb the U.S. Embassy in Paris, France, and North Atlantic Treaty Organization (NATO) headquarters in Brussels, Belgium, on September 13, 2001, were foiled. Also aborted was an al-Qaida plan to attack the U.S. Embassy in Sarajevo, Bosnia, on October 8, 2001. During fall 2001, several national warnings were issued by U.S. government officials of major impending terrorist attacks in the United States, presumably by U.S.-based al-Qaida members.

Also, during fall 2001, various incidents of biological terrorism involving anthrax-tainted letters took place in the United States. Five people died as a result of these unconventional incidents. The source of these biological weapons is still unknown. At this stage of the investigation, it is uncertain whether the anthrax attacks are the work of domestic or foreign terrorist groups, such as al-Qaida.

There is a growing concern of a worst-case scenario. For instance, an aerosolized release of 100 kilograms of anthrax spores in an enclosed setting is projected to be able to cause over 100,000 deaths. Given these apprehensions, the potential threat of smallpox, another form of biological weapon, has also attracted public attention. Extremely infectious and associated with a high mortality rate, a possible outbreak of smallpox would be much more devastating than anthrax attacks. A glimpse of the ominous future was provided in summer 2001, when a government-sponsored, simulated smallpox attack (called "Dark Winter") in Oklahoma City, Oklahoma, demonstrated that such an incident could result, for example, in smallpox exposure of millions of people in 25 states.

Already on high alert as a result of the September 11 attacks, the anthrax scare incidents, and the warnings of further terrorist assaults on the United States, American security officials from the Federal Bureau of Investigation (FBI) and the CIA, have joined agencies of other nations, such as Pakistan's Inter-Services Intelligence, in probing the possibilities of al-Qaida possessing weapons of mass destruction. It is noteworthy that as early as May 1998, bin Laden issued a statement entitled "The Nuclear Bomb of Islam," in which he proclaimed that it is the duty of Muslims to employ even unconventional capabilities, including the use of nuclear weapons.

U.S. coalition intelligence operatives in Afghanistan discovered credible evidence related to al-Qaida's intensive efforts to obtain weapons of mass destruction. For instance, authorities found documents in al-Qaida's safe houses in Kabul related to methodologies in the use of biological, chemical, and nuclear weapons. The discovery of laboratory equipment, bio-terrorism manuals, and chemical and biological training facilities elsewhere in Afghanistan is an additional ominous illustration of the intentions of bin-Laden's network to resort to super-terrorism.

Bin Laden and his lieutenant al-Zawahiri declared several times before and after the September 11 attacks that they will use the unconventional weapons only in an extreme "emergency situation." Nevertheless, in light of al-Qaida's proven brutal record and the Taliban's threats about America's destruction, unconventional attacks against the United States are more likely prospects than before.

U.S. government officials must continue to be on heightened alert in light of such mass destruction threats such as nuclear-related terrorist attacks. These nuclear terrorism dangers include: a crude explosive device designed to spew radioactive material, a truck bomb attack against an operating U.S. nuclear power plant, and a jetliner crashing into a plant containing lethal stockpiles of nuclear waste.

Another imminent threat to U.S. national security is the challenge of cyber terrorism. This new medium of communication, command and control, supplemented by unlimited paralyzing and destructive electronic keyboard attacks on civilian and military critical infrastructure nerve centers, can be no less devastating than mass destruction attacks. Suffice to mention several catastrophic scenarios of cyber terrorism, such as altering formulas for medication at pharmaceutical plants, "crashing" telephone systems, misrouting passenger trains, changing pressure in gas pipelines to cause valve failure, disrupting operations of air traffic control, triggering oil refinery explosions and fires, scrambling the software used by emergency services, "turning off" power grids, and detonating simultaneously numerous computerized bombs around the world.

These potential unconventional risks, coupled with conventional threats on land, sea, and air, starkly underscore the vulnerability of the United States at home and abroad. Despite its crushing military setbacks in Afghanistan, al-Qaida's multinational network still remains a major challenge to American security concerns as well as to the entire international community.

It is not surprising, therefore, that the unfolding post-September 11 developments have attached unprecedented attention nationally and globally to the threats posed by terrorism. In addition to the significant political and strategic aspects of the challenges of terrorism, there have been profound economic consequences. The "Day of Infamy" resulted in the following press headlines:

- Business Grinds to Near-Halt After Terrorist Attacks
- Does a Disaster Await Markets?
- Attacks Trigger Nationwide Office Evacuations
- Attacks Cast Shadow over Boardrooms
- World Bank, IMF [International Monetary Fund] May Cancel Meetings
- Overseas Stocks Plunge
- Wall Street Comes to a Halt
- Fed Ready to Support Banks
- Exxon, Chevron Freeze Gas Prices
- Wall Street Fears for Employees
- Telecom Networks Stressed, but Operating

Although technically unsophisticated terrorist acts, the September 11 incidents had an enormous worldwide economic impact, particularly in the airline, tourism, and hospitality sectors. In the United States, the following severe economic ramifications have resulted from the September 11 events:

- $50-$80 billon in potential insurance claims (property, casualty, life insurance, business interruption, workers' compensation, and disability)
- Billions of dollars in clean-up costs and repairing infrastructure (telephone lines and electrical cables)
- Billions of dollars lost in company revenues
- Billions of dollars of reduced market capitalization for U.S. companies on U.S. stock markets
- Reduced tax intakes by state and federal authorities
- Military and law enforcement outlays

- Support to selected industries such as airlines (including a $15 billion stabilization package and $5 billion in potential outlays for improving aviation security)

- Increased private sector expenditures on security measures, data storage, multiple sites, and emergency preparedness

- $40 billion dollars in federal emergency funding in the wake of the attacks

- Billions of potential federal, state, and local funds to be allocated to security, emergency preparedness, and health matters

- Potential federal and state government outlays to stimulate the economy following the attacks

In the future, potential U.S. business interests targeted by terrorists may, for instance, include the Clearing House Interbank Payment Systems (CHIPS), a computer network that links 59 of the world's largest banks operated by the New York Clearing House. Approximately $292 trillion passed through the CHIPS system in 2000. Although no attacks were reported at CHIPS on September 11, a number of banks connected to the system lost service for several hours.

It is against the foregoing background as well as the growing realization that terrorism is a clear and present danger to the viability of economic development in the 21st century, that we decided to focus this book on the impact of the September 11 attacks on the U.S. government, Corporate America, and U.S. labor.

Chapter 1, "Terrorism and Business: Historical and Contemporary Perspectives," provides a context as to the nature of terrorism in terms of its meaning and consequences from ancient to modern times. The chapter analyzes the dangers posed by terrorism to American business at home and abroad, leading to the current post-9/11 era. An assessment of U.S. business victimization indicates that every corporate sector has been affected by terrorism during the past four decades. These corporate targets were selected by substate and state-sponsored terrorists because of their symbolic visibility as well as their built-in vulnerability. The grim outlook is that the personnel, facilities, and operations of Corporate America will continue to remain a primary target in the future for many reasons, including the continued existence of an international network of terrorist groups, such as al-Qaida, with easily accessible multiple U.S. business targets at home and abroad.

Chapter 2, "The Economic Costs to the United States: An Overview," presents an overview of the U.S. economy leading up to the September 11 incidents. It examines the economic costs to the United States arising from the September attacks, the anthrax attacks that shortly followed, and U.S. military activities in Afghanistan. Economic indices, business trends, consumer sentiments, unemployment figures, credit policy, and stock market results are then reviewed. Analyses by the Federal Reserve (Fed) and other sources are used to relate the various implications on multiple regions. New York City and Washington, D.C., which were most directly affected by the attacks, are examined in detail. Although the chapter predominantly discusses the consequences of the terrorist incidents upon the United States, the global impact is also examined.

Chapter 3, "Terrorism and Corporate America: Impact on Selected Sectors," chronicles the effects and responses of the U.S. business community to the attacks. More particularly, the chapter discusses matters such as: the general impact on business; corporate earnings results for the third quarter of 2001; consequences on future investments; transactions cancelled or delayed; sourcing, inventory, and logistics issues relating to potential terrorist disruptions to manufacturing and distribution; security and risk issues in the new business environment; and corporate debt and bankruptcies.

Chapter 3 also assesses the effect of the September 11 terrorist incidents on specific U.S. industries. Some sectors were negatively affected, others less so. Numerous industries are evaluated: aviation; hotels, conventions, and tourism; insurance; real estate; energy; technology; media and entertainment; transportation; and others.

Chapter 4, "War on Terrorism: The Role of Industry," highlights the products and services of companies in specific industries (or subsectors) that may undergo further demand as the U.S. government and the business community are increasingly mobilized in the war on terrorism. The following goods and services are discussed: defense; security equipment, technology, and services; diverse technology products and services; pharmaceuticals and forensics; germ detection and remediation; transportation; and "survivalist" and miscellaneous merchandise.

Chapter 5, "Terrorism and the Impact on U.S. Labor," covers multiple matters relating to the effect of terrorism on U.S. labor in the post-September 11 setting. The diverse relevant issues include: the physical consequences of terrorism on the U.S. workforce; the emotional ramifications of terrorism on U.S. labor; diverse employer, governmental, and non-governmental assistance offered to U.S. workers victimized by terrorism; the effect of terrorism on the National Guard, military reserves, and prospective recruits; the new paradigm for U.S. workers; and the impact of terrorism on employers in the post-September 11 era.

Chapter 6, "Terrorism and U.S. Government Responses," reviews the multidimensional measures that the U.S. government has undertaken in the wake of the post-September 11 environment. This chapter discusses the $40 billion emergency funding measures and other approved government funding measures. It highlights the $15 billion Airline Transportation and Systems Stabilization Act, the aviation security law, other aviation security measures, calls for support by other transportation industry segments, and governmental responses to the insurance industry crisis. Moreover, Bush administration and congressional initiatives relating to expanding U.S. capabilities against bio-terrorism are also detailed.

Chapter 6 also discusses selected security and investigative actions undertaken by the government, such as: creating the Office of Homeland Security; passage of the Uniting and Strengthening America by Providing Appropriate Tools Required to Intercept and Obstruct Terrorism Act of 2001 (USA Patriot Act); selected law enforcement and judicial anti-terrorism actions; steps taken to counter terrorist funding activities; Securities and Exchange Commission's investigation of terrorists' participation in illegal stock and funding activities; the improvement of Capitol Hill security; and miscellaneous anti-terrorism activities of the departments of State, Treasury, Defense, and Justice, and agencies of the intelligence community. Finally, this chapter discusses: federal government assistance to state governments economically disadvantaged as a result of the September 11 attacks; a variety of U.S. forms of foreign aid as well as international cooperation in the war against terrorism; and a review of additional government funding measures, including the Fiscal Year 2002 Budget.

The lessons learned from the forthcoming chapters are set forth in the "Conclusion." It is pointed out, for instance, that despite the initial security improvements undertaken by the U.S. government and Corporate America in the aftermath of the September 11 attacks, numerous challenges remain. The U.S. government and the U.S. business community must, therefore, expend greater efforts to fight the scourge of terrorism at home and abroad.

Chapter I

Terrorism and Business:

Historical and Contemporary Perspectives

I Introduction

On September 11, 2001, Americans were stunned to witness the unprecedented drama of terrorists striking such a devastating blow at the symbols of the nation's commercial and military power. Despite this horrific experience the reality is that terrorism directed against U.S. business at home and abroad did not begin on the "Day of Infamy."

The purpose of this chapter is to provide a brief historical and contemporary context leading to the September 11 trauma and its economic consequences. The overview focuses on the conceptual meaning of terrorism, its development throughout the centuries, and the nature of the threat to American business at home and abroad.

II The Nature and History of Terrorism

A Definitional Focus

The historical record indicates that there is no universal consensus on a definition of terrorism. Every sovereign state reserves to itself the political and legal authority to define terrorism in the context of domestic and foreign affairs. Yet, some governments speak with a bewildering variety of voices on the meaning of terrorism. The United States is a case in point.

Under the U.S. federal system, each state determines what constitutes an offense under its criminal or penal code. States have defined terrorism generically as a crime. Also, specific statutes covering other selected criminal acts are identified as terrorism. For instance, the State of Washington, in its anti-terrorism provisions, defines a "terrorist act" as an act that is intended to:

"(1) intimidate or coerce a civilian population; (2) influence the policy of a branch or level of government by intimidation or coercion; (3) affect the conduct of a branch or level of government by intimidation or coercion; or (4) retaliate against a branch or level of government for a policy or conduct of the government."

In the U.S. Congress, it is also evident that no agreement has been reached on defining terrorism. During the past several decades, Congress has held numerous hearings, considered bills, adopted resolutions, and passed laws on terrorism. Yet, thus far, a comprehensive working definition that addresses the different forms of terrorist attacks has not emerged from Congress.

Similarly, the executive branch, partly as a result of the very nature of its jurisdictional diversities, has not developed a coordinated position on the meaning of the term. Since the 1980s, for example, the Federal Bureau of Investigation (FBI) has defined terrorism as "the unlawful use of force or violence against persons or property to intimidate or coerce a government, the civilian population, or any segment thereof, in the furtherance of political or social objectives."

The Department of State has adopted another definition, which is contained in Title 22 of the United States Code, Section 2656f(d), stating that "the term 'terrorism' means premeditated, politically motivated violence perpetrated against noncombatant targets by subnational groups or clandestine agents, usually intended to influence an audience." Additionally, "the term 'international terrorism' means terrorism involving citizens or the territory of more than one country" and "the term 'terrorist group' means any group practicing, or that has significant subgroups that practice, international terrorism." This description of terrorism has been adopted by the U.S. government since 1983. The definition is incorporated in the State Department's report, *Patterns of Global Terrorism 2000*, published in April 2001.

The term terrorism has also invariably been considered as the "poor man's warfare" or "asymmetric warfare" in which state and nonstate adversaries avoid direct engagement with military forces. Instead, they devise and carry out strategies, tactics, and weapons to exploit perceived weaknesses. As a result of the September 11, 2001, attacks, other concepts have been advanced to characterize terrorism, including "acts of war," "war crimes," "crimes against humanity," and "crimes against peace."

Regardless of the various descriptions of terrorism, there seems to be an agreement related to several key components, such as the nature of the act (e.g., unlawful); perpetrators (e.g., individuals, groups, states); objectives (e.g., political); intended outcomes and motivations (e.g., fear and frustration); targets (e.g., individuals, business, government, and non-goverment); and methods (e.g., hijackings).

On the basis of these elements, it is reasonable to adopt the following definition for the purpose of this book: Terrorism is the calculated employment or the threat of the use of violence by individuals, sub-national groups, and state actors to attain political, social, and economic objectives in violation of law. Acts of terrorism are intended to create an overwhelming fear in a target area larger than the immediate victims attacked or threatened.

From Ancient to Modern Terrorism

Terrorism, as a cost-effective tool of low-intensity conflict that projects psychological intimidation and physical force in violation of law, has ancient roots. Examples are the attacks mounted by the Jewish religious extremists, known as the Zealot Sicarii, against the Romans in occupied Judea as well as the martyrdom missions of the Muslim Hashashin (assassins), targeting the Crusaders in the Middle East. The former were active for 70 years in the first century and the latter between the 11th and 13th centuries. Their experience proved the effectiveness and durability of terrorism, even when the tools are rather primitive.

In subsequent periods, such as between the 16th and late 18th centuries, several European maritime states employed pirates, or privateers, to terrorize the seas for the purpose of advancing foreign policy objectives. By the time of the Reign of Terror, 1793-1794, during the French Revolution, terrorism from "above" and "below" was commonplace. A variety of European groups, nourished by left- and right-wing ideologies and militant nationalism, attained some tactical successes. Resorting to regicide and other terrorist methodologies such as bombings, terrorists assassinated a considerable number of European rulers and officials, including Tsar Alexander II in 1881. Although not intended by the perpetrator, the murder of the Austrian Archduke in Sarajevo drew the European powers into World War I. The period between World War I and World War II also witnessed waves of terrorist attacks in different regions of the world, such as Asia and the Middle East, where nationalist groups fought for their liberation from colonial rule.

It was not until the late 1960s that terrorism became a constant fixture of international life. Rapid developments in technology, communications facilities, and inexpensive and rapid travel contributed to the proliferation of indigenous international terrorist groups and to the intensification of ideological and political violence (e.g., the rise of Palestinian terrorism resulting from the Arab defeat of the Six-Day War of 1967).

For the past 4 decades contemporary terrorist groups utilized a wide range of tactics in order to achieve their political, social, economic, or strategic objectives. These methods of operation have included arson, bombings, kidnappings, hijackings, facility attacks, destruction of property, slaughter of innocent people, and assassinations. The terrorist arsenal comprises not only explosives and arms, such as guns, but also more sophisticated weapons, such as antitank rockets and ground-to-air missiles.

As technological developments offer new capabilities for terrorist groups, the modus operandi of terrorist organizations may subsequently alter. According to various intelligence reports, at least a dozen terrorist groups have shown an interest in acquiring or actively attempting to obtain biological, chemical, or nuclear weapons. It is conceivable that a highly motivated and desperate terrorist group with sufficient technological and financial assets will attempt to improve its bargaining leverage by resorting to mass destruction violence.

A determined terrorist group would be willing to take numerous risks in acquiring and using such weapons. Because the confrontation is seen by many groups as an "all-or-nothing" struggle, in case of failure of their objectives, terrorists are prepared to bring the government to submission. More particularly, terrorists would use these weapons of mass destruction and, in the process, bring devastation and destruction to many lives, including their own.

The prospects of success for such a terrorist organization would be enhanced if it had previously demonstrated sophisticated technological capabilities and a strong willingness to incur high risks involved in achieving their objectives. Even if there is some skepticism about the credibility of the threat, no rational government would likely risk an unconventional incident. The danger is that if one sub-national body succeeds in achieving its goals, then the temptation for other terrorist groups to use, or threaten to use, similar weapons may become irresistible.

In view of these considerations, the arsenal of tomorrow's terrorist might include biological, chemical, and nuclear instruments of massive death and destruction potential. These weapons are capable of producing from several thousand to several million casualties in a single incident. Such attacks could also cause governmental disruption of major proportions, adverse economic implications, and widespread public panic.

Although no major biological, chemical, or nuclear terrorist incident has occurred, the historical record of the past 40 years provides evidence of terrorist groups involved with some types of unconventional operations. For instance, the Aum Shinrikyo, the Japanese terrorist doomsday cult, mounted a sarin gas attack on the Tokyo, Japan, subway in 1995. The attack resulted in 12 deaths and over 5,000 injuries. Aum Shinrikyo was seeking more lethal weapons at the time its leaders were arrested. During fall 2001, the United States was victimized by bio-terrorism, as illustrated in anthrax-tainted mail disseminated in different parts of the country. The attacks have resulted in 5 deaths and affected other Americans.

While the probability of nuclear terrorism remains low in comparison to biological and chemical terrorism, the human, physical, psychological, and economic consequences of such mass destruction terrorism could be enormous. If a nuclear bomb is stolen (or built by a terrorist group with sufficient resources and capabilities), an explosion in a major city of about 1 kiloton (one twentieth of the explosion capacity of the Hiroshima attack) would cause more than 100,000 fatalities and economic damage totaling in the billions of dollars.

There are several specific reasons why the frequency and severity of terrorism will increase during the twenty-first century. First, terrorism has proved very successful in attracting publicity, disrupting the activities of government and business, and causing significant death and destruction. Second, arms, explosives, supplies, financing, and communications are readily available to terrorists. Third, an international support network of groups and states exists that greatly facilitates the undertaking of terrorist activities. Fourth, certain conditions, such as religious extremism or perceptions that the "cause" is lost, could provide terrorists with an incentive to escalate their attacks dramatically by resorting to weapons of mass destruction.

III   Terrorism Against America

Introduction

The United States is a principal target of terrorism. Not only do domestic extremist groups commit acts of terrorism at home, but also, international groups carry out attacks against many American targets abroad. Attacks by foreign terrorists on U.S. soil occurred less frequently.

During the 1970s indigenous and foreign terrorist campaigns in the United States resulted in 600 attacks against civilian and military targets. The success of the counter-terrorism activities of the FBI and law enforcement agencies, coupled with changes in the global political environment, reduced the frequency of terrorism in the United States in the 1980s. During that decade, the number of terrorist incidents reached 220, a two-thirds decrease from the 1970s.

The 1990s marked an escalation of spectacular incidents of terrorism in the United States. One dramatic terrorist attack was the 1993 bombing of the World Trade Center by Middle East terrorists (killing 6 people and injuring 1,042) and the aborted plot to destroy New York landmarks. In 1995, American perpetrators with ties to para-military militias, destroyed a federal building in Oklahoma City, Oklahoma, killing 168 and injuring 674 people. At the time, the Oklahoma City bombing was the worst terrorist incident ever to take place in the United States.

Another noteworthy terrorist attack on U.S. soil was the 1996 bombing in Atlanta, Georgia, host of the Summer Olympic Games, in which 1 person was killed and more than 100 were wounded. At the beginning of the 21st century, the United States was most heavily attacked by al-Qaida terrorists on September 11, 2001. The human toll is estimated to be 3,300 killed or missing and presumed dead, with thousands more wounded.

Throughout the 1970s and 1980s, U.S. cultural, diplomatic, economic, and military interests abroad were major targets of terrorism. In the 1990s, a similar threat developed. For instance, in 1996 there were 296 acts of international terrorism; approximately one fourth of them were directed against U.S. targets. During those approximately 75 incidents, 24 U.S. citizens died while 250 were wounded. By 2000, the number of anti-U.S. terrorist attacks abroad rose to 200, killing 19 U.S. citizens.

The United States has been the most popular single target of international terrorism. American citizens—officials, diplomats, military officers, business people, and children—have been victimized by both state-sponsored terrorism (e.g., Libya, Iraq, Iran, Sudan, and Syria) and sub-state groups, including Marxist-oriented (e.g., Germany's Red Army Faction), nationalists (e.g., Provisional Irish Republican Army [PIRA]), Islamic fundamentalism (e.g., al-Qaida), Palestinian (e.g., Abu Nidal Organization), and ideological mercenaries (e.g., Japanese Red Army).

Among the most significant international terrorist incidents directed against the United States or involving Americans during the past two decades are: the 1979 take-over of the U.S. Embassy in Tehran, Iran, during which American diplomats were held hostage for 444 days; the bombing of the U.S. Embassy and the Marine headquarters in Beirut, Lebanon, in 1983;

the 17-day hijacking of TWA Flight 847 in 1985; the 1988 destruction of Pan Am Flight 103 over Scotland; the truck bombing at the Khobar Towers near Dhahran, Saudi Arabia, in 1996; the attack on the U.S. Embassies in Kenya and Tanzania in 1998; and the suicide bombing against the USS *Cole* in the Yemeni port of Aden in 2000.

Terrorist Attacks Against Business Targets in the United States

The following section provides an historical and contemporary overview of the victimization of Americans—with special emphasis on business community targeting—perpetrated by domestic and foreign terrorists during attacks undertaken in the United States.

There have been occasional outbreaks of terrorism in the United States during the past 200 years carried out by both domestic and foreign groups. Some of the earliest "home-grown" groups included: vigilantes, originally organized to keep law and order in the lawless Western frontier; the Ku Klux Klan during the post-Civil War period; and the Molly Maguires, whose primary interest was vengeance against the anti-Irish-Catholic Scotch, Ulster, Welsh, and English Protestants based in Pennsylvania during the 1870s.

In the turbulent 1960s a proliferation of radical groups with violent tendencies carried out attacks. The Weather Underground, the New World Liberation Front, the George Jackson Brigade, the Symbionese Liberation Army, the Black Liberation Army, and the Black Panther Party were among the most active of such left-wing groups in the United States. During the same period ethnic and nationalist groups (e.g., the Jewish Defense League [the JDL], Armenian movements, Puerto Rican Armed Forces of National Liberation, Omega 7-Cuban Nationalist Movement, and the Cuban National Liberation Front) operated in the United States and Puerto Rico. The capabilities and tactics used by these groups proved to be less effective than their counterparts in other regions around the world.

During the 1970s, terrorist campaigns in the United States targeted the police, military, business, and other victims in over 600 attacks. In justifying their operations, terrorists communicated a multitude of rationalizations. For instance, in a statement claiming credit for the bombing of the Gulf Oil Building in Pittsburgh, Pennsylvania, in June 1974, the Weather Underground explained that the attack was to punish the corporation for "financing the Portuguese in Angola, stealing from the poor in the United States and exploiting the people and resources of 70 countries." The JDL targeted Soviet facilities, residences, companies, and installations of Eastern European countries in the New York area to protest Soviet Bloc policies toward their Jewish minorities and to Israel.

In addition to terrorism perpetrated by indigenous groups in the 1970s, foreign nationalist groups were also active in the United States. For example, the Croatian group Otpor (Resistance) hijacked TWA Flight 724 from New York to Paris, France, in 1976. The operation was conducted to attract attention to its separatist goal of independence from Yugoslavia.

During the 1980s, the United States experienced fewer terrorist incidents domestically than abroad. According to FBI data, terrorist acts within the United States declined drastically after the first few years of the decade. In the 1980s, the total number of terrorist activities on U.S. soil of indigenous and foreign origin, reached an estimated 220, approximately one third that of the previous decade.

The major reasons for this declining trend were the successes of proactive operations of the FBI and effective cooperation between law enforcement agencies in the United States and abroad. The prosecution of terrorists, such as the 1986 indictment by a federal jury in Boston, Massachusetts, of 8 radicals involved in a 9-year series of bombings, bank robberies, and murder, was also a contributing factor in the decline of domestic terrorism during the 1980s. Another impetus for the decline was a social phenomenon—the general loss of revolutionary fervor in the United States during this period.

Nevertheless, domestic terrorist groups operating in the United States during the 1970s were also active to some extent during the 1980s. The Weather Underground and the Black Panther Party were involved in the Brinks armored car robbery in 1981 in Nyack, New York. Also, the JDL engaged in violence against its perceived enemies in this decade.

In addition to these and other domestic groups, a variety of new organizations committed to ideological and political violence emerged during the 1980s. Examples of U.S. terrorism during this decade include reactionary right-wing movements advancing anti-Semitic and white supremacist causes (e.g., Aryan Nation) as well as anti-government and anti-tax beliefs. Another active group was the Evan Mecham Eco-Terrorist International Conspiracy (EMETIC), desiring to preserve the ecological systems by attacking perceived despoilers of the ecology through acts of sabotage ("ecotage"). Mention should also be made of the Animal Liberation Front (ALF) and related groups, dedicated to the elimination of animal use in medical research and industry. Animal rights groups in the United States have usually confined attacks to destruction of property, rather than targeting humans. An exception, however, was the attempted murder of the president of U.S. Surgical Corp. by means of a bomb.

During the 1980s several foreign terrorist groups continued their operations in the United States. For example, the PIRA maintained a gun-running ring in 1982. A Sikh terrorist organization's plan to destroy an Air India aircraft at Kennedy Airport in 1986 was thwarted. Unfortunately, the terrorists succeeded in such an operation in Canada in 1995.

There was some evidence that foreign governments, such as Libya and Iran, established an infrastructure in the United States to aid in carrying out terrorist acts. One example of such a possible act of state-sponsored terrorism was the 1989 San Diego pipebomb attack on the car of the wife of Captain Will Rogers, the commanding officer of the USS *Vincennes*. In 1988, the ship had inadvertently shot down a civilian Iranian airliner resulting in numerous deaths.

In the 1990s several domestic anti-business incidents were recorded. These events included the bombing by skinheads of the Elite Tavern, a homosexual bar in Seattle, Washington, and the arson attacks on several Chicago department stores by members of the ALF.

The most dramatic terrorist event of the decade—and the deadliest terrorist attack occurring on U.S. soil up to the September 11, 2001, incidents—was the bomb blast on April 19, 1995, that destroyed the 9-story Alfred P. Murrah federal building in Oklahoma City. This devastating attack, perpetrated by 2 American terrorists, claimed 168 lives, including 19 children, and wounded 674 people. The explosion emanating from the detonation of a truck-based, 4,800-pound ammonium nitrate fuel oil bomb, destroyed the federal building while severely damaging or destroying 25 other buildings. Another 300 buildings were damaged and window glass was shattered in a 10-block radius.

Aside from indigenous domestic terrorist activity, the phenomenon of international Islamic groups operating in the United States in the 1990s became evident. Seeking to achieve common political, social, economic, or strategic objectives that transcend national differences, these terrorists, existing under the banner of radical Islam, struck at the United States on February 26, 1993. As indicated above, a devastating car bomb explosion occurred in the parking garage at the World Trade Center in New York City, killing 6 people and injuring 1,042 others. The bomb, consisting approximately of 1,200 pounds of explosives, resulted in a crater of 150 feet in diameter and 5 stories high. The attack caused considerable damage to the garage and hundreds of vehicles were demolished. The Vista Hotel, located directly above the detonation site, was badly damaged.

The economic costs were enormous. The property damage to the World Trade Center amounted to over $500 million. The building was closed for 1 month to complete extensive structural repairs. In addition, serious disruption to the activities of some companies resulted from the attack.

The perpetrators, and some of the organizers, of this incident were arrested, convicted, and are currently serving their sentences. They include people of several nationalities: Egyptians, Iraqis, Jordanians, Palestinians, and U.S. citizens.

Following the 1993 World Trade Center terrorist attack, members of the international radical Islamic network once again posed a significant threat to American security interests. In June 1993, a group of terrorists consisting of Egyptians, Sudanese, a Jordanian, and a Puerto Rican were apprehended by the FBI in an aborted plot directed at a number of New York City landmarks and various political figures. The terrorists had targeted the United Nations, a New York federal building, the Lincoln and Holland tunnels, Egyptian President Hosni Mubarak (during his 1993 visit to New York), and at least 2 U.S. political figures. The conspirators were subsequently convicted and sentenced for their criminal activities.

The multi-pronged New York City terrorist plot that was thwarted in 1993, the attack on the World Trade Center in 1993, the bombing in Oklahoma City in 1995, and the most recent assault of September 11, 2001, have underscored most dramatically the vulnerability of the United States to the threat at home originating from both domestic and international terrorism with resulting dire human, political, social, and economic implications.

Terrorist Attacks Against U.S. Business Overseas

The historical record demonstrates that the American business community abroad—including its personnel, facilities, and operations—has been a primary target of terrorism during the past 4 decades. As the most powerful free enterprise system in the world, the United States has become particularly vulnerable to ideological, theological, and political violence nationally, regionally, and globally. There are many factors contributing to this situation, including the fact that the United States maintains extensive cultural, political, economic, and military presence overseas. Also, a considerable number of foreign terrorist groups and state sponsors of terrorism oppose American values, policies, and actions. This reality, coupled with other globalization trends such as technological advancement in weaponry and communications, has resulted in the expansion of international terrorist operations against American business wherever it operates outside the United States.

According to the State Department's Office of the Coordinator for Counter-Terrorism statistics, some 30% of all international terrorist attacks against America during the period 1968 through 1989 were directed against American business. This trend also continued during the 1990s.

It is expected that U.S. business abroad will also be targeted in the future. One reason for this likelihood is the fact that many of the root causes of terrorism are perceived by potential perpetrators as being unresolved, and, thereby, necessitate a target, such as American business, to strike. Another reason is the inevitable emergence of new political, social, and economic problems that will encourage terrorism.

An examination of the historical experience of American business abroad during the past several decades indicates that specific rationalizations were advanced by terrorist groups to justify their attacks. For instance, on January 22, 1971, the People's Revolutionary Front in the Philippines declared that the bombing of the Manila headquarters of Caltex demonstrated "the anger of the Filipino people against American imperialism." Other rationalizations were made for attacks on the offices of Honeywell, IBM, and the Bank of America in Milan, Italy, on June 3, 1972. These terrorist actions were carried out by the perpetrators—as described in the terrorists' leaflets—in support of the "struggle of the Vietnamese people against American imperialism" and the victories "of the revolutionary and Communist Army in Vietnam." The Black September Organization (formed by the Palestine Liberation Organization) damaged an Esso oil pipeline near Hamburg, Germany, on February 22, 1972. The action was perpetrated because the terrorist group accused the U.S. company of "helping the Israelis."

In the 1980s other specific explanations were offered by terrorist groups to justify targeting American business overseas. After bombing the showroom of Litton Industries in Belgium, on October 2, 1984, the left-wing Communist Combatant Cells (CCC) stated that the attack was conducted to protest the company's contract with the North Atlantic Treaty Organization (NATO) for intermediate-range ballistic missiles. On April 2, 1986, the Arab Revolutionary Cell (ARC) claimed credit for the mid-air bombing of TWA Flight 840. The ARC stated that the attack was in retaliation for "all the American imperialist attempts to bring our Arab masses to their knees . . . the last of which was the failed attempt to attack Libya."

During the following decade additional rationalizations were advanced to justify targeting U.S. business abroad. In 1991, the National Liberation Army (ELN), a pro-Cuban terrorist group in Colombia, targeted the Cano-Limon Convenas oil pipeline—490 miles of oil duct jointly owned by Ecopetrol of Colombia and a consortium of foreign oil companies, including U.S. Occidental and Royal Dutch Shell—and related oil camps and pumping facilities. The ELN charged that foreign oil interests were violating Colombia's sovereignty. Also, by attacking the oil pipeline, the ELN proclaimed that it succeeded in undermining Colombia's foreign investment climate.

In 1991, particularly following the start of Operation Desert Storm, Iraq and its sub-state supporters called for a Jihad (Holy War) against the United States and allied interests worldwide. About 170 terrorist incidents were recorded against the coalition members, most targeting Americans. Numerous low-level attacks were conducted against U.S. business interests around the world. In Kuala Lumpur, Malaysia, the ticket offices of American Airlines and Northwest Airlines were attacked on January 25, 1991, with a warning: "Bush kills Muslims. Death to all Americans." Around the same period, in Sydney, Australia, the American Chamber of Commerce was firebombed, followed by a caller's statement: "War must stop. Leave Arabs alone. This is only the beginning."

On March 16, 1991, in Izmir, Turkey, a Turkish auto parts company that carries General Motors (GM) and Detroit Diesel products was bombed. The perpetrators, Dev Sol (Revolutionary People's Liberation Party, a Marxist group) asserted: "American imperialism continues its worldwide massacre. The final one is the massacre of the people of the Middle East . . . U.S. get out of the Middle East."

During spring 1991 similar messages were communicated by terrorists against numerous other American companies, including American Express, Bank of Boston, Bank of New York, Coca-Cola, Chase Manhattan Bank, Citibank, Ford, Kentucky Fried Chicken, McDonald's, and Proctor and Gamble. Fortunately, the terrorist attacks against U.S. business interests overseas during this period were conducted using primitive means.

By the end of the 1990s, U.S. involvement in former Yugoslavia provided another element that terrorists used to claim justification for attacks on American business interests abroad. On April 17, 1999, a group called, Enraged Anarchists claimed responsibility for bombing a GM-Detroit Motors car dealership in Athens, Greece. The building was spray-painted with the following message: "The bombings in Kosovo are a polite offer of the favorite company Detroit Motors."

Persons protesting NATO's military action against Yugoslavia in selected cities in Western Europe called for belligerent actions to be taken against NATO interests, "War to be waged against the war." Such a call to violence was undertaken by arsonists on May 20, 1999, when terrorists attempted to set fire to a Blockbuster Video store in Sicily, Italy. In Prague, Czech Republic, violent demonstrators, organized by the Global Street Party—a loose association of anarchists and radical environmentalists opposed to capitalism, war, social inequality, and globalization—attacked 2 symbols of American "socio-economic imperialism," McDonald's and Kentucky Fried Chicken outlets.

An analysis of American business victimization by domestic and international terrorist attacks abroad illustrates that nearly every type of business sector engaged in by U.S. companies overseas has been targeted. A wide range of U.S. industries that were affected by terrorism overseas were: financial and banking; energy; aviation; automobile and tires; technology, industrial, and defense; mining and engineering; tourism and hospitality; franchises and beverages; pharmaceutical and consumer products; retail; service firms; and other business categories.

These U.S. business targets were singled out because of their symbolism such as the "American way of life" visibility as well as for other practical reasons, including vulnerability of target considerations. The U.S. enterprises attacked overseas ran the gamut from Fortune 500 companies to small firms. The following is a partial list of U.S. companies, from different sectors, that were victimized by terrorism overseas during the past 40 years:

- Automotive and Tires: Chevrolet (Mexico), Chrysler (Argentina), Dunlop Tires (Argentina), Firestone (Argentina), Ford (Chile), General Motors (Uruguay), Goodyear (Argentina), and Goodrich (Philippines).

- Aviation: Bell Helicopter International (Iran), Pan American Airlines (United Kingdom), and Trans World Airlines (Lebanon).

- Energy: Caltex-Mobil (Lebanon), Chevron (Sudan), Esso (Uruguay), Exxon (Sardinia), Gulf (the Netherlands), Houston Oil (Colombia), Mobil (South Africa), Standard Oil (Lebanon), Texaco (Guatemala), and Texas Petroleum (Colombia)

- Financial and Banking: American Express (Germany), Bank of America (Italy), Bank of Boston (Argentina), Bank of New York (Italy), Citibank (Greece), Diners Club (Colombia), First National

Bank of Chicago (Lebanon), and First National City Bank (Argentina).

- Franchises and Beverages: Burger King (Honduras), Coca-Cola (France), 7-Eleven (Panama), Kentucky Fried Chicken (Peru), McDonald's (Turkey), and Pepsi-Cola (Argentina)

- Media: Associated Press (Lebanon)

- Mining and Engineering: Bolivian-U.S. Mining (Bolivia), Fisher Engineering (Iran), Southern Peru (Peru), and Minnesota Mining and Manufacturing (Spain)

- Pharmaceutical and Consumer Products: Colgate-Palmolive (Mexico), Johnson & Johnson (Mexico), Park-Davis (Argentina), and Squibb (Argentina)

- Retail: Sears, Roebuck & Co. (Brazil), and Woolworth (Germany)

- Service Firms: Mail (DHL Worldwide Express, Chile), Advertising (McCann-Erickson, Turkey), and Insurance (American Life Insurance, Turkey)

- Technology, Industry, and Defense: Bechtel (Indonesia), Dow Chemical (Greece), Grumman (Iran), Honeywell (Italy), IBM (Germany), ITT (Uruguay), Kodak (Turkey), Owens-Illinois Glass (Venezuela), Rockwell International (Iran), Sylvania Electronic (Mexico), Union Carbide (Mexico), and Xerox (Argentina)

- Tourism and Hospitality: Avis (Italy), Hertz (Spain), Intercontinental (Jordan), Marriott (Sri Lanka), Ramada (Turkey), and Sheraton (Argentina).

Many types of violence were directed against the foregoing and other U.S. business personnel, facilities, and operations from the 1960s through the 1990s. The modus operandi of dozens of terrorist groups included: threats, thefts, robberies, break-ins, bombings, kidnappings, hostage-taking, assassinations, hijackings, sabotage, and armed attacks.

While thousands of business-related incidents were recorded in the past four decades, a number of international terrorist plots were prevented due to effective intelligence and law enforcement efforts. One of the best known aborted operations was the 1995 plan of the al-Qaida affiliated group to destroy a dozen U.S. airline flights on Asian-Pacific routes. The three terrorists involved in the plot were arrested overseas, brought to the United States, and convicted in federal court.

The rare success in aborting this potentially horrific terrorist attack was in sharp contrast to the continuing victimization of U.S. business abroad. The brutal historical record as well as the potential for future attacks indicate a grim outlook for corporate security interests. One indicator of costly future trends in terms of human life and property is the current wave of anti-U.S. violent demonstrations, resulting from American military operations against the Taliban regime in Afghanistan and bin Laden's al-Qaida leadership and infrastructure in that country. Clearly, these protesters, mostly radical Islamic activists, are creating an extreme anti-American environment that is likely to encourage acts of terrorism directed not only against U.S. diplomats and military personnel but also against American business activities overseas.

Illustrative of the anti-U.S. propaganda and psychological warfare that inevitably could contribute to such an eventuality are the following slogans and themes communicated on November 1, 2001, in Indonesia, the most Muslim-populated country in the world: "America is a Terrorist"; "Bush has waged a war toward Muslims by using the term crusade"; "American equal Jewish, they're dirty dogs, ultimate devils"; "Demand severance of diplomatic relations with the U.S."; and "If the U.S. continues attacking Afghanistan during Ramadan, Muslims in Indonesia will wage Jihad (Holy War)."

These virulent diatribes as well as pre-September 11 anti-American expressions as enunciated by bin Laden, al-Qaida, and others, are poison that terrorists have used to fuel their aggression against U.S. targets domestically and internationally. The language and ideologies upon which they rest were the basis for the heinous, multi-pronged attacks carried out by 19 terrorists on September 11, 2001, against symbols of American military and business power—the Pentagon and the World Trade Center. Moreover, such messages should serve as serious warnings to U.S. interests of possible future terrorist attacks against the United States at home and abroad.

Chapter 2

The Economic Costs to the United States:

An Overview

I Introduction

Shortly after the World Trade Center and Pentagon attacks, Federal Reserve (Fed) Chairman Alan Greenspan aptly remarked, "Nobody has the capacity to fathom fully how the effects of the tragedy of September 11 will play out in the economy." Yet, as President Bush stated, "[M]ake no mistake about it, this has affected our economy in a big way."

Eleven weeks since the attacks—November 20, 2001—there is already considerable evidence of the ramifications of the incidents on U.S. economic indices, Corporate America, U.S. consumers, and the world economy.

This chapter provides an overview of the economic costs to the United States resulting from the September 11 terrorist incidents, anthrax attacks during autumn 2001, and U.S. military activities in Afghanistan in the fall 2001. Also discussed is the state of the U.S. economy in the period leading up and subsequent to the World Trade Center and Pentagon attacks. Attention is given to economic indices, business trends, and consumer sentiments. Unemployment figures, credit policy, and stock market results during fall 2001 are analyzed. The impact of the terrorist attacks on particular regions in the United States is examined. Analyses by the Fed and other sources are presented to capture the distinct consequences on many regions, in particular New York City and Washington, D.C.—locations most directly impacted by the attacks. While the chapter predominantly covers the implications of the terrorist incidents on the United States, the global impact is evaluated as well.

II The State of the U.S. Economy

The Economy Before September 11, 2001

Prior to September 11, 2001, the United States was on the brink of recession: growth had slowed, manufacturing was contracting, orders of technology equipment—especially telecommunications products—were down, business investment had declined, lower corporate profits were exhibited, Standard & Poor's (S&P) 500 index had fallen 13% since summer 2001, unemployment was rising, and consumer spending was weak.

United States gross domestic product (GDP) expanded at an annual rate of only 0.3% during the second quarter of 2001. The Industrial Production Index fell almost 5% in the year following its zenith in September 2000. In August 2001, U.S. factory capacity utilization was just 76%, the lowest level since July 1983, when the United States was recovering from the 1981-82 recession. From January-July 2001, 1.4 million people had already been laid off. In August 2001, unemployment was 4.9% (more than 1% above its level in August 2000). A Labor Department survey of 353 industries found that 44% of businesses were still hiring in August 2001, the worst showing since the last recession, in 1990-91. The University of Michigan's index of consumer confidence fell from 91.5 in August 2001 to 81.8 in September 2001, the weakest level since November 1993.

Following the terrorist attacks, a number of economic indicators and activities in Corporate America strengthened the view that a short recession might be unavoidable. Professor Paul Krugman of Princeton University agreed with the premise that the U.S. economy was already in a precarious position prior to the World Trade Center and Pentagon attacks. Likewise, the Council of Economic Advisers' R. Glenn Hubbard argued that bin Laden may get too much credit for a recession that likely commenced during the second quarter of 2001. It is useful to highlight that since World War II, the average recession in the United States lasted eleven months, although some lasted only five months, with none over sixteen months.

The Economy After September 11, 2001

The September 11, 2001, terrorist incidents strengthened the likelihood that the United States is heading into a recession. The attacks damaged confidence and lessened demand, leading companies to reduce production, eliminate business units, freeze investments, and dismiss workers. Furthermore, concerns about the speed of economic recovery, catastrophic terrorist events, anthrax attacks, employee safety, the effectiveness of U.S. military actions in Afghanistan, and confusion on the scope and length of the U.S. war on terrorism also negatively influenced the U.S. economy.

On October 31, 2001, the Commerce Department reported that during the third quarter of 2001, GDP was particularly gloomy, as it reached -0.4%. The drop in GDP was another signal that the economy was under severe constraints in terms of growth. Another quarter of declining GDP will result in the U.S. economy technically reaching the definition of a recession—two consecutive quarters of declining economic growth. During fall 2001 a number of private and government economists stated that the United States has been in recession since the second quarter of 2001.

The Commerce Department reported that sales of durable goods (other than defense)—products expected to last a minimum of three years—declined 8.5% in September 2001, to $165.4 billion. The drop was the fourth consecutive decline and sales were at their lowest level since August 1996. The principal reduction was observed in the aircraft business where the four hijackings of September 11, 2001, significantly undermined prospects for commercial airlines for the near term.

During the same month, the U.S. trade deficit declined to $18.7 billion—on $95.99 billion in imports and $77.29 billion in exports—from $27.1 billion in the month before. The factors influencing these results were reduced demand for U.S. goods, declining U.S. demand for oil, and payments from foreign insurers based on September 11 claims.

During October 2001, U.S. manufacturing activity, as measured by the National Association of Purchasing Management Index, declined to 39.8 from 47 in September 2001. The October 2001 figure was the lowest mark in almost eleven years. Industrial capacity for September 2001 stood at only 75% of total prospective output, the worst level in eighteen years; it declined to 73.1% in October 2001. The Fed's industrial production index declined by 1.1% in October 2001, the biggest monthly decline in almost a decade.

Business (non-farm) productivity, a measurement of how much employees produce for every hour worked, increased during the third quarter of 2001 by 2.7%. The figure was one of the few positive economic features associated with the third quarter of 2001. During the first and second quarters of 2001, productivity rose by 0.1% and 2.2%, respectively. The producer prices for finished goods declined 1.6% in October 2001.

In the third quarter of 2001, business inventories declined at an annual rate of $50.4 billion. In the first and second quarters of 2001, business stockpiles fell at annual rates of $27.1 billion and $38.3 billion, respectively. The National Association of Purchasing Management's October 2001 index declined to 46.2 from 46.6 in the previous month.

For September 2001, the Commerce Department also reported new home sales dropped 1.4%, to a yearly level of 864,000. This decline likely would have been greater but for extremely low interest rates. The National Association of Realtors reported that existing home sales for September 2001 fell 11.7% to a yearly rate of 4.89 million homes. Also, the Commerce Department announced that the median price for new homes in September 2001 dropped 5.1%; while the previous 2 months also witnessed declines reaching 4.7% in total. News about the housing market was more discouraging in October 2001. Housing starts reached an adjusted annual rate of 1.55 million units, down 1.3% from September 2001.

Consumer spending data during fall 2001 is helpful to gain a better gauge of the economy. Consumer prices fell 0.3% in October 2001 with declining energy prices (which dropped 6.3%) and hotel prices (which declined 1.8%) contributing to the decline. During October 2001, producer prices declined by 1.6%, the biggest one-month decline in 55 years, due in large part to falling automobile and gasoline prices.

During September 2001, consumer spending dropped by 2.2% due to the initial shock of the World Trade Center and Pentagon attacks. By October 2001, principally in response to automotive manufacturers' incentives and zero financing loans, consumer spending rose 7.1%.

According to RCT's National Retail Traffic Index, for the weeks ending September 8-October 20, 2001, the number of consumers visiting malls remained under levels for the September-October 2000 period. Online sales, excluding auctions, from the week ending September 23, 2001, through October 21, 2001, hovered or exceeded $800 million per week, indicating that consumer spending had not evaporated.

Due to zero interest rate offers by automobile manufacturers, sales of new cars and light trucks during October 2001 reached record figures equal to an annual level of 21.3 million units. In October 2001, the month when many retailers reduce prices to make way for winter merchandise, retail sales increased by 0.9%, following no rise in retail sales in September 2001. Among retailers that experienced sales growth during October 2001 were: Wal-Mart (up 6.7%), Costco (up 6%), TJX (up 4%), and Kohl's (up 13.5%). Meanwhile, retailers that suffered declines in sales during October 2001 were: the Gap (down 17%), Federated Stores (down 8.7%), Kmart (down 4.4%), and Sears (down 4.4%). From January-October 2001, discount stores and department stores combined for about 71% and 18%, respectively, of consumer outlays, while warehouse stores and luxury stores comprised just around 9% and 2%, respectively, of shoppers' purchases during the same period.

In October 2001, bank regulators announced that between May-June 2001, almost 10% of syndicated loans, equaling nearly $200 billion, were designated as adversely rated. Also, lenders nationwide reported that the amount of non-performing assets and higher charge-offs (the figure a credit loses on a bad loan) rose in September 2001 over September 2000 levels.

Princeton's Professor Krugman suggested that the terrorist attacks could have a large negative psychological impact on consumers and investors. Likewise, Professor Jeremy Siegel of the University of Pennsylvania was concerned that terrorism could significantly undermine consumer confidence. Initial data on surveys of confidence and buying intentions were misleading, suggested Stephen Slifer of Lehman Brothers, as patriotism and faith in America were not based on economic factors.

Against this backdrop, consumer sentiment rebounded unexpectedly in October 2001 from a fall after September 2001's terrorist attacks, according to a University of Michigan survey. Its figure for consumer sentiment in October 2001 was 82.7, an increase from the September 2001 level of 81.8, yet still below the pre-attacks figure of 83.6. Another indicator, consumer expectations for the future, also rose from 73.5 in September 2001 to 75.5 in October 2001, stemming partly from Fed interest rate cuts leading to lower interest rates for mortgages and car loans. Yet, people's outlook of present economic conditions declined to 94.0 in October 2001 from 94.6 in September 2001.

In a survey of consumers conducted in October 2001, the Conference Board found that 52% of Americans believed that the September 11 attacks would push the economy into recession. Nevertheless, the survey reflected that 90% of Americans did not intend to postpone buying appliances, cars, and homes while 80% stated they would proceed with pending financial investments.

The Consumer Federation of America and the Credit Union National Association projected that during the 2001 holiday season, 57% will spend as much money on gifts as in 2000, 28% less than in 2000, and 13% more than in 2000. As those predictions are generally in line with estimates during the 2000 holiday season, they were not as negative as some initially expected.

With regard to wages, the Labor Department announced in October 2001, figures for the Employment Cost Index for the third quarter of 2001, which rose 1%.

Unemployment

The unemployment rate rose to a four-year high of 4.9% in August 2001, and remained at that level in September 2001. During October 2001, 415,000 jobs were eliminated, raising the unemployment level from 4.9% to 5.4%, a five-year high. In that month jobs in retail trade and hotels declined by 81,000 and 46,000, respectively.

In some areas of the United States, unemployment shifted upward very rapidly throughout all of 2001. For instance, in California's Santa Clara County and San Francisco during December 2000, unemployment figures were 1.3% and 2.5%, respectively. By October 2001, the jobless rate had more than doubled to 6.4% in Santa Clara County and 6% in San Francisco. The relatively sparsely populated states of Alabama, Arkansas, Kentucky, Louisiana, Mississippi, and Tennessee tallied over 36,000 job losses during the first 9 months of 2001.

To comprehend the scope of job losses during fall 2001, the following facts are useful. From September 11, 2001, through November 7, 2001, U.S. companies cut nearly 250,000 jobs. Among the manufacturing, airlines, technology, retail, services, and other companies experiencing large job cuts were: Boeing, 30,000; American Airlines, 20,000; Starwood Hotels & Resorts, 12,000; United Technologies, 5,000; Sears, 4,900; Eastman Kodak, 4,000; Honeywell International, 3,800; BellSouth, 3,000; Unisys, 3,000; Textron, 2,500; R.R. Donnelley & Sons, 2,400; AT&T, 2,400; EMC, 2,400; Advanced Micro Devices, 2,300; Applied Materials 2,000; Phelps Dodge, 1,400; American Standard, 1,000; CommerceOne, 700; Reuters, 500; and KPMG Consulting Inc., 400.

In October 2001, Goodyear Tire & Rubber Co. announced plans to lay off up to 1,400 workers, or 5% of its North American manufacturing work force, at five U.S. plants due to lower tire sales and uncertainty about the economy. These layoffs were in addition to reductions of 7,800 workers announced earlier in 2001.

In October 2001, Credit Suisse First Boston announced its intention to eliminate 2,000 jobs, or 7% of its workforce, during the next fiscal year. Also, Merrill Lynch projected that during the fourth quarter of 2001, it would eliminate 10,000 jobs, or 15% of its workforce. During fall 2001, it was expected that Bear Stearns would reduce its staff force by 830 workers, or 7.5% of its employees.

Reagan National Airport, in Arlington, Virginia, was closed for several weeks following the September 11, 2001, attacks. During part of that time, the airport was used as a makeshift state unemployment office for thousands of people formerly employed in the transportation, tourism, and hospitality sectors. Northern Virginia technology firms MicroStrategy Inc. and Net2000 Communications Inc. announced they were laying off hundreds of workers at the end of September 2001, citing economic uncertainty caused by the terrorist attacks.

Between March-October 2001, almost 900,000 jobs were eliminated in the United States, the biggest job loss for a March-October period since the 1990-1991 recession. Mike Kiernan of the Working for America Institute estimated that more than 400,000 jobs were lost from September 11, 2001, to mid-October 2001. According to the Hotel and Restaurant International Employees Union, nearly 100,000 of its members have either lost their jobs or had their hours cut since September 11, 2001.

In September 2001, the Labor Department announced that mass layoffs—worker dismissals involving a minimum of 50 employees—reached 1,316 cases, totaling 158,859 jobs. The number of large layoffs was the highest since 1995 and 41% higher than September 2000 figures. This type of layoff affected 2 states, California and Nevada, most severely, resulting in 54,267 and 10,762 dismissals, respectively, in September 2001. From January-September 2001, mass layoffs affected 1.7 million workers.

According to the Labor Department, 93,000 jobs were slashed from manufacturing payrolls in September 2001, extending a 14-month streak that saw employment in that sector fall by 1.1 million. Large declines were recorded by makers of semiconductors, computers, and telecommunications. The nation's service sector eliminated 102,000 jobs in September 2001. Wholesalers also eliminated 21,000 jobs, while retail establishments reduced 44,000 workers, primarily at restaurants and bars. Personnel supply companies lost 18,000 jobs. Health services was the sole industry that experienced job growth, 29,000 in September 2001.

First-time jobless claims rose to 535,000 during the last week in September 2001, the highest figure in nine years. This number included almost 11,000 new claims in New York and Virginia related to the destruction of the World Trade Center and the shutdown of Reagan National Airport.

The number of workers filing new claims for unemployment benefits approached a 9-year high during the week of October 8, 2001, as the September 11, 2001, attacks compounded the economic damage from a factory slump. During the week of October 15, 2001, new claims for unemployment benefits rose by 8,000 to 504,000, the second-highest figure in almost a decade.

Workers stayed unemployed longer than before September 11, 2001, as witnessed by 3.65 million people continuing to draw unemployment benefits in the week ending October 6, 2001. The number of people still receiving unemployment benefits reached 3.72 million during the last week of October 2001. The total number of persons receiving unemployment in the United States during the week ending November 3, 2001, rose to 3.826 million, an 18-year high.

The initial jobless claims during the week ending November 3, 2001, dropped by 46,000 to 450,000. During the week ending November 10, 2001, new jobless claims declined by 6,000, to reach 444,000. Other analysts predict that the unemployment rate may reach as high as 6.5% in 2002.

Future Economic Outlook

Most economic benchmarks for fall 2001, Anthony Karydakis of Banc One Capital Markets suggested, are indicative of a very poor economic condition for this period. Likewise, James Glassman of J.P. Morgan Chase Securities remarked that despite the fact that in fall 2001, the economy was not technically considered to be in recession, in actuality, economic indicators and company behaviors indicate such a status.

On October 20, 2001, Greenspan stated, "We are looking at a[n economic] situation which is by no means as bad as numbers of us were fearful it might turn out to be. But it [the economy] also has not exhibited a sharp snapback, which has been typical of what happens when you get a major hurricane or natural disaster." In a speech before the National Association of Manufacturers more than a week later, President George W. Bush remarked that he was "deeply concerned" that economic indicators were signaling that the economy was heading toward recession.

Growing company layoffs and shutdowns may further accelerate unemployment, resulting in reduced consumer spending, and further impinging on a weakened U.S. economy during fall 2001 and winter 2002. Moreover, continuing disruptions to business and governmental activities due to terrorism threats and military incursions in Afghanistan and elsewhere would negatively affect the economy. For instance, Mark Keller of A.G. Edwards surmised that if U.S. military responses are protracted, then the economy will be adversely affected.

Allen Sinai of Decision Economics predicted that the economic downturn would be particularly stark from fall 2001 through spring 2002. According to a survey of senior executives conducted by the National Association of Manufacturers, a majority anticipated that their respective sectors would be in recession from the last quarter of 2001 through the initial quarter of 2002.

Other economists predicted that significant fiscal spending, particularly in defense, and loose monetary policy, along with a stable financial system, may spur a recovery by the second quarter of 2002. According to some calculations, during 2002, fiscal spending may reach about 1.5% of GDP. Professor Robert J. Barro of Harvard University asserted that the possibility of greater military spending in 2002 and beyond would buttress GDP accordingly: an additional $1 in defense spending would lead to a $0.60 to $0.70 rise in GDP. Macroeconomic Advisers of St. Louis projected that every $1 of tax cuts and additional spending would result in $1.50 of economic growth 18 months hence.

III Federal Reserve Credit Policy and Performance of Stock Markets

Federal Reserve Credit Policy

Following the World Trade Center and Pentagon attacks, central banks in the United States, Europe, and Japan injected significant amounts of cash in order to ease financial markets and reduce chaos in the event of possible runs on banks by a panicky public.

On September 13, 2001, 2 days after the terrorist incidents, the Fed considered whether to cut interest rates immediately. After careful consideration, the Federal Open Market Committee (FOMC) determined that financial markets were too disrupted and economic outlook too uncertain to adequately assess the justification for such a policy move. Also affecting its decision was the fact that at the time, the U.S. stock markets were closed while the bond market had reopened after a 2-day shutdown.

On September 17, 2001, the FOMC decided to lower its target for the federal funds rate by 50 basis points to 3%. Also, the Fed approved a 50 basis points reduction in the discount rate to 2.5%. The Fed promised to continue to supply unusually large volumes of liquidity to the financial markets, as required, until more normal market functioning is restored. Prior to this

0.5% cut, the Fed pumped almost $100 billion into the banking system to help keep financial markets functioning.

On October 2, 2001, the FOMC decided to lower its target for the federal funds rate by 50 basis points to 2.5%. In a related action, the Fed approved a 50 basis point reduction in the discount rate to 2%. The Fed observed that business and household spending had weakened, although long-term projections for the economy were positive. This interest rate cut was the second since the World Trade Center and Pentagon attacks and the ninth in 2001.

At its next scheduled meeting on November 6, 2001, the FOMC once again reduced the target for the federal funds rate by 50 basis points to 2.0%, its lowest level since 1961. In addition, the Fed undertook to lower the discount rate by 50 basis points to 1.5%. The Fed's rationale for its decision was "uncertainty and concerns about the deterioration in business conditions both here and abroad are damping economic activity." This decision marked the Fed's tenth interest rate cut in 2001. In a sign of coordinated monetary policy, the European Central Bank lowered its key financing rate from 3.75% to 3.25% on November 7, 2001. The same day, the Bank of England decreased its key rate from 4.5% to 4%.

The frequency and size of the interest rate cuts may cause the Fed, with the federal funds rate at 2.0%, to hold future rate reductions to 0.25%. As some economists suggested, larger cuts may result in the Fed facing the same problem that the Japanese central bank faces: with official short-term interest rates very low (near zero), it is very difficult to use monetary policy to encourage economic activity. Decisions made at the next two FOMC meetings (in mid-December 2001, and late January 2002) will enable Fed watchers to get a better handle on how the Fed plans to proceed.

Lower interest rates have in turn enabled lenders to lower mortgage rates. Such circumstances have encouraged consumers to purchase homes, apply for new mortgages, and refinance existing mortgages. The Mortgage Bankers Association of America reported that the number of mortgage applications submitted during the first week of November 2001 reached record levels; about 75% of those were for refinancings. During this period, the average interest rate nationally on a 30-year fixed-rate mortgage for loans under $275,000 was 6.45%, down from 6.56% in the last week of September 2001. For 15-year fixed-rate mortgages, the national average in the first week of November 2001 was 5.94%, the lowest level in a decade.

On October 4, 2001, the U.S. Treasury held an unscheduled $6 billion auction of 10-year notes in order to reduce shortages resulting from disruptions to trading floors, back-office operations, and communications systems on Wall Street in the aftermath of the attacks. The auction raised the supply of 10-year notes by more than 20%, resulting in the prices of the notes to decline, and yields to increase to 4.5%.

The Treasury Department's decision in late October 2001 to discontinue the sale of 30-year bonds was an additional attempt by the government to push down long-term borrowing rates as well as to implement plans to finance national debt with shorter-term instruments. Due to this development, prices on 30-year bonds advanced significantly. It is expected that the Treasury's decision will ultimately induce the demand for 10-year Treasury notes, which yield less than 30-year bonds. Also, 10-year Treasury notes are projected to play a larger role than in the past in establishing corporate bond and mortgage rates.

The impact of the World Trade Center and Pentagon attacks on the value of the U.S. dollar is informative as well. On September 10, 2001, the U.S. dollar was trading at 121.04 yen, the Euro traded at 89.50 cents, and the British pound at $1.4550. On the day of the attacks, the U.S. dollar's value fell to 119.2 yen, and the Euro rose against the U.S. dollar to 91.5 cents. Once fears over the attacks abated and U.S. responses to terrorism took form, the Fed and other central banks intervened, and the U.S. dollar rebounded.

Yet, on November 12, 2001, concerns of possibly another aviation terrorist attack that day—an American Airlines Flight 587, en route from Kennedy Airport in New York to Santo Dominigo, Dominican Republic, crashed in the Queens borough of New York, killing 260 onboard and 5 on the ground—affected trading in the U.S. dollar, in part. The dollar closed at 120.39 yen, the Euro traded at 89.47 cents, and the British pound was at $1.4543.

Following news that the Northern Alliance had captured the Afghan capital of Kabul, and that Taliban troops were fleeing the city on November 13, 2001, the U.S. dollar strengthened against the Japanese yen to 121.67, the Euro to 88.09 cents, and the British pound to $1.4411. Also that same day, information was disclosed by U.S. government officials that the crash of American Airlines Flight 587 was due to a mechanical malfunction, and not a terrorist incident. In about 8 weeks following the most destructive terrorist incident in U.S. history, U.S. currency was at almost precisely the same value against major currencies as it was on the day of the attacks.

Performance of Stock Markets

Following the September 11, 2001, terrorist incidents, economists, market strategists, and businesspeople had different perspectives on future stock market returns. Hugh A. Johnson of First Albany Corporation projected sub-par stock returns through 2005. Professor Sendhil Mullainathan of the Massachusetts Institute of Technology foresaw that any future shifts would also need to consider that stocks were overvalued prior to the terrorist attacks. Warren Buffet, chief executive officer (CEO) of Berkshire Hathaway, said that one's viewpoint of the stock market should not be altered due to the terrorist attacks: if one thought that stocks were over-valued before the incidents, then that perspective should likewise continue even in light of the attacks.

Joseph J. Mezrich of Morgan Stanley said that in previous crises, such as the onset of World War II, the Cuban missile crisis, the oil shocks of the 1970s, and the Persian Gulf War, the upheaval initially left investors more risk-averse than they were before the crisis. Historically, stock valuations rose when the government resolved a problem decisively; they remained low during longer crises, like the Arab oil embargo of 1973-74. Other analysts, including Birinyi Associates, suggested that subsequent to significant shocks, such as the John F. Kennedy assassination, 1973 oil embargo, and World Trade Center bombing (1993), the stock market (using the Dow Jones Industrial Average, [DJIA]) initially declines, although an increase later occurs within half a year. An exception to this rule was the Pearl Harbor attack during which the DJIA fell by about 9.5% within 6 months after the bombing. This section will answer whether similarities between the September 11, 2001, terrorist incidents and the Pearl Harbor incident are valid, too, in terms of the impact on DJIA levels.

With the reality of terrorism, conflict in Afghanistan, and possible future U.S. incursions overseas ingrained in the American psyche for some time to come, stock market analysts' commentaries are filled with such discussions. For instance, David Memmott of Morgan Stanley commented in October 2001 that the absence of additional major terrorist incidents was an encouraging sign and reflected an upswing in the market. Another perspective, that of Jeffrey Kleintop of PNC Advisors, suggested that advances in the market fueled by investors' perceptions that the Taliban will be defeated quickly were overly optimistic factors. Ken Sheinberg of SG Cowen explained that the market is highly sensitive to negative economic, military, and terrorism-related developments.

It is worth noting that stock market analysts reduced their earnings estimates for months prior to the September 11, 2001, terrorist attacks. In fact, some argued that the stocks were overly expensive before the attacks, with the S&P 500 index trading at 22 times projected earnings on September 10, 2001, above the traditional 15 to 17 multiples that the index often exhibits.

On September 10, 2001, the DJIA was 9,605.51, the S&P 500 index was 1,092.54, and the Nasdaq Composite Index was 1,695.38. Due to the September 11, 2001, terrorist incidents, damage to telecommunications and infrastructure, dislocation of personnel, and the need for a mourning period, U.S. stock markets remained closed until September 17, 2001. Elsewhere, stock markets declined dramatically on news of the event, closing on September 11, 2001, in following way: London's FTSE 100 declined 5.7% to 4,746; Frankfurt's DAX fell 8.49% to 4,273.53; Paris's CAC-40 dropped 7.39% to 4,059.75; Toronto's 300 declined 4.03% to 7,048.8; Mexico City's Bolsa decreased 5.55% to 5,531.02; and Sao Paulo's Bovespa fell 9.18% to 10,827.96. In morning trading on September 12, 2001, Tokyo's Nikkei 225 dropped 5.04% to 9,773.71 and Hong Kong's Hang Seng fell 8.04% to 9,579.65.

On the last day of the trading week following the World Trade Center and Pentagon attacks, September 14, 2001, London's FTSE 100 declined 3.8% to 4,755.70; Frankfurt's DAX decreased 6.29% to 4,115.98; Paris's CAC-40 dropped 4.97% to 3,909.49; Toronto's 300 declined 2.98% to 6,890.85; Sao Paulo's Bovespa fell 2.64% to 10,034.40; Tokyo's Nikkei 225 rose 4.12% to 10,008.89; and Hong Kong's Hang Seng increased 0.90% to 9,655.45.

As a result of uncertainty about the markets, the Securities and Exchange Commission (SEC) temporarily relaxed some rules that prohibited certain types of trades by companies and individuals. The return of trading at major U.S. stock exchanges on September 17, 2001, provided a patriotic triumph in the sense that a pillar of the U.S. economy—investment in stocks—would not be destroyed by terrorism. Exceptionally heavy volume—2,369,340,000 on the New York Stock Exchange (NYSE) and 2,189,192,800 on the Nasdaq—and significant declines—the DJIA dropped 684.81 points, or 7.13%, and the Nasdaq composite index fell 115.82, or 6.83%—exemplified the negative implications of the World Trade Center and Pentagon attacks on investor sentiment.

The 5 most active stocks on the NYSE declined as follows: General Electric (down $4.20 to $35.15), EMC (down $0.20 to $13.75), Disney (down $4.33 to $19.25), AOL Time Warner (down $4.41 to $30.00), and Cendant (down $3.36 to $14.40). Likewise, the 5 most active stocks on the Nasdaq on September 17, 2001, fell: Cisco (down $0.47 to $35.15), Intel (down $2.48 to $23.59), Oracle (down $0.45 to $11.01), Microsoft (down $4.67 to $52.91), and Sun Microsystems (down $0.44 to $9.85).

Spurred by the four hijackings and their subsequent havoc of September 11, 2001, it is not surprising that the NYSE- and Nasdaq-listed companies that lost the most (on a percentage basis) on September 17, 2001, were principally airlines and firms in the travel business. Among them were: (1) NYSE: America West (down 65.1%, or -$5.60, to $3.00), U.S. Airways (down 52.1%, or -$6.50, to $5.57), Continental Airlines (down 49.4%, or -$19.59, to $20.05), Delta Airlines (down 44.6%, or -$16.61, to $20.64), UAL/United Airlines (down 43.2%, or -$13.32, to $17.50), Sabre Holdings (down 40.9%, or -$8.42, to $12.76), and AMR/American Airlines (down 39.4%, or -$11.70, to $18.00); (2) Nasdaq: Mesa Air (down 62.3%, or -$9.28, to $5.62), Travelocity (down 43%, or -$9.46, to $12.56), Priceline (down 39.8%, or -$1.99, to $3.01), Northwest Airlines (down 36.7%, or -$7.20, to $12.42), Atlantic Coast Airlines (down 35.8%, or -$9.50, to $17.02), and Expedia (down 33.8%, or -$12.25, to $24.00).

In contrast to the aforementioned declines, defense, technology, and security companies on the NYSE and Nasdaq did exceptionally well on September 17, 2001, as the prospective conflict in Afghanistan and the need for greater military, security, telecommunications, and anti-terrorism capabilities, and spending in those sectors became evident to investors. As such, some of the corporations in this category were: (1) NYSE: Level-3 Communications (up 38.1%, or $24.00, to $87.00), Raytheon (up 26.8%, or $6.65, to $31.50), Teledyne (up 18.2%, or $2.62, to $17.00), Northrop Grumman (up 15.7%, or $12.86, to $94.80), Lockheed Martin (14.7%, or $5.63, to $43.95); (2) Nasdaq: InVision (up 165.3%, or $5.14, to $8.25), Visionics (up 93.2%, or $3.98, to $8.25), CompuDyne (up 57.6%, or $4.75, to $13.00), Polycom (up 33%, or $6.31, to $9.30), and Kroll Inc. (up 28.8%, up $2.08, to $9.30).

For the five days after trading resumed following the World Trade Center and Pentagon attacks, the DJIA incurred its biggest weekly percentage decline since 1933, falling 14.3%, or 1,369.70, to 8,235.81. Likewise, the Nasdaq composite index declined substantially, 16.1%, or 272.19 points, to 1,423.19, while the S&P 500 index fell 11.6%, or 126.74 points, to 965.80. Ed Yardeni of Deutsche Bank Alex Brown explained that there was extensive panic selling in the week following the attacks.

Experiencing significant declines for the week were airplane manufacturer Boeing, which lost 30.74% and closed at $30.10, and avionics equipment-maker Honeywell, which dropped by 30.53% and closed at $24.80. In contrast, the stock of videoconference equipment-maker, Polycom, rose 43% during the week and closed at $27.37.

A positive upward shift in the markets occurred during the trading week ending September 28, 2001. The stock market DJIA rose 166.14 points, or 1.9%, on September 28, 2001, with a weekly gain of 7.4%, its best week since 1984. At the same time, the day marked the end of the third quarter, the DJIA's worst since the crash of 1987. The S&P 500 index dropped 15% for the third quarter of 2001, also the largest decline since 1987. Bad news also touched the Nasdaq as the composite index fell 30.65% during the third quarter, closing at 1,498.80.

On October 2, 2001, the Fed announced a 0.5% interest rate cut and investors responded by advancing the DJIA by 1.29%. The following day, the major stock indexes attained their highest closing since the September 11, 2001, terrorist attacks as technology stocks soared following the Bush administration's proposed economic stimulus package and positive news from Cisco. The Nasdaq composite index rose 5.9%, its largest percentage gain since April 2001. Also, the DJIA advanced 1.9%, or 173.19 points, to 9,123.78, placing it above 9,000 for the first time since the incidents. The S&P 500 index jumped nearly 2%, or 20.95 points, to 1,072.28, only 1.9% under its pre-attack close of 1,092.54.

For the week ending October 5, 2001, a number of positive stimuli—the Fed's 0.5% cut in its benchmark interest rate to 2.5% and President Bush's proposal on an economic stimulus package—influenced the market, pushing it in a positive direction. The DJIA gained 272.21 points, or 3.1%, to 9,119.77; the S&P 500 index increased 30.44 points, or 2.9%, to 1,071.38; and the Nasdaq composite index rose 106.50 points, or 7.1%, to 1,498.80. The S&P 500 index figure and the Nasdaq composite index level were within 2% and 5%, respectively, of pre-attack marks. Also, positively affecting the market was Dell Computer's announcement that it would meet third-quarter 2001 forecasts. The company gained 21.75% for the week, closing at $22.56.

By October 11, 2001, the S&P's 500 index surpassed its pre-attack level of 1,092.54, by rising 16.44, or 1.5%, to 1,097.43. The Nasdaq composite index also advanced above its September 10, 2001, level, 1,695.38, by climbing 75.21, or 4.6%, to 1,701.47. In addition, the DJIA rose 169.59, or 1.8%, to 9,410.45, yet still nearly 2% below its close of 9,605.51 prior to the incidents.

Tim Heekin of Thomas Weisel Partners and John Powers of Robertson

Stephens explained that the success of the U.S. military strikes, no major terrorist retaliation, and possible economic recovery in 2002 caused investors to look favorably on stock investing. Also, investors were spurred by General Electric meeting analysts' 2001 third-quarter expectations, and news that Yahoo, PepsiCo, Genetech, and Abbott Laboratories either met or exceeded analysts' expectations for 2001 third-quarter projections.

On October 16, 2001, the Nasdaq composite index rose 1.52%, or 25.76 points, to 1,722.07. The S&P 500 index rose 0.69%, or 7.56 points, to 1,097.54. The DJIA advanced 0.39%, or 36.61 points, to 9,384.23. Stocks cascaded following remarks by Fed Chairman Greenspan about continuing uncertainty in the economy. That same day, more anthrax exposures in the U.S. Congress led to closure of the House of Representatives for several days. Matthew Johnson of Lehman Brothers explained the day's stock market decline by stating that consumer confidence severely waned following the discovery of anthrax in and around the U.S. Congress.

For the trading week ending October 19, 2001, the DJIA fell 140.05 points, or 1.5%, to 9,204.11; at that time, the index was down 14.67% for 2001. The Nasdaq composite index dropped 32.09 points, or 1.88%, to 1,671.31; the composite was down 32.35% for the year. The S&P 500 index fell 18.17 points, or 1.66%, to 1,073.48; the composite was down 18.69% for 2001. Poor earnings reports, such as from SBC Communications and Pharmacia, continued concerns about anthrax attacks (e.g., following the anthrax-related deaths of 2 U.S. Postal Service workers), and public impatience with the pace of the U.S. and the Northern Alliance's military advances in Afghanistan were among issues weighing negatively on investors during October 15-19, 2001. Positive factors included market perceptions of further interest rate cuts and the attractiveness of lower credit for consumers who were considering acquiring homes or automobiles.

With reference to individual companies, for the trading week ending October 19, 2001, Home Depot was down 3% (down 11.6% for 2001), General Electric declined 4.5% (down 22.3% for 2001), Intel fell 3.4% (down 19.7% for 2001), Citigroup rose 1.8% (down 10.2% for 2001), AT&T declined 11.2% (up 36.9% for 2001), IBM rose 1.8% (up 20.8% for 2001), and Microsoft accelerated 2.7% (up 33.5% for 2001).

For the trading week ending October 26, 2001, investors aggressively purchased stocks even though negative news, including disappointing 2001 third-quarter reports and worsening economic statistics—orders for durable goods and sales of existing homes declined while claims for state unemployment rose by 504,000—abounded. Surprisingly, then, the DJIA gained 341.06 points, or 3.7%, to 9,545.17; the S&P 500 index increased 31.13 points, or 2.9%, to 1,104.61; and the Nasdaq composite index rose 97.65 points, or 5.8%, to 1,768.96. Incidentally, the Nasdaq composite index reached a new post-attack high during the week.

During the trading week terminating November 2, 2001, the main U.S. stock indices fell initially before rallying on Friday. Overall, the DJIA declined 221.63 points, or 2.3%, to 9,323.54; the S&P 500 index dropped 20.51 points, or 1.9%, to 1,084.10; and the Nasdaq composite index rose 23.23 points, or 1.3%, to 1,745.73. Among the factors impacting the trading week were news of: a very disappointing unemployment rate for October 2001 of 5.4%, a 0.5% gain from the previous month; continued poor 2001 third-quarter earnings reports (United Airlines' parent company, UAL, and US Airways Group Inc. lost $1.15 billion and $766 million, respectively); declining economic indicators (construction and consumer spending fell); additional anthrax cases; warnings of possibly imminent major terrorist attacks; the likelihood of Argentina's default on debt; and a tentative accord between Microsoft and the Justice Department relating to antitrust issues. The aforementioned final factor occurred on November 1, 2001, and pushed the Nasdaq composite index up 56.10 points, or 3.3%, to 1,746.30 (above pre-attack levels); the DJIA rose 188.76 points, or 2.1%; and the S&P 500 index rose 24.32 points, or 2.3%, to 1,084.10.

In the trading week ending November 9, 2001, the nation's key stock markets rose significantly. More specifically, on November 9, 2001, the DJIA gained 284.46 points, or 3.05%, to 9,608, making its first close above the pre-attack level of 9,605.51. During this week, the S&P 500 index increased 36.21 points, or 3.34%, to 1,120.31; and the Nasdaq composite index rose 82.75 points, or 4.74%, to 1,828.48. Among the factors that investors weighed were: the Fed cut interest rates by 0.5% to 2%, leading many investors to switch to equities as money market and bond yields declined further; initial unemployment claims rose less than expected; productivity figures were better than expected for the third quarter of 2001; a great likelihood of passage of the congressional stimulus package emerged; and potential difficulties arose in undertaking the Compaq Computer and Hewlett-Packard merger.

On November 13, 2001, the DJIA rose 2.1%, or 196.58 points, closing at 9,750.95, the S&P 500 index reached 1,139.09, up 1.9%, or 20.76 points, and the Nasdaq composite index catapulted 2.8%, or 51.98 points, to 1,892.11. The sharp advances that day were spurred, in the main, by news that the Northern Alliance had entered Kabul, Afghanistan, as the Taliban troops largely deserted the city. Also, further information was provided by U.S. government officials implying that the American Airlines Flight 587 that crashed in Queens on November 12, 2001, was probably not due to a terrorist attack.

The stock of American Airlines' parent company, AMR Corporation, declined 9%, or $1.64, to $16.49, due to the impact of the American Airlines Flight 587 crash that day. In addition, strong third quarter of 2001 results from various companies, such as Home Depot, and upbeat forecasts by others, including Texas Instruments, aided in the positive results on U.S. stock markets.

For a perspective on declines in U.S. stock markets during 2001, from January-November 13, 2001, the DJIA dropped 1,035.90 points, or 9.6%; the S&P 500 Index fell 181.19 points, or 13.72%; and the Nasdaq composite index declined 578.41 points, or 23.41%. During this time frame, the 10 largest U.S. mutual funds (by largest asset holdings) had a loss along the following lines: Fidelity Magellan (-12.6%), Vanguard 500 Index (-12.9%), American Investor Co. America (-5.6%), Fidelity Growth & Income (-10%), Fidelity Contrafund (-14.8%), American Growth (-14.5%), American New Perspectives (-10.5%), American Euro Pacific (-14.6%), and American Century Ultra (-17.2%).

Internationally, stock markets have generally fared even worse than U.S. stocks during the January-November 13, 2001, period. More specifically, the Dow Jones World Index (excluding the United States) fell 35.38 points, or 22.55%; London's FTSE 100 declined 945.4 points, or 15.19%; Frankfurt's DAX fell 1486.64, or 23.11%; the Paris CAC-40 declined 1,360.74, or 22.96%; and Tokyo's Nikkei 225 dropped 3,755.13, or 27.24%.

Prior to the September 11, 2001, terrorist incidents, the price of gold per troy ounce (Comex spot price) was around $273. By late September 2001, as often is the case in times of political and military shocks, the price of gold per troy ounce rose to slightly above $293. By November 13, 2001, the price of gold reached $278.30, an increase of $0.90 partially due to anxiety about the crash of American Airlines Flight 587. As such, 2 months following the World Trade Center and Pentagon terrorist attacks, the price of gold is up only about $5, around 2%, more than its price on September 10, 2001.

In the trading week ending November 16, 2001, the DJIA closed at 9,866.99 points, the S&P 500 stock index reached 1,138.65, and the Nasdaq composite index ended at 1,898.58. On the last day of that trading week, all 3 indices declined by less than 0.1%, though they were approaching important benchmarks: the DJIA nearing 10,000; and the Nasdaq composite index approaching 2,000. The S&P's 500 index was still quite a distance from 1,500. The week demonstrated that investors were buoyed by U.S. military advances, retail prices for October 2001 rising by 7.1%, and the prospects for an economic recovery in mid-2002.

In closing, less than 10 weeks after the September 11 incidents, the S&P 500 index, the DJIA, and the Nasdaq composite index all reached levels above their lowest levels following the attacks.

IV The Economic Impact on Specific Regions of the United States

Overview

Although it is too early to ascertain the full extent of economic ramifications of the September 11, 2001, terrorist attacks, the Fed's Beige Book (Beige Book) of October 24, 2001, which summarized economic and business information from the Fed's 12 districts—Atlanta, Boston, Chicago, Cleveland, Dallas, Kansas City, Minneapolis, New York, Philadelphia, Richmond, San Francisco, and St. Louis—from September 1-October 15, 2001, is instructive. A more detailed review of the Beige Book's finding for the 2 Fed Districts most directly affected by the World Trade Center and Pentagon events—New York and Philadelphia (includes Washington, D.C.)—is set out below.

For the Second District—New York—the Beige Book reports:

> Economic conditions in the Second District have weakened since the last report. It is unclear how much of the weakening may be attributed to the material disruptions and aftermath of the September 11 terrorist attack. The disaster's impact was particularly evident in Manhattan real estate, retail trade, and tourism. Many businesses in the District are facing downward price pressures from weakening demand and lower commodity prices. Labor markets have shown signs of deteriorating since the last report. Department stores report that sales fell well below plan during the week of the attack, though they have recovered modestly in each of the past few weeks . . . . [H]ome sales in and around New York City have slowed drastically since the last report, and both apartment prices and rents have fallen by an estimated 10%. In general, contacts note that the high end of the market has been most affected. Contrary to initial post-attack expectations, Manhattan's office market has not tightened—availability rates at the end of September were slightly higher than a month earlier. Hotels, taxi drivers, and Broadway theaters experienced a steep falloff in business in mid-September, but activity has reportedly recovered somewhat in the weeks

since. Finally, bankers again report weaker loan demand, tighter credit standards, and moderately higher delinquency rates in the latest survey, taken in early October.

For the Third District—Philadelphia—the Beige Book reports:

Business activity in the region slowed in mid-September following the attacks in New York and Washington and picked up slowly late in the month and in early October. Manufacturers reported declines in shipments and orders in October compared with September. Retail sales have moved up after being extremely slow in mid-September, but they have been just level compared with a year ago. Auto sales also moved up, but remain below last year's pace. Bank loan volumes rose slightly in September, with gains in business and residential real estate loans, but consumer credit has been flat. Travel and tourism activity remains weak, although it has improved since mid-September . . . . [B]usinesses in the District have mixed views, and all indicate that they face greater uncertainty than usual. Manufacturers forecast increases in orders and shipments during the next 6 months. Retailers, however, expect sales in the remaining months of the year to be even with or to fall below last year's results. Auto dealers also anticipate a slowdown in sales. Commercial bank credit officers expect continued slow growth in commercial and industrial lending, but they are uncertain what course consumer lending will take. They expect residential real estate lending to ease.

In a study by Economy.com on the impact of the attacks on U.S. cities, the company concludes that not a single city of the top 318 metropolitan areas will benefit economically from the terrorist attack.

New York City Area

The human and financial damage inflicted on New York City as a result of the September 11, 2001, terrorist assault on the World Trade Center was significant but incalculable. This is particularly so for the physical pain and mental anguish of the victims, survivors, and their families and friends. Professor Al Parish of Charleston Southern University described the impact of the attacks in terms of destruction as a combination of a natural disaster, like a hurricane, with a Pearl Harbor-like incident.

Estimates on what it will cost to repair infrastructure damage in downtown New York City total $7.4 billion: replacing destroyed subway lines, $3 billion; utility repairs, including 300,000 telephone lines, one phone-switching station, and 36 miles of electrical cable, $2 billion; and rebuilding the Port Authority Trans-Hudson (PATH) New York/New Jersey station below the World Trade Center, $2.4 billion.

New York City Comptroller Alan G. Hevesi estimated in early October 2001 that the attacks caused $34 billion in property damage, including 13 million square feet of Class A office space. At least 22 buildings were destroyed or severely damaged in the catastrophe. Comptroller Hevesi projected cleanup and rescue at $14 billion, and other continuing costs in fiscal 2002 and 2003 at a minimum of $31 billion.

Economy.com predicted that New York City will lose nearly $90 billion in output during the next three years. It may be until the middle of 2003, Economy.com suggested, before growth may reach the pre-September 11, 2001, level of output. Other sources placed the total lost output to the New York City economy from the terrorist incidents at $16.9 billion.

According to a preliminary study by the Fiscal Policy Institute, issued on September 28, 2001, the New York City economy projected that 108,500 jobs, 2.4% of total employment, would be lost within the first month after the terrorist attacks. The output of these workers is $16.853 billion, and their compensation is $6.723 billion. Also, the institute predicted that the greatest job impacts would be in the securities, retail trade, and restaurant sectors. Other workers likely affected, the Institute surmised, include those in the tourism and business travel sectors.

Due to the attacks, over 100,000 workers have been shifted to temporary or permanent offices in midtown Manhattan, Long Island, New Jersey, and elsewhere.

To alleviate the financial costs of the terrorist attacks, in early October 2001, New York Governor George Pataki (Republican) requested the federal government to furnish $54 billion in incentives, tax breaks, and subsidies. Also, New York City sought to raise $1 billion to help pay for its recovery through a sale of one-year notes from the New York City Transitional Finance Authority.

Washington, D.C., Area

The September 11, 2001, terrorist attack on the Pentagon immediately transformed Washington, D.C., into a main target of terrorists. Mayor Anthony A. Williams (Democrat) said in September 2001 that the impact of the attacks and their consequences were significant. The District of Columbia government notified the White House Office of Management and Budget that it expected to lose $200 million in revenue over the next 2 years because of the September 11 attacks; half of it in the next 6 months, as a result of depressed hotel and sales taxes.

Due to the terrorist incidents and expected declines in tourism, the Washington, D.C., area, with its $10 billion in annual revenue in the hospitality services, predicted to lose an estimated $2 billion in revenue during the last few months of 2001. About 12,500 D.C. hotel workers were expected to have lost their jobs by November 2001.

According to the Washington Convention & Tourism Corp., Washington, D.C. lost $10 million a day in travel business because Reagan National Airport remained closed for several weeks. The closure of National was particularly harmful because about 23% of visitors to the city arrived through that airport. The attacks caused the loss of 2,000 jobs in and around the airport and the loss of $330 million in direct economic activity in Virginia. Since the airport's closure, half of Washington, D.C.'s 25,000 hotel employees have lost their jobs. Even with the reopening of the airport in October 2001, an overall drop in travel to the nation's capital was expected.

In mid-November 2001, Gaylord Entertainment Co. of Nashville, Tennessee, disclosed that it was reconsidering whether to proceed with a planned $560 million hotel and conference center in Prince George's County, Maryland, in light of depressed tourism and unfavorable financial markets in the aftermath of the World Trade Center and Pentagon attacks.

In mid-October 2001, Maryland and Virginia officials announced that tax revenue had declined significantly in recent months. They warned that further economic damage caused by the September 11, 2001, attacks would force deep program cuts. Virginia released figures that reflect revenue is down 10% of the pace needed to maintain a balanced budget.

Some analysts, including Professor Stephen Fuller of George Mason University, suggest that in the post-September 11 world, there is some bright news for the Washington, D.C., area. The positive aspects to the Washington, D.C., area stem from the billions of dollars that the Bush administration plans to spend on the war on terrorism, partly for services provided by local defense contractors, security companies, technology companies, and biotechnology firms. Also, as the command center for the battle against terrorists, including the base of the Office of Homeland Security in Washington, D.C., the region's government employees, consultants, lawyers, lobbyists, and financiers will have sufficient work for many years to come. Yet, some may find the potential physical risks of working in Washington, D.C., particularly in the White House or Congress, as too great and may move elsewhere.

Prior to September 11, 2001, the Washington, D.C., region received about $25 billion in federal contracts. This figure should significantly rise with greater financial resources dedicated to reducing the risks of terrorism. George Mason's Fuller argued that the federal government's contribution to the Washington, D.C., area economy—about 32% of gross regional product (GRP) in 2000—should actually alleviate drains on the region because government and other outlays related to the war on terrorism will reach $5 billion.

In Northern Virginia, a high concentration of defense and information technology firms foresee further federal spending benefiting their bottom line. Among companies that may benefit is CACI International Inc. of Arlington, Virginia, an information technology firm working with the Defense Department. CACI, which projects revenues of $563.8 million in 2001, saw its stock catapult from $9 a share on September 17, 2001, to a high of $70.98 on November 7, 2001. Anteon Corporation, which assisted the Federal Emergency Management Agency (FEMA) in building a new computer system for processing disaster information, should benefit from this trend. In Montgomery County, Maryland, there are various defense contractors, biotechnology firms, and pharmaceutical companies that could gain revenue as a result of the war on terrorism.

Professor Fuller predicted that 79,000 jobs may be added in Washington, D.C., in 2002. He suggested that while more than 20,000 tourism industry workers may have lost their jobs, the buildup in defense- and security-oriented work will more than offset those job losses. Mark Vinter of First Union Corp. argued that tourism layoffs will outnumber the job gains in the anti-terrorism effort. In Maryland, unemployment applications increased 21% in the three weeks after the incidents, and unemployment rose to 4% in September 2001, from 3.9% in August 2001.

To conclude on a positive note, in late October 2001, the Washington, D.C.-Baltimore, Maryland, bid to host the 2012 Summer Olympics proceeded to the second round of U.S. candidate applicants (the others cities are New York; San Francisco, California; and Houston, Texas).

Other Regions

Among areas hard-hit due to the World Trade Center and Pentagon attacks is Las Vegas, Nevada. The city relies very heavily on air travel. Before the September 11, 2001, terrorist attacks, it had the fastest economic growth of any American city. Subsequently, tourism has declined significantly. Cancellations by 78,000 conventioneers in the first few weeks following the attacks resulted in a loss of $78.7 million in anticipated spending, excluding gambling.

Concerns about faltering economic conditions and the specter of terrorism spread throughout North Texas. The region already suffered from a lengthy telecommunications slump that led to 15,000 job losses and 5,000 employee reductions by American Airlines in the Dallas area. At a Harley-Davidson plant in Kansas City, Missouri, 300 people were added to the workforce in October 2001. At the same time, however, Sprint Corp. eliminated 3,000 jobs in the Kansas City area.

The tourism sector in Louisiana, which employs 120,000 people of whom 65,000 are in New Orleans, suffered from fewer visitors than at pre-attack levels. Initial losses in New Orleans' French Quarter run to $37 million.

Seattle is suffering from the prospect of nearly 20,000 Boeing layoffs in the area. Such costs could trigger an additional 34,000 jobs lost from Boeing suppliers, subcontractors, and others. Workers at the Port of Seattle are apprehensive about the future, as the September 11, 2001, attacks have exacerbated the downturn in port activities. Also, the technology slump, including the dot-com meltdown, further aggravated Seattle's economy.

In Cincinnati, Ohio, the home of Procter & Gamble and Delta Air Lines' second biggest hub, the September 11, 2001, terrorist incidents negatively impacted the city's travel and hospitality industry, resulting in 1,500 job losses. The terrorist incidents also delayed the opening of additional Cincinnati-area locations by Fidelity Investments and DHL Worldwide Express.

V   International Impact

The timing of the disaster struck at the worst possible time of the business cycle as the United States, Europe, and Japan were falling into concurrent slumps. According to Horst Kohler, the managing director of the International Monetary Fund (IMF), prior to the September 11, 2001, attacks, "The global situation was weak, with a synchronized downturn across all major regions."

Examples of the worldwide economic downturn prior to the attacks on the World Trade Center and Pentagon included: Japan's Nikkei stock index declined, as Japanese companies slashed jobs and wages; East Asian exports fell (the Philippines had its worst export figures in 21 years during August 2001) and foreign direct investment in East Asia waned; economic hardship worsened throughout Latin America, particularly in Mexico, Brazil, and Argentina; European companies slashed jobs (Ireland lost 10,000 technology jobs, and France's Alcatel cut 20,000 jobs), delayed mergers and acquisitions, and closed business units; and developing countries suffered from low commodity prices (e.g., coffee and cocoa) and weak demand.

According to the Organization for Economic Cooperation and Development (OECD), a group of 30 advanced industrialized countries, the terrorist attacks caused "a severe shock to the world economy." As a result, the OECD reduced its projection for economic growth among its members by one half for 2001, from 2% to 1%.

Likewise, some economists reduced their 2002 growth forecasts worldwide by several percentage points, projecting multi-billion dollar losses of economic output. World Bank chief economist Nicholas Stern predicted that the terrorist incidents would harm international trade and investment and, ultimately, reduce growth rates of developing countries by approximately 1%. Credit Suisse First Boston projected that economic growth worldwide would decline an average of 1.5% in both 2001 and 2002, the worst 2-year totals in over 50 years.

In late October 2001, the World Trade Organization (WTO) projected that during 2001, world trade would grow by 1%-2%, significantly less than the 7% growth forecast by the institution in May 2001. During 2000 world trade increased by 12%.

ABN Amro reduced its forecasts for economic growth for most Asian nations during 2002 by 2%-4%. According to different reports, other than the economies of India and China, no Asian country's economy is expected to grow more than 3% in 2001. Merrill Lynch reduced its projection for growth in Asia (excluding China and India) to less than 1% in 2001 and about 4% in 2002, compared with the forecast of 1.6% and 4.5%, respectively, before the terrorist incidents. The United Nations (UN) predicted that the terrorist attacks would slice 2.4% from Asia's GDP (excluding Japan and China) in 2001, the equivalent of approximately $50 billion in lost economic activity.

The Bank of Japan warned that prolonged declines in U.S. private consumption would further adversely affect the Japanese economy. In September 2001, unemployment in Japan rose to 5.3%, the highest level since World

War II. The Japanese government pressured Japanese banks to write off about $500 billion in non-performing loans.

Taiwan reported that its exports declined 43% in September 2001. During the third quarter of 2001, Taiwanese exports were 4.2% lower than during the third quarter of 2000. Korean exports of semiconductors dropped by 63% in September 2001. Also, during the third quarter of 2001, Singapore experienced a 5.6% decline in growth, the weakest quarterly performance in over 30 years.

The economic ramifications of the September 11, 2001, terrorist attacks on Europe were multi-fold. After the terrorist incidents, some European companies cancelled or delayed investments, eliminated business units, revised business plans, cut employees, and sought additional funding to stay solvent. In October 2001, HypoVereinsbank announced that 9,000 jobs would be eliminated during 2002. The German insurance conglomerate announced that terrorist-related claims would reach $1.3 billion.

With Europe's economy already weak since spring 2001, the attacks could lead the continent into a recession. Some economists have significantly reduced their forecast for Euro-zone GDP growth in 2002 to 1.1%. Robert Lind of ABN Amro said that economic activity across Europe would decline during fall 2001. Meanwhile, the European Central Bank projected an economic recovery in the Euro zone sometime in 2002.

Indications of sluggishness in European investment include Finnish and Italian stock market results which declined by 46.37% and 29.76%, respectively, during the first 10 months of 2001. Also, European consumer confidence has significantly waned. For example, in September 2001, the German business sentiment Info index dropped to near a 28-year low of 85. Negative perspectives are due, in part, to Germany's growing unemployment numbers, which reached 3.9 million, or 9.5%, in October 2001. During the second quarter of 2001, economic growth in Germany was flat. The German growth rate is expected to decline slightly during the third and fourth quarters of 2001.

Canada, the largest trading partner of the United States, underwent a difficult autumn 2001 in economic terms. For instance, in October 2001, the Canadian dollar reached a low against the U.S. currency, plunging to 63.34 U.S. cents. Also, Canadian employers undertook massive job cuts since the September 11, 2001, attacks, including: Nortel, 20,000; Air Canada, 5,000; Bombadier, 3,800; and Quebecor, 2,400. Delays at U.S.-Canadian border crossings due to heightened security have adversely affected the flow of $1 billion in goods, including critical component parts for the automobile industry, that transverse the border each day.

Mexico's dependence on the U.S. economy—over 80% of Mexico's manufactured goods are exported to the United States and 60% of Mexico's foreign investment originates from the United States—will adversely affect the Aztec nation if the United States suffers a recession. Already, following the attacks, U.S. tourism to Mexico declined by some 50%. U.S.-Mexican trade suffered due to delays along the border. Projections for economic growth in Mexico in 2001 have been cut to under 1%. On the bright side, Mexico, America's fourth biggest supplier of oil, may benefit from additional U.S. consumption if supplies from the Persian Gulf are interrupted.

Across Latin America, there was evidence of the negative economic consequences of the September 11, 2001, terrorist incidents. For example, the vital tourism industry declined in Central America and the Caribbean, placing further strains on foreign reserves and raising unemployment. Transnational companies delayed investments in the Southern Cone mining regions as well as throughout Latin America's industrial and consumer sectors. Indeed, in fall 2001, "Latin America is entering one of the most difficult periods it has faced in many decades," says Enrique Iglesias, president of the Inter-American Development Bank.

Following the attacks, Argentina's three-year plus recession worsened. Some analysts predicted that despite the $8 billion IMF emergency package in August 2001, a default by Argentina of $130 billion in central government debt and $20 billion in provincial government debt seemed almost inevitable. By November 1, 2001, Argentine President Fernando de la Rua requested Argentine and foreign lenders to swap about $100 billion in bonds for lower yielding securities, effectively triggering new debt renegotiation discussions.

Lloyds Bank reduced Brazil's economic growth forecasts for the fourth quarter of 2001 from 2% to zero. Within a week of the September 11, 2001, events, Spain's Telefonica Moviles—citing the negative impact of the attacks—announced that the company would not go forward with its planned $875 million investment in Celular CRT Participacoes, a Brazilian mobile telephone company. Yet, a strengthening of the Brazilian real vis-à-vis the U.S. dollar and an upswing in Sao Paulo's Bovespa in mid-November 2001 portend well for Brazil.

Developing nations, particularly those in sub-Saharan Africa, Alan Gelb and Ian Goldin of the UN predicted, would suffer greatly in the aftermath of the September 11, 2001, events. The economists said that the economy in developing countries during 2002 would decline more than had the attacks not taken place. As a result, up to an additional 3 million people will be forced into poverty and 20,000 African children will die due to the economic downturn engendered from the World Trade Center and Pentagon incidents.

The success of November 2001 at the Doha, Qatar, meeting of the WTO, including commitments to negotiate by January 2005 accords on eliminating agricultural export subsidies as well as other developments, illustrated that international terrorism may undermine, but cannot defeat, international commerce.

Chapter 3

Terrorism and Corporate America:
Impact on Selected Sectors

I   Introduction

The aftermath of the World Trade Center and Pentagon attacks and the danger of a slumping economy led some corporations to reduce costs, fire employees, cancel acquisitions, delay transactions, and postpone investments. Yet, other companies proceeded differently by pursuing opportunities, completing purchases, and, in essence, continuing to hedge their risks by conducting business, even if not, as usual.

This chapter initially analyzes a number of matters that Corporate America has focused on in light of the September 11, 2001, terrorist incidents, anthrax attacks, and their aftermath during fall 2001, including: the conduct of business; a review of corporate earnings results for the third quarter of 2001; future investments; a review of transactions cancelled or delayed; sourcing, inventory, and logistics issues to keep in mind as potential terrorist disruptions to manufacturing and distribution matters are weighed; security and risk; and corporate debt and bankruptcies.

Subsequently, the chapter discusses the effect the fall 2001 terrorist attacks had on a number of specific industries. Some sectors were negatively affected, others less so. Among the industries that are examined are: aviation; hotels, conventions, and tourism; insurance; real estate; energy; technology; media and entertainment; transportation; and additional sectors.

II Issues Affecting Corporate America in Post-September II Era

Introduction

Assessing the ramifications of the September 11, 2001, terrorist attacks on corporate earnings is difficult and ultimately somewhat imprecise for industries other than those for which a direct impact is simple to deduce—airlines, tourism, hospitality (hotels, conventions, and restaurants), and insurance. After all, differentiating the fallout of the incidents from the drag on an already declining economy is complex. In addition to the most negatively affected sectors as noted above, industries that probably will be adversely impacted include real estate, energy, technology, media and entertainment, and public and private mail carriers.

Diverse sectors of the economy will be affected, inter alia, by consumer anxiety and business apprehension about the costs of terrorism to individuals, companies, and the nation. The additional costs of fighting terrorism, for both the private and public sectors, will also weigh on the rapidity of the recovery by sectors. Also, heightened distribution and transportation costs connected with increased security, delays, new methodologies for formerly routine office activities (such as in screening and opening mail), and the specter of terrorism will adversely impact most sectors to some degree.

Among the sectors that may exhibit additional levels of business as a direct or indirect result of the military, security, health, and other responses to terrorism that the U.S. government and companies are undertaking include: defense; security equipment, technology, and services; diverse technology products and services; pharmaceuticals and forensics; germ detection and remediation; and business aviation, charter planes, trains, buses; and "survivalist" merchandise. These segments of the economy are also detailed in Chapter 4.

Prior to the September 11, 2001, terrorist incidents, the economy was sluggish, and corporate results were poor. After the terrorist attacks, sharp profit declines were expected for the third quarter of 2001. According to a First Call/Thomson Financial survey of Wall Street analysts, earnings should also drop 23% in the fourth quarter of 2001.

For some corporations, terrorism was a principal cause for the losses during the third quarter of 2001. For others, a weakening economy was the key factor. While for other firms, it was both. A prominent issue was whether some companies will try to include other losses under the September 11, 2001 banner. Tobias Levkovich of Salomon Smith Barney and Sean Ryan of Fulcrum Global Partners suggested that some companies may, indeed, use the terrorist incidents as an excuse for failing to hit their expected numbers.

The September 11, 2001, terrorist attacks could make it simple for business to massage the results they present. In the pronouncements of 150 warnings of earnings shortfalls during the last two weeks of September 2001, nearly two-thirds pointed to the attacks as a factor in the decline, according to First Call/Thomson Financial.

The negative ramifications to the economy may not be limited to the third quarter of 2001. However, many companies took their largest earnings reduction in that quarter. The main impact of the attacks could be on declining revenue during the fourth quarter of 2001.

In order to make 2002 results appear better than expected, businesses may load losses into 2001 by:

- Reducing values on physical assets, which will lessen depreciation charges in the future

- Exaggerating troubled debts and subsequently raisingprofits when debtors pay their obligations

- Charging approaching restructuring costs immediately

- Postponing deals so that they are consummated in later quarters and reflected in 2002 revenues

The likelihood of such expansive accounting is greater now than it was before the October 2001 ruling of the Emerging Issues Task Force of the Financial Accounting Standards Board (FASB) that no expenses stemming from the September 11, 2001, attacks should be listed separately. The FASB's rationale was that the terrorist events were so extraordinary that they were pervasive and financially impacted almost every company. Thus, trying to draw a line between those expenses that could be labeled extraordinary and others that could not be so labeled would be impractical and not helpful to investors, suggested David Zion of Bear Stearns.

Corporate Earnings Results for the Third Quarter of 2001

According to *Business Week* and S&P's Compustat, corporate earnings for the third quarter of 2001 were the worst in 25 years. The 900 entities followed by *Business Week* suffered an average 55% decline in earnings as compared to the third quarter of 2000. Compustat reported that some of the hardest-hit sectors were: technology (semiconductors, telecommunications, electronics, computers, and peripherals), airlines, automotive, media, and steel. Among companies that lost the most money during the third quarter of 2001 were: Lucent Technologies ($7.3 billion), Agere Systems ($3.3 billion), AT&T ($2.2 billion), Motorola ($1.4 billion), and UAL/American Airlines ($1.1 billion). The decline in the airline sector was partly due to effects of the September 11 attacks.

Moreover, the 5 industries with the largest decline in market value (based on companies in the S&P 500 index) between September 10, 2001, and October 5, 2001, were: semiconductor equipment (-22.3%), metal mining (-21%), photo/imaging (-20.6%), lodging/hotels (-19.2%), and airlines (-18.4%). U.S. Airways Group had the fourth largest percentage drop of stocks on the New York Stock Exchange (NYSE) during the third quarter of 2001 (preferred shares and securities that began the quarter at less than $5 a share are excluded). U.S. Airways Group declined $19.65, from $24.30 on June 29, 2001, to $4.65 on September 28, 2001, a decline of 80.7%.

On the bright side, Compustat reported that third quarter profits for 2001 in a number of industries were above figures for the third quarter of 2000: drug distribution (up 109%), savings and loans (rose 64%), construction and real estate (increased 60%), petroleum services (accelerated 54%), and aerospace and defense (up 53%).

Among companies that made the most money during the third quarter of 2001 were: General Electric ($3.2 billion), ExxonMobil ($3.2 billion), Citigroup ($3.2 billion), Philip Morris ($2.3 billion), and Pfizer ($2.1 billion).

The leading 5 industries that gained the most market value (based on companies in the S&P's 500 Index) between September 10, 2001, and October 5, 2001, were electronic defense (40.7%), greeting cards (19.5%), insurance brokers (18.1%), cellular services (15%), and gold (11%). Directly, or tangentially, these sectors were impacted by the September 11 incidents.

Future Investments

Shortly following the World Trade Center and Pentagon attacks, various companies announced that they would put on hold their previously planned investments. Manpower Inc., the nation's largest supplier of temporary workers, canceled plans to open 40 new offices. Eastman Chemical, a leading supplier of material for plastics and paint, announced that new investments would be postponed. C.R. England Inc., a family-owned trucking company with 2,500 tractor-trailers, stated that the attacks would discourage the firm from making further investments in the immediate future. Park Place Entertainment Corp. delayed construction of an additional $450 million hotel tower at its Caesar Palace location in Las Vegas, Nevada.

The economic downturn that hit the nation in 2000 was spurred primarily by reductions in business investment, not consumer spending, some economists suggested. Currently, by waiting or avoiding additional investment, thousands of companies appear to be pushing the economy further downward. Nariman Behravesh of DRI-WEFA, stated that in all sectors, executives are too uncertain about the future to undertake new investments. During fall 2001 and beyond, whether management will delay investments will depend, in part, on U.S. military successes in Afghanistan, potential additional terrorist attacks at home, consumer confidence, economic stagnation, availability of capital, and stock market performance.

Further investment may be delayed because presently corporate spending on equipment and buildings still far exceeds the amount of cash that companies are generating internally. Through the second quarter of 2001, the financing gap, the difference between capital spending and internal company funds, was running at an annual rate of $251 billion. A large financing gap means that companies have to borrow heavily to support investment.

Businesses that pursued deals and investments during September-November 2001, in the aftermath of the twenty-first century's "Day of Infamy," included:

- The discount retailer Wal-Mart Stores announced intentions to spend $10 billion during 2002 for additional stores.

- The drugstore retailer Walgreen disclosed plans to invest nearly $1.3 billion on 475 stores and activities in 2002.

- The financial services institution Deutsche Bank agreed to buy Zurich Scudder Investments, a money management firm, for $2.5 billion in cash and assets.

- The technology company VeriSign Inc. announced it would merge with Illuminet Holdings, a telecommunications services firm, in a deal valued at $1.2 billion.

- The municipal bond retailer, Lebenthal & Company, was acquired by MONY Group in a deal valued at about $25 million.

- Oil and gas giants Phillips Petroleum Co. and Conoco Inc. agreed to a merger with $35 billion market value, 58,000 employees, and $53 billion in sales.

Given Imaging Ltd., a medical-imaging company, had an initial public offering (IPO) on the Nasdaq with trading up 3.9% above its $12 offering price, to $12.47 on the first day of trading, October 4, 2001. Other companies that had IPOs in October 2001 included TheraSense Inc., a diabetes-monitoring company, and Principal Financial Group, an investment and insurance company. During November 2001, the number of IPOs rose significantly, with companies such as Weight Watchers International, DJ Orthopedics, and BAM Entertainment offering their shares on public markets. It is projected that 24 companies will issue IPOs in December 2001.

Transactions Cancelled or Delayed

The September 11, 2001, terrorist incidents caused some companies to reconsider the appropriateness or timing of certain investments and transactions. Less than a week after the attacks, Berkshire Hathaway apparently cited a clause in a contract enabling termination of the agreement in the event of "war or armed conflict." More specifically, it was reported that Berkshire Hathaway rescinded its offer to purchase up to $500 million of Finova Group's 7.5% senior-secured notes. A number of airlines contacted Boeing Co. to request delaying the delivery of several dozen airplanes, valued in total at several billion dollars.

Some contracts have clauses enabling a party to walk away from a transaction in case of material adverse change, force majeure, or impossibility of performance. Yet courts tend not to reward a party that does not want to proceed with a contract because its performance has become more difficult or would be unprofitable. Likewise, some courts have also ruled that act-of-war clauses do not apply where risk can be anticipated when the agreement was signed.

The attacks also derailed very advanced merger negotiations between Keefe, Bruyette & Woods and BNP Paribas in a deal expected to be worth between $300 million to $400 million. It was reported that the parties may resume discussions in the future. Keefe, Bruyette lost 67 of 224 employees during the World Trade Center attacks. Also, the attacks apparently interfered with initial merger discussions between the investment firms of Lehman Brothers Holdings Inc. and Lazard LLC.

Hewlett-Packard's acquisition of Compaq Computer, General Motor's negotiation relating to its possible sale of Hughes Electronics, the possible spin-off of AT&T's cable business, and the merger of Land O'Lakes Inc. and Purina Mills Inc. were delayed due to the terrorist events.

In light of the World Trade Center and Pentagon attacks, a number of companies delayed the launch of products, including: Gillette Co.'s new line of children's toothbrushes; GloxoSmithKline's drug Paxil; and the films "Big Trouble" and "Collateral Damage."

According to a Duke University/Financial/Executives International mid-October 2001 survey of nearly 700 chief financial officers, 26% said they would postpone investments because of the September 11 attacks, 71% responded it would not affect planned spending, and 3% stated that the incidents would spur additional capital spending.

Sourcing, Inventory, and Logistics

Disruptions to distribution systems immediately following the World Trade Center and Pentagon incidents caused a number of companies to re-examine just-in-time inventory techniques (which involves delivery of parts to the assembly line only when they are needed). Still, the use of international and multiple domestic sources for manufacturing and the prevalence of just-in-time practices will make it arduous to modify these currently ingrained elements of production.

In responding to such potential threats, a number of corporations are increasing inventories and building additional storage facilities. While raising the levels of inventories may force increased costs in such outlays, they may, concurrently, buffer firms by allowing for ample supplies of key components even in case of a major terrorist attack.

According to Joseph Martha and Sunil Subbakrisha of Mercer Management Consultants, manufacturers, retailers, and suppliers will be well advised to take into consideration a few strategies regarding sourcing, inventory, and logistics issues, such as:

- Inventory Management. Manufacturers will need to carry more buffer inventory in order to hedge against supply and production-line disruptions.

- Sourcing. Manufacturers should be more selective about where their critical parts are coming from. A sourcing strategy will have to vary by location.

- Transportation. Manufacturers and retailers should consider broadening their shipping arrangements.

It is noteworthy that increased security in transportation systems, particularly in shipping and trucking, is causing: higher costs; interference with tight production schedules as supplies are not delivered as expected; closing or decreasing production routes; and accelerating delays. Since the September 11, 2001, attacks, trucks are subject to greater scrutiny by national, state, and local law enforcement officials. Also, truckers' licenses and transportation manifests are examined more closely. Bridges, tunnels, and highway toll facilities are under expanded surveillance.

Federal Aviation Administration (FAA) aviation restrictions instituted following the World Trade Center and Pentagon attacks affected various companies. FedEx Corp., which handles nearly 3.3 million packages daily, had its air operations grounded in the United States for more than two days. To respond to this interruption in its normal business practices, FedEx rented additional trucks to transport some packages. In addition, the anthrax attacks significantly impeded the U.S. Postal Service to deliver mail to specific regions during fall 2001.

Risk

The ramifications of September 11 include heightened risk with regard to physical and economic matters. For instance, the cost of reducing risks at offices and businesses through adding new security guards, purchasing surveillance equipment, acquiring metal and bomb detection equipment, buying detectors of chemical and biological agents, acquiring machines that can irradiate mail, and training security and office employees will affect competition and profitability. Industries and companies that fail to respond to terrorist risks may save capital by not purchasing anti-terrorism products and services, but they will also run a higher risk of human and financial costs if an incident does occur.

Companies that do not undertake security measures and adopt emergency preparedness procedures may lose customers. Clients may avoid doing business with companies that have sub-par, or worse, nonexistent, security measures. Firms that invest in security products and services, such as airlines that fortify cockpit doors before their competitors do, or shopping malls that place security officers at all entrances, may tout these measures to current and prospective clients. Some consumers may view additional security as a sign that a particular location, such as shopping malls, is a potential terrorist target.

The unpredictability of terrorist attacks and their negative consequences in physical, psychological, and financial terms may also raise the price of risk. According to Professor Howard Kunreuther of the University of Pennsylvania, manifestations of terrorist activities, such as those of September 11, 2001, will force executives to increasingly weigh untraditional hazards and political violence in their business and risk calculations. Such deliberations, Middlebury College's David Collander and others explained, will be complex because incidents of terrorism have generally not been heretofore analyzed by U.S. executives when considering domestic transactions. In turn, the scope of uncertainties will make decision-making difficult for executives and investors, Alan Ackerman of Fahnestock & Company stated. Ross Perot Jr., president and chief executive officer (CEO) of Perot Systems Corp., observed that terrorism is a risk that businesses will have to weigh.

Yet, U.S. companies often do weigh political risk issues—terrorism, expropriation, inconvertibility of currency, and contracts with a government entity—when conducting business overseas, particularly in emerging markets. Some entities purchase political risk insurance from private companies, national entities (e.g., Overseas Private Investment Corporation), or international organizations (e.g., Multilateral Investment Guarantee Agency). The specter of terrorism may even cause selected foreign investors to consider the risk of terrorism when calculating whether to undertake an investment in the United States. The future will show whether companies will find it necessary and financially feasible to obtain political risk insurance.

Analogously, the insurance industry, hit with potentially $80 billion in property, casualty, and other claims as a result of September 11, may altogether not offer terrorism coverage in the United States. Alternatively, insurance companies may cap potential damages and set premiums at exorbitant levels to lessen the formidable risks associated with insuring terrorist events.

In addition, the risk premium attached to business transactions involving high levels of uncertainty could rise as a result of terrorism, explained Professor Allan Meltzer of Carnegie Mellon University. The risks and costs related to the growing threat of terrorism are exemplified by steps that corporations and organizations are taking to counter these challenges.

The NYSE will likely establish a second trading floor on a different power and communications grid than on the exchange's main floor. Other contingency plans might include shifting trading to other stock exchanges in the United States or abroad. The threats to physical facilities such as stock exchange floors may lead to greater use of electronic markets and greater reliance on technology than was the case before the attacks—perhaps based in more fortified and remote locations.

Oppenheimer Funds, whose 598 employees at Two World Trade Center survived, had its computers backed up every evening at a remote location, a Denver, Colorado, office. Due to New Jersey-based backup measures, Dow Jones—based at One World Financial Center (all of its 800 employees there survived)—had its web sites, e-mail, and news wire services functioning even in the aftermath of the attacks. Two World Trade Center-based Aon Corp. suffered no data losses due to backup systems. Tragically, about 175 Aon employees were killed during the attacks.

In light of the damage inflicted during the September 11, 2001, terrorist attacks, previously hesitant companies are investing in expensive backup sites, data storage software and services, and emergency/contingency planning. A number of banks and securities firms adopted some, or all, of these measures following the bombings of the World Trade Center in 1993. Thus, damage caused by the September 2001 attacks was not less pervasive in some respects due to the existence of data storage capabilities.

To maintain several locations at once can raise costs for business if they are unoccupied or not sublet other than in emergency situations. If employees are dispersed in the name of reduced centrality, with little damage resulting if one of several sites is attacked, there exists a downside—though minor—of reduced company cohesion. After all, daily human contact among peers tends to nurture cooperation among workers that videoconferences, e-mail, and other technological advances cannot completely replicate.

Instead of establishing duplicate, fully functional sites for use in case of a disaster, some entities request key personnel to regularly bring key computer diskettes and data home for safekeeping. In the future, it would be wise for businesses to spend greater attention and funds on data storage, backup sites, contingency planning, and security software in light of the devastating consequences of catastrophic terrorist attacks.

Another measure that companies may utilize in order to reduce possible attacks against office buildings is the adoption of multiple electronic means to conduct business: online payments, web sites, participation in electronic business-to-business exchanges (B2B), online sourcing and procurement, electronic data interchange (EDI), and in the financial world, electronic trading markets. Unfortunately, cyber terrorism and non-political cyber attacks are possible threats to electronic business (E-Business).

Security

Some have likened investments on security measures to funds allocated to reducing pollution in that they are both socially helpful but economically unproductive. Such a perspective seems to neglect the often-quoted adage—penny rich, pound foolish. After all, improved aviation security at U.S. airports, coupled with better intelligence and law enforcement capabilities on September 11, 2001, probably would have prevented some—if not all—of the nineteen hijackers from boarding the four aircrafts that fateful day. Instead, and ignoring the advantage of hindsight, inadequate security at the three airports—Dulles, Newark, and Logan—enabled the perpetrators access to the planes with their subsequent horrific impact: over 3,300 deaths, billions of dollars of property damage, significant declines in financial markets, and the negative impact on various industry sectors, including airlines, insurance, tourism, and hospitality.

According to Cushman and Wakefield Inc., the real estate firm, about 50% of multi-tenant commercial buildings will invest in better security, such as: using computerized access control systems, video surveillance systems, bomb-detection devices, and x-ray equipment.

Boeing Co.'s improved security measures include: establishing barriers on roads leading to unfenced buildings and forbidding workers from wearing or using company logos while traveling overseas. Some companies, such as Eastman Kodak, have the rationale that the improved security measures are best not discussed as any developments may be countered by potential perpetrators.

An example of the sensitivity of security issues in the aftermath of the attacks was the decision by Hewlett-Packard to have its San Francisco and Los Angeles employees remain at home on the day of the incidents—two scheduled destination points of the hijacked planes.

The American Chemistry Council, the industry association for over 180 chemical companies, is cognizant of the potential threats to the chemical sector. After all, toxic and volatile chemicals could kill thousands during an explosion or fire at a manufacturing plant or storage facility. With this in mind, chemical companies have accelerated vigilance against possible attacks by: maintaining readily accessible hazardous materials teams, fortifying plants and storage facilities, raising the training and skills of security officers, and acquiring additional vapor suppression machines.

The Washington, D.C., area's metro and bus system is undertaking a variety of anti-terrorism measures, including: improving security at bus garages and rail yards; increasing the number of police officers patrolling stations, trains, and buses; and installing additional equipment.

Interaction with Law Enforcement, Investigative Authorities, and Other Government Entities

In the wake of the September 11, 2001, terrorist incidents, coupled with the anthrax attacks in fall 2001, it is expected that there will be greater exchanges between industry, on the one hand, and law enforcement and investigative authorities, on the other, in terms of security measures as well as suspected terrorist investigative matters.

Given the increased attention that the Fed, Treasury Department, U.S. Customs Service, Securities and Exchange Commission (SEC), Commodity Futures Trading Commission, Federal Bureau of Investigation (FBI), and Central Intelligence Agency (CIA) will pay to the funding sources of terrorists, businesses in all sectors, particularly financial institutions and securities firms, will likely face greater scrutiny of their activities. This in turn may require heightened diligence in investigating domestic and international clients and partners to ensure that entities with whom one conducts business with are not fronts for domestic or international terrorists. Although such investigative activities may likely prove time-consuming and costly, they may become prudent practice for firms that want to keep a clean bill of health— and potentially avoid government sanctions at the same time.

Companies may face accelerated contact with law enforcement and investigative officials regarding possible illegal activities of clients, such as customers at banks. Under such circumstances, the American Banking Association instructs, it is imperative that banks receive valid legal documents— subpoena, search warrant, or summons—prior to releasing any confidential information. With the added investigative capabilities that law enforcement acquired as a result of the enactment of an October 2001 anti-terrorism law, there is a likelihood that further interaction between the government and business will arise.

Because terrorists are expanding the use of electronic communications— cell phones, pagers, e-mail, Voice-Over-Internet-Protocol (VOIP), and instant messaging—it is probable that Internet Service Providers (ISPs) and telephone companies will witness a rise in inquiries from investigative authorities. Furthermore, the FBI may require ISPs to collaborate and permit the agency to install monitoring software such as DCS1000 (previously known as Carnivore) to trace suspected terrorists' Internet activities.

Furthermore, there is heightened emphasis by industry to exchange information with government entities, including law enforcement, health, safety, and emergency preparedness officials. This improved collaboration can be seen as the government consults with: the defense industry to craft superior weapons; the telecommunications sector to build better communications equipment; the software and hardware sectors to craft improved cyber security capabilities; the pharmaceuticals industry to develop drugs and vaccines aimed at defending against biological agents; and germ-detection companies and bomb detection manufacturers to provide products that can spot the presence of pathogens and bombs, respectively.

Corporate Debt and Bankruptcies

The higher levels of corporate debt and registered bankruptcies since 2000 will marginally be aggravated in the short term. Corporate debt (indebtedness as a percentage of net worth) has escalated from 73% in 1995 to 77% in 2000.

During the first seven months of 2001, the level of corporate debt in default was almost twice the whole amount of corporate debt in default in 2000. Excessive corporate debt in 2001 is no longer limited to telecommunications companies; it is harming technology, retail, lodging, leisure, and transportation companies. In addition, syndicated bank loans that are likely to be in default rose to 5.72% during the second quarter of 2001, an increase over the 3.25% figure during 2000.

Less than four weeks after the September 11, 2001, terrorist incidents, Standard & Poor's downgraded $162 billion in debt issued by 45 corporations while it upgraded $44 million in debt issued by only 9 firms. As a result, yields on corporate bonds, particularly junk bonds, have risen dramatically while bond prices have fallen sharply.

In 2000, 176 public companies filed for Chapter 11 bankruptcy protection with total pre-petition assets valued at $94 billion. From January-September 2001, companies with $163 billion of total pre-petition assets requested bankruptcy court protection. As a result of the September 11, 2001, terrorist events, coupled with increased layoffs, loan defaults, cash crunches, and worsening economic indicators, business failures are expected to accelerate. Chapter 11 bankruptcy provisions enable companies to continue to operate while in bankruptcy; Chapter 7 results in the liquidation of company assets.

In fall 2001, Renaissance Cruises of Fort Lauderdale, Florida, and Aladdin Gaming LLC, a Las Vegas, Nevada, hotel casino, two large companies in the tourism and hotel industries, filed for Chapter 11 bankruptcy. Also, in October 2001, Polaroid Corporation, which invented instant photography but could not adjust to the digital era, filed for Chapter 11 bankruptcy. Another one-time market leader, Bethlehem Steel, filed for Chapter 11 bankruptcy protection in October 2001 due to increased foreign competition, high pension and health care costs, and massive market declines.

During November 2001, Burlington Industries Inc., a leading textile company; ANC Rental Corp., owner of Alamo and National rental cars; and Net2000 Communications Inc., a telecommunications firm, filed for Chapter 11 bankruptcy. As with the other companies that filed for bankruptcy, the role of the September 11 attacks in the ultimate decline of the companies is fairly tenuous. At best, the business climate in the aftermath of the attacks aggravated an already poor situation. As Net2000 chairman and CEO Charlie Thomas explained, the terrorist incidents further dissuaded investors to pursue participation in companies already facing a credit crunch. In the case of ANC Rental, with declining airport travel in fall 2001, rental car demand was down as well.

III Aviation

Overview of U.S. Airlines

Prior to September 11, 2001, many airlines were already facing financial difficulties. The fallout from the attacks caused U.S. airline carriers to suffer the sharpest decline in 30 years. In September 2001, the number of miles flown by paying passengers dropped by about 35% and passenger traffic dropped 25% from September 2000 levels.

According to Deutsche Bank Alex Brown, the decline in traffic at major airports during September 2001 was significant: -33.7% for American Airlines, -33.4% for US Airways, -32.7% for Delta Air Lines, -31.5% for United Airlines, -31% for Continental Airlines, -30.7% for Northwest Airlines, -21.6% for Southwest Airlines, -21% for America West, and -18.7% for Alaska Air.

Due to declining air travel following the four hijackings of two American Airlines and two United Airlines flights on September 11, 2001, Delta Air Lines announced in late September 2001 that it was laying off 13,000 employees. Also, the company disclosed that it was cutting 15% of its schedule, effective November 1, 2001.

Most of the other major airlines announced a 20% cut in operations. Northwest Airlines originally announced that it would lay off 2,800 flight attendants, but eventually 2,500 Northwest attendants chose to take voluntary furloughs. In September 2001, US Airways announced it would close reservation centers in Indianapolis, Dayton, Syracuse, and San Diego.

Airline and union officials announced in late September 2001, that the number of layoffs in the airline industry were under 100,000, largely because thousands of employees took voluntary furloughs. In addition, encouraged by some new incentives, more than 1,000 airline workers took early retirement. Hundreds of pilots plan to go temporarily into the Air National Guard or the Air Force Reserve.

The gravity of the downturn facing the airline sector was brought to prominence on October 18, 2001, when United Airlines Chairman James Goodwin wrote to the air carrier's 100,000 workers, "In the wake of the horrific events [of September 11, 2001] we are in nothing less than a fight for our life," as the airline was losing $20 million a day. News of Goodwin's letter severely hurt United Airlines' stock price, which fell 9.6% to $16.85 on October 17, 2001. Shortly afterwards, Goodwin was replaced as chairman of United Airlines.

Like other regional airlines, Atlantic Coast Airlines, based at Dulles International Airport in the Washington, D.C., area, fared better than larger carriers. While large airlines such as United Airlines need planes to be about 80% full to turn a profit, commuter airlines require an average of only about 50%. Nevertheless, Atlantic experienced a decline in passengers in September 2001 to 45.7% capacity from 57.2% in September 2000. Still, by early October 2001, Atlantic's passenger loads rose to 51% capacity.

To deal with new government and other requirements necessitated by the September 11 terrorist attacks, airline executives are increasing security, retraining workers to distinguish between fake and legitimate identifications, and searching suitcases. Airlines must also enforce more stringent rules, such as the carry-on limit of one suitcase and one small bag. Due to heightened security, airline passengers will likely spend significantly more time at airport check-ins and gates than they did before the current terrorist crisis. Airlines, in turn, have become more accommodating to passengers than they used to be. For example, some provide free coffee and newspapers in the airline terminals before flights.

To attract travelers, a number of airlines announced in October 2001 free round-trip tickets, while other slashed fares by as much as 50% or offered to double the frequent-flier miles awarded. For example, Delta Air Lines said that it would give away 10,000 round-trip tickets to New York City from fall 2001 through spring 2002. Meanwhile, United Airlines slashed its unrestricted business fares by 25%-50% for flights through December 31, 2001. American Airlines said it is offering double miles for frequent fliers through November 15, 2001.

The crash of American Airlines Flight 587 in the borough of Queens in New York City on November 12, 2001—apparently due to a mechanical failure—did little to help the already weak airline industry. The General Accounting Office (GAO) estimates that the airlines could lose $6.5 billion to $10.5 billion by December 31, 2001, due to the attacks. Given the difficulties facing the industry, it is foreseeable that a number of airlines may file for bankruptcy protection, cease operations completely, or merge. An in-depth discussion of the aviation stablization law, aviation insurance proposals, and aviation security measures appears in Chapter 6.

Foreign Airlines

Not only have U.S. airlines suffered dramatically from the aftermath of the September 11, 2001, terrorist incidents, but the financial ramifications have been particularly severe for international carriers as well. As a result, at foreign airlines unprofitable routes were cancelled, planes were grounded, and jobs were cut. Airlines worldwide are projected to lose between $7 billion and $11 billion in 2001.

At Air Canada, reservations declined by 30% and plane occupancy fell by 50% several weeks following the September 11, 2001, terrorist attacks. This decline led to 5,000 job cuts, the grounding of 84 aircraft, and the reduction of flight schedules by 20%. In late October 2001, the Canadian government provided $45 million to Air Canada to compensate the carrier for losses sustained in the aftermath of the September 11 incidents. In mid-November 2001, the second largest Canadian airline, Canada 3000, filed for bankruptcy and eliminated 4,800 jobs.

Varig, the national airline of Brazil, announced layoffs of 1,700 employees. The Mexican state-owned airline operator, Aeromexico, plans to fire employees and abate flights by up to one fifth.

The Japan Travel Bureau announced that 78,600 flights from Japan to the United States during September-October 2001 were cancelled. Japan Air Lines, which earns about 40% of its revenue on trans-Pacific flights, expects to lose $150 million from canceled flights in September and October 2001.

In mid-November 2001, Japan Airlines and Japan Air System, announced that they will form a holding company next year, with full consolidation of operations expected in 2004. All Nippon Airways lost 30% of its international traffic volume in the last 3 weeks of September 2001.

Elsewhere in Asia, Korean Airlines reduced its number of flights, grounded planes, and lowered its projected employee hires. The Korean government provided $191 million to Korean Air and another national airline, Asiana Airlines, as well as $11 million in tax exemptions in 2002 in order to soothe the $400 million in losses the airlines suffered in the aftermath of the September 11 incidents. Ansett Australia, which is owned by Air New Zealand, filed for bankruptcy in September 2001. The New Zealand carrier is seeking a $350 million rescue package from public and private shareholders.

In Europe, Swissair received $281 million from the Swiss government to pay past-due bills, airport fees, and other costs prior to its merger with Crossair. Also, Swissair will reduce 25% of long-range flights and 3,000 catering jobs. UBS and Credit Suisse provided $812 million to Swissair primarily to aid the airline in acquiring a 70% stake in Crossair.

In October 2001, British Airways and Virgin Atlantic announced plans to reduce routes, ground planes, and fire 7,000 and 1,200 workers, respectively. Likewise, Aer Lingus announced plans to eliminate 2,500 workers and obtain a loan from the Irish government to aid the airline. Air France will decrease its flights to the United States by one fifth in winter 2001. Alitalia, the Italian carrier, announced it would ground some planes, suspend flights, and reduce its staff by 2,500 positions.

The German airline Lufthansa announced it would reduce the number of flights to North America. These fewer flights will result in grounding 28 airplanes and decreasing seating capacity by 20%. Also, Lufthansa will impose a surcharge of $16 on round-trip tickets in order to pay for tighter security and costlier insurance. Scandinavian Airlines System announced it would cut up to 1,100 jobs and decrease capacity by 12%.

In early October 2001, Sabena filed for protection from creditors and obtained a $115 million bridge loan from the Belgian government. By early November 2001, Sabena ceased operations.

On October 10, 2001, the European Commission (EC) agreed to permit EC member states to aid European airlines, such as Sabena, to recover from the September 11, 2001, terrorist events. The EC's Transportation Commissioner, Loyola de Palacio, explained that airlines could be compensated for losses arising from the cancellation of flights to and from the United States during the four days after the terrorist incidents. Also, Palacio said that airlines would receive assistance for costs related to heightened security measures and rising insurance premiums. However, the EC refused to allow government support for losses that predated the incidents.

Airports

Most commercial airports are experiencing severe revenue declines due to reduced flights and fewer passengers following the September 11, 2001, terrorist incidents. Reduced traffic, in terms of planes and passengers, have abated aircraft landing fees and resulted in declining income from parking-lot operators, airport stores and restaurants, and car rental and ground transportation concessions.

In the first two weeks following the attacks, sales at airport shops and food eateries dropped by nearly 40%. For their part, airports are adverse to allowing tenants, such as retailers and restaurants hit hard by the downturn in travel, to postpone rent payments. The Airports Council International (ACI) predicted that due to the terrorist incidents, U.S. airports may lose $3 billion and 10,000 jobs at airport shops and restaurants.

The financial losses of Washington, D.C., area airports since the day of the incidents through September 30, 2001, are telling. Dulles International Airport and Baltimore-Washington International Airport lost about $5 million and $4.7 million, respectively, during this nearly three week period. The latter airport incurred $487,000 in unanticipated security costs, with additional security-focused requirements reaching another $1.3 million.

Reagan National Airport was the last airport reopened after the September 11, 2001, attacks. The closure of Reagan National Airport for several weeks resulted in idling thousands of airline, other transportation, hospitality, and tourism workers as well as costing millions in revenues for airlines and the airport.

Adam Whiteman of Moody's Investors Service commented that the majority of large U.S. airports already carry $1.1 billion in debt. Michael Lexton of Bear, Stearns warned that reduced air travel would make it difficult for airports to pay bondholders.

Further expenses have attached to airports as they must comply with additional security steps outlined by the FAA. The American Association of Airport Executives and the ACI seek to obtain a rapid solution for airports' financial problems by winning direct federal reimbursement for the cost of FAA-mandated security measures put in place after the attacks.

IV   Hotels, Conventions, and Tourism

Hotels

According to Smith Travel Research, in the ten days following the September 11, 2001, terrorist incidents, the lodging industry lost $700 million in revenue. Yet, the U.S. hotel occupancy rates rebounded from the first week following the World Trade Center and Pentagon terrorist incidents (September 16-22, 2001), when it reached 52.3%, to the week of October 14-20, 2001, when hotel occupancy stood at 63%. The rise in hotel occupancy during these 2 periods was exhibited in various cities, such as: Boston, Massachusetts (from 46.3% to 68.5%); New York (from 54.6% to 75.1%); San Francisco, California (from 42.2% to 60.6%); and Washington, D.C. (from 41.8% to 64.9%). Likewise, revenue per available room increased from $38.68 to $51.72.

Despite the moderate upsurge in subsequent business, hotels have experienced significant difficulties due to the aftermath of the attacks. In late September 2001, Marriott International Inc. announced plans to fire workers and reduce hours for up to 20% of its 3,900 headquarters staff in Bethesda, Maryland. Marriott estimated that revenue per room would decline by 7%-10% in the third quarter of 2001 due to declines in business travel. The terrorist incidents, which destroyed the Marriott World Trade Center hotel and severely damaged the Marriott Financial Center hotel, should further damage the company's bottom line. Also, Cedant Corporation, owner of Days Inn, Super 8 hotels, and Avis rental cars, lowered its earnings projection on September 28, 2001, for the remainder of 2001 and all of 2002, blaming the consequences that the terrorist attacks were having on the travel industry.

In the Washington, D.C., area, the local hospitality industry—including hotels, restaurants, and caterers—felt the effects of scaled-back business as people canceled plans to travel to the nation's capital. It is expected that the Washington, D.C., area hospitality business could lose an estimated $2 billion in revenue from September 11, 2001, through December 31, 2001.

The District of Columbia projected a loss of $80 million in restaurant and hotel room taxes between October 2001 and March 2002. In mid-October 2001, occupancy rates at Washington, D.C., hotels were 20% below projected figures. The September 11, 2001, terrorist incidents caused declining revenues from out-of-town visitors across the hospitality and tourism sectors.

DoubleTree Hotel and Executive Meeting Center in Rockville, Maryland, suffered $1 million in canceled business in the month following the attacks. To reduce such losses, some travel agencies, hotels, and restaurants focused on local and "friends and family" business, such as weddings, weekend getaways, and local corporate meetings. Lansdowne Resort and Conference Center in Leesburg, Virginia, marketed to local biotechnology and defense contractors that may require more expansive settings for corporate engagements.

Business at Atlantic City, New Jersey, casinos and hotels remained brisk in the initial weeks following the September 11, 2001, terrorist attacks. Unlike the nation's largest gambling destination, Las Vegas, Nevada, which is largely dependent on air travel for tourist transportation, Atlantic City—the second-largest gambling site in the United States—is reached primarily by car or bus; only 3% of its visitors arrive by plane. By comparison, in late September 2001, hotel occupancy at properties in Atlantic City (Caesars and Bally) was about 90% while in Las Vegas it was 75%. The American Gambling Association predicted that gambling destinations that are not heavily reliant on air travel should persevere even with declining tourism in fall 2001.

In Los Angeles, California, the Wilshire Grand Hotel expected an occupancy rate for October 2001 to reach only 48%; in October 2000 the occupancy rate was 75%. Due to the downturn in business, up to 285 hotel jobs were eliminated or hours were curtailed.

Choice Hotels International initiated a $10 million promotional campaign aimed at generating travel, calling on Americans not to let terrorists interfere with the fundamental right to travel. Patriotically, Days Inns donated 2,000 free rooms in the New York City and Washington, D.C., metropolitan areas to families of the victims and emergency crews aiding in the recovery efforts.

In order to stimulate activity in the U.S. hotel and lodging industry, the American Hotel & Lodging Association proposed to Congress in October 2001 to implement a number of measures, such as:

- Restore the deduction for travel expenses of a spouse accompanying an employee on a business trip to 100%.

- Reinstate the deduction allowed for business meals and entertainment to 100%.

- Temporarily cut or defer federal payroll administration tax payments equally affecting the employer and employee contributions.

- Extend the eligibility requirements for the Small Business Administration's Economic Injury Disaster Relief Program.

- Aid states that have difficulty processing and paying unemployment and worker compensation claims resulting from the attacks.

Conventions

Business leaders, developers, and government officials are concerned about the possibility of fewer tourists and conventioneers than was projected to use Washington, D.C.'s planned $756 million convention center and 1,000-room, $30 million hotel. The convention center, with 1 million square feet of space, is planned to open in spring 2002. In fall 2001, some meeting planners expressed concerns about holding events in Washington, D.C., in 2003 and beyond.

With many people concerned about traveling, a substantial number of conventions and conferences were canceled or rescheduled in the first 4 weeks following the September 11, 2001, terrorist attacks. For example, the Internet World Conference at the Jacob K. Javits Convention Center in New York City was rescheduled from October 2001 to December 2001. The importance of the convention and special-events industry is especially evident in New York City, where it generates about $4 billion in revenues a year. The largest American computer conference, the Comdex trade show in Las Vegas, Nevada, proceeded as scheduled in November 2001.

Convention organizers reacted to numerous cancellations of events by offering discounted or free air and train travel, hotel accommodations, and show tickets. Other incentives included promises of additional security, seminars regarding the threats of terrorism, and in the last resort, declining reimbursements for payments made by those already registered.

If the United States engages in a prolonged military conflict coupled with occurrences of other aviation terrorist attacks, travel will likely decline, resulting in high vacancies at hotels. Such circumstances would, in turn, result in conventioneers meeting at local or regional destinations, rather than at locations necessitating the use of airplanes.

Tourism

In Florida, tourism is the biggest sector of the state economy, sourcing about one fifth of the total Florida economy, or $50 billion a year. In 2000, more than 70 million tourists came to Florida. The decline in tourism in Florida in the aftermath of the September 11, 2001, terrorist events has been staggering. This is particularly so in Miami, where 96% of tourists that visit the city, including its foreign tourists who comprise 55% of total visitors, arrive by plane. For instance, whereas Miami Beach hotels were 60% occupied in September 2000, a year later, some hotels had occupancy rates of 10%. The hotel occupancy rate in September 2001 in Orlando, Florida, the second-biggest hotel market in the United States, dropped to 45% from 62% in August 2001.

With numerous flight, hotel, and rental car cancellations to the Sunshine State, many Floridian stores and restaurants suffered as well. During the first few days after the terrorist incidents, Miami lost about $15 million of tourism revenue daily. By October 2001, the projected losses were closer to $10 million of tourism revenue a day. During fall 2001, an estimated 5% of the 130,000 workers in the tourism business in Miami-Dade County lost their jobs.

Florida Govenor Jeb Bush (Republican) urged Floridians to travel in-state to make up for the shortage of out-of-state guests. Other state and local tourism authorities appealed to Florida residents to travel in-state. To complement these marketing tactics, many hotels gave significant discounts to Florida residents.

Hawaii's deserted beaches reflected the fact that more than 25% of the state's economy is supported by tourists who travel by air. Gov. Benjamin J. Cayetano (D) called the situation, "the worst economic crisis" in state history. Hopefully, attractive airline and hotel packages appearing in fall 2001, will entice holiday vacationers.

Since the September 11, 2001, terrorist attacks, the number of tourists visiting Washington, D.C., declined, particularly at the Smithsonian, the most visited museum complex in the world. On September 23, 2001, only 22,000 people visited the Smithsonian museums on the Mall, compared with 75,000 on September 23, 2000. At the Air and Space Museum, there was a drop of more than 75% of visiting tourists in the weekend following the attack. This drop in visitors affected restaurants, gift shops, and employees at the locations.

The Corcoran Gallery of Art, which was closed for a short period after the attacks, saw a decline of about 50% in visitors between early and late September 2001. Attendance at George Washington's residence in Mount Vernon, Virginia, experienced a 50% drop in visitors during September 2001 compared to September 2000. The shortfall of 18,500 people also caused a $360,000 decrease in revenues.

The White House suspended public tours since mid-September 2001, through the time of this writing, mid-November 2001. Less than 3 weeks after the attacks on the World Trade Center, New York's Empire State Building reopened to the public.

During fall 2001 there was an 11% decline in foreigners seeking visas to the United States. This decline was attributed to fear of future terrorist attacks and economic hardship overseas.

American tourism overseas—to Germany, India, Canada, and Mexico—declined dramatically since September 11, 2001. According to the Travel Business Roundtable, about one quarter of the persons who planned to fly during the Thanksgiving holiday changed their minds; 40% of those persons planned to stay at home and 60% expected to drive.

It is too soon to determine how long and how many persons will be apprehensive about traveling by commercial airlines due to the four hijackings in September 2001. To be sure, numerous security breaches at U.S. airports in fall 2001—guns, knives, and other weapons brought onboard planes—certainly have not soothed passengers' concerns. Even passage of full-scale aviation security legislation approved in November 2001 will, in practice, take much time to improve airline security.

V Insurance

Due to claims arising from the September 11 terrorist attacks, the insurance industry will suffer losses estimated at between $50 billion and $80 billion, the costliest insurance loss in U.S. history. This amount will be paid in part by primary insurers (companies such as State Farm). Another portion will be paid by reinsurers (such as Lloyd's of London). Reinsurance is essentially insurance for insurance companies, enabling primary insurance companies to share the risk with other insurance companies.

The scope of the insurance claims will likely include: life, property, casualty, workers' compensation, business interruption, and disability claims. Property and casualty losses are estimated at between $40 billion to $70 billion. It is foreseen that life insurance costs will run at between $3 billion and $6 billion. With reference to disability pay, initial estimates suggest claims will reach under $100 million.

Business interruption claims could reach $5 billion because many buildings in the World Trade Center complex area are damaged or inaccessible. Workmen's compensation claims might reach $500,000 per claim. United Airlines and American Airlines whose aircraft were crashed by terrorists on

September 11, 2001, may face massive liability in excess of the insurance coverage (typically $1.5 billion to $2 billion per plane). The September 2001, aviation recovery law contained clauses that American Airlines and United Airlines limited damage awards stemming from the attacks.

The World Trade Center attacks exposed U.S. and European insurers and reinsurers to potentially huge claims, including: General Reinsurance ($1.25 billion), Munich Reinsurance ($907 million), Swiss Reinsurance ($722 million), XL Capital Ltd. ($700 million), Allianz ($620 million), General Electric ($600 million), and American International Group ($500 million).

New York Life Insurance Co. expects to pay close to $100 million in life insurance claims related to the September 11 attacks. Following the World Trade Center and Pentagon attacks, thousands of Americans sought the need for life insurance. Insurance.com reported that queries about life insurance rose 68% above normal levels during the first half of October 2001.

According to the American Council of Life Insurers, individual life insurance policies in the United States generally do not contain terrorism exclusions. However, such exclusions exist in agreements for individuals who travel to places where terrorism is prevalent.

With regard to disability insurance for the September 11 victims, UnumProvident Corp. announced in fall 2001 that it would likely pay $30 million in disability claims. Hartford Financial Services Group reported that through October 2001, it received few disability claims related to September 11.

While insurers contend that they have sufficient capital to handle sporadic bombings, another massive terrorist attack could bankrupt some insurers if they do not have exclusions in insurance contracts to protect themselves. Due to such financial threats, in fall 2001 the insurance industry initiated various proposals to Congress for federal aid and assistance in case of further terrorist incidents. Governmental responses to the calamities affecting the insurance industry are addressed in Chapter 6.

Subsequent to the September 11, 2001, terrorist incidents, some insurers increased rates by 50% to 100% for particular shippers and owners of large commercial property coupled with stiffer policy terms. Workmen's compensation rates are expected to rise by at least 20% in 2002.

Among the highest rate hikes are those involving the airlines, where underwriters raised premiums by up to 400%. Fortunately for the airlines, the September 2001 airline stablization legislation allows for the federal government to pay any rise in commercial insurance as well as be responsible for third-party liability insurance for terrorism for half a year. The Council of Insurance Agents and Brokers announced that rates for insurance policies covering property damage are rising by some 30% to 50%.

According to Conning and Co., premiums for property and casualty policies increased by 4.5% from 1999 to 2000 and are expected to rise by 7.2% in 2001 and 7.7% in 2002. Premiums for large property owners are projected to rise 25% to 35% in 2002. Also, it is expected that in 2002 and beyond, few policies will provide coverage for terrorism events.

Some insurance companies reduced their maximum liability on a variety of policies. The ramifications of such actions to the insurance industry may include recalculation of how to cover major office buildings. While some insurers may stop writing terrorism policies, others may sell high-priced protection geared to cover terrorism.

A great concern to insurance industry leaders is the ability of property and casualty companies to obtain reinsurance to protect them against the cost of future terrorist attacks. Because reinsurance firms took the largest hit from the attacks, they may drop terrorism coverage, reduce maximum liability levels, or raise premiums on such policies by several hundred percent in 2002.

Major reinsurers announced that they will not renew terrorism coverage without the presence of a government support plan in place by December 31, 2001. Insurers said that they will not insure terrorism risks unless they have reinsurance coverage. In January of each year, roughly 70% of commercial policies with terrorism provisions expire. About 90% of all commercial policies are renewed on January 1, 2002.

In November 2001, some insurance companies contacted clients informing them that their policies will be cancelled on January 1, 2002. Insurers also contacted states to enable them to avoid offering terrorism coverage after December 31, 2001.

Some real estate professionals surmised that lending and other transactions will not proceed until large commercial developments receive terrorism insurance. Larry A. Silverstein, who acquired the lease to operate the World Trade Center in July 2001, sought $7.2 billion from insurers for the destruction resulting from the attacks. The figure is twice the amount insurers say he can claim. Silverstein maintained that he is entitled to collect twice on the policies because the 2 planes hitting the World Trade Center constituted separate occurrences.

Due to Silverstein's assertion relating to the level of insurance coverage applicable in this case, Swiss Reinsurance Co. filed suit in October 2001 against him. In its filing, Swiss Reinsurance claimed that the company and other insurers of the real estate complex should be liable for solely $3.5 billion, as the 2 hijacked airlines constituted only 1 insurable event.

Robert Hartwig of the Insurance Information Institute suggested that U.S. insurers observe how European insurers responded to the threat of terrorism. Following Irish Republican Army bombings in London in the early 1990s, global reinsurers, such as Munich Re and Swiss Re, refused to fully cover terrorist risk to commercial property. Rather, insurers capped claims for terrorist damage of buildings and their contents.

While Asian insurance companies had limited exposure to the September 11, 2001, attacks, they may benefit from the overall rise in premiums already underway in the industry. Also, Asians are increasingly interested in business, travel, and life insurance as the calamities of the fall 2001 attacks have heightened awareness of the potential effects of terrorism.

Government responses to the insurance crisis stemming from the September 11 incidents are covered in Chapter 6.

VI Real Estate

Introduction

The World Trade Center and Pentagon incidents reduced analysts' projections about construction of commercial buildings for 2001 and 2002. For instance, Robert Murray of the Construction Information Group predicted that the level of commercial office construction will decline in 2001 by 16% and 2002 by 9%. These figures are less optimistic than projections made prior to the attacks, when declines of only 14% and 4%, for 2001 and 2002, respectively, were expected.

During the third quarter of 2001, the vacancy rates for class A and B office space was 11.8%; a year earlier the figure stood at 9.6%. The economic downturn coupled with the massive job losses were principally responsible for greater availability of class A and B office space. The burst in the technology bubble affected San Francisco and Boston particularly hard in the third quarter of 2001, when vacancy rates reached 17.6% and 16.5%, respectively, in contrast to levels of 4.8% and 4.7%, respectively, a year earlier.

New York

All seven buildings in the World Trade Center complex fell or partially collapsed. One Liberty Plaza, the 4 World Financial Center buildings, and 11 other buildings sustained damage during the terrorist incidents. As a result of the attacks, about 29 million square feet (30% of the office space in Manhattan's downtown financial district) was affected, including 13 million square feet in the World Trade Center complex. As of October 2001, about 8.2 million square feet of commercial space was available in the Wall Street area, although a large portion does not include modern telecommunications wiring and layout that are in line with some financial firms' requirements. Partly due to the damage resulting from the World Trade Center attacks, the vacancy rates for class A and B office space in Manhattan during the third quarter of 2001 dropped to 4.3% from 7.4% during the third quarter of 2000.

The World Trade Center complex, built on a 16-acre site, was constructed at a cost of about $1.5 billion. Cushman & Wakefield predicted that redevelopment of the area would necessitate a developer to charge rents of $60 a square foot (about 30% higher than expected market rates), commencing 2006. New York State authorities may need to issue and guarantee some $7 billion in bonds in order to cover any new project at that location.

The owner of the World Trade Center—the Port Authority of New York and New Jersey (Port Authority)—awarded a 99-year lease to Larry A. Silverstein in a deal valued at $3.2 billion. Initially, it was reported that the lease contained a provision that enables Silverstein to be free from the duty of paying rent in the event of a terrorist attack, with control shifting to the Port Authority. Subsequent information suggested that Silverstein still owes the Port Authority $116 million annually in lease payments.

The five largest tenants at the North Tower (One World Trade Center) were: Empire Blue Cross Blue Shield, Marsh & McLennan, Sidley Austin Brown & Wood, Bank of America, and Dai-Ichi Kangyo Trust. At the South Tower (Two World Trade Center), the five main tenants included: Morgan Stanley, Guy Carpenter, Fiduciary Trust Co. International, Oppenheimer Funds, and AON Corp. Additionally, many foreign banks and boutique investment firms were housed at the Twin Towers. The human toll of the attacks is detailed in Chapter 5.

The damage and destruction inflicted upon buildings, infrastructure, and office equipment during the attacks caused companies to move, share space, or make do with their offices. As a result, the demand for new offices caused upward pressure on already high New York City rents, leading some companies to relocate elsewhere. One alternative is New Jersey, where 10 of the biggest 18 companies formerly based at the World Trade Center relocated in fall 2001.

The proximity of Jersey City to Wall Street, coupled with modern, technology-laced buildings with rents up to 70% lower and with smaller taxes than in Manhattan, has made Jersey City very attractive. About 32,000 displaced workers conduct their duties from offices in Jersey City. Moreover, Goldman Sachs & Co. intends to have a New Jersey-based 40-floor office building completed in 2003.

Tenant defections from lower Manhattan to midtown Manhattan, New Jersey, or Connecticut will adversely affect Brookfield Properties Corp., the largest private office landlord in lower Manhattan. It was reported that Brookfield received $50 million in insurance to help reconstruct four buildings damaged during the attacks.

By late October 2001, nearly 50 former World Trade Center tenants reported that they were moving their operations to midtown Manhattan. The financial firms that plan to relocate from lower Manhattan include Lehman Brothers, Morgan Stanley, and Bear Stearns. Other entities that are reported to be leaning to moving from the area include CIBC World Markets, Gruntal & Co., and possibly the Nasdaq Stock Market.

In October 2001, Lehman Brothers announced that it will buy from Morgan Stanley a partially completed, 32-story, one million square-foot office building in the Times Square area. Lehman will pay approximately $650 million, with occupation of the building occurring at the end of 2001. Lehman owned or leased over one million square feet in two buildings at the World Financial Center. Lehman may ultimately use, lease, or sell part of the space following its repair, which is expected to be completed in fall 2002.

Also in October 2001, Morgan Stanley obtained office space in Manhattan's East Side, at 3rd Avenue and 49th Street, for approximately 700 employees. Previously, these employees were based at the World Trade Center.

Over 100,000 employees relocated to offices in New York, New Jersey, and Connecticut. For example, Merrill Lynch sent some of its 9,000 employees based in lower Manhattan to offices in Jersey City, New Jersey. The New York Board of Trade moved to backup offices on Long Island, New York. Citicorp Asset Management, which had 2,500 workers at the World Trade Center complex, moved 1,100 employees to locations in midtown Manhattan; Rutherford, New Jersey; and Stamford, Connecticut.

Alternatively, about 70 tenants based among the locations that were harmed during the September 11, 2001, incidents acknowledged that they will keep offices in lower Manhattan. Other entities that announced that they will maintain a presence in the area include the Federal Reserve Bank of New York, Deutsche Bank, Goldman Sachs, Merrill Lynch & Co., and Dow Jones & Co.

Initially following the attacks, some companies shared office space. The NYSE, which was not damaged in the attacks, permitted the American Stock Exchange to trade equities on its floor. The New York City office of the law firm of Cleary, Gottlieb, Steen & Hamilton, formerly based at One Liberty Plaza, has housed employees at 9 temporary locations in the city, including at other law firms.

Pentagon

The September 11, 2001, terrorist attack on the Pentagon and subsequent fire destroyed or damaged over 4 million square feet of office space. It was projected that it will take years to mend the damage done during the attack. The incident also resulted in over 4,800 Pentagon workers being dislocated from their offices. Within a week of the attack, arrangements were made to house nearly 3,200 workers at two office buildings in Crystal City, Virginia. Other temporary offices included locations in Washington, D.C., Maryland, and Virginia.

Future Developments

Companies with decentralized real estate set-ups—various units spread out among disparate cities or regions—may become a growing trend among selected firms that seek to reduce the impact of a massive terrorist attack. A company that has already adopted the decentralized paradigm—the origin of which is not at issue for this purpose—is the Swiss bank UBS. UBS also owns the PaineWebber securities brokerage firm. More specifically, UBS has offices in midtown New York, brokerage activities in New Jersey, and a trading center in Connecticut.

Some architects and urban planners, such as Steven Johnson, argued that in light of possible massive terrorist attacks during this century, it is preferable to avoid building skyscrapers huddled together along endless blocks. Instead, it is preferable to construct disparate office developments separated by parks and sports stadiums. After all, by establishing distinct city nodes of up to 100,000 people, it is possible to respond and isolate a small section of the city in case of a biological terrorist attack.

Firms such as Comdisco offer an important service when a company's offices are damaged during a disaster, such as a terrorist bombing. Comdisco operates facilities with mainframes and services that replace lost equipment. For a subscription fee, plus a disaster assessment that may reach millions of dollars, firms can move their workers temporarily to Comdisco's centers.

Within weeks of the attacks, 3,000 employees from lower Manhattan moved into various Comdisco locations. Comdisco owns the huge warehouse in Long Island City, New York, where the New York Board of Trade maintains its emergency trading floor. As part of a bankruptcy court auction, Comdisco announced in October 2001 the sale of its disaster recovery business to SunGuard Data Systems Inc. for $825 million.

Other companies, such as owners of telecom hotels—office buildings with extensive telecommunications equipment and technology-friendly facilities—have received a jolt in interest in the New York-New Jersey area in the weeks following the World Trade Center and Pentagon terrorist incidents. These telecom hotels, in concert with data storage centers, were heavily marketed in the past few years to technology-thirsty dot-coms and telecommunications companies.

During fall 2001, some employees have become nervous about working at their company offices. Across the nation, more people are requesting to work from home, wanting to avoid buildings that could be potential targets and preferring to stay close to their families at a time of heightened anxiety.

Before the attacks, telecommuting was seen as a stagnating trend, as bosses decided it was too difficult to manage a network of dispersed, remote workers. Also, employees felt stigmatized if they were not seen around the office. But the September 11 attacks have caused many workers to reevaluate their priorities, and some companies are exploring this option.

Companies now view home-based employees as a defensive measure if their offices become inaccessible. For instance, hundreds of workers from American Express Co., which maintained its headquarters and additional offices in Manhattan damaged during the terrorist incidents, are now working "virtually," as the company sets up temporary locations in New Jersey and Connecticut. Firms located outside New York, such as Charles Schwab Corp., based in San Francisco, California, and ABN Amro North America, based in Chicago, Illinois, are exploring telecommuting options with great vigor.

The above shift could result in a slight reduction in traditional commercial leasing to smaller-scale commercial developments as well as technologically enhanced residential models. Also, consultants advising on establishing virtual offices and the companies that assist in establishing their telecommunications networks should benefit from this trend.

General Growth Properties Inc., one of the largest mall owners nationwide, closed its 146 regional malls on September 11, 2001. Traffic plunged during the first few days following the attacks but rebounded rather rapidly. By the weekend of September 24-25, 2001, traffic had returned to within 5% of year-earlier levels.

The threat of terrorism on U.S. soil adds further challenges to landlords of large-scale retail centers, such as shopping malls. Landlords of such developments must balance the need for great security measures without concurrently scaring away customers who might perceive such steps as confirming that shopping malls are imminent terrorist targets. Against this backdrop, some shopping centers have hired additional security guards, improved safety and security training for property management staff, tightened restrictions on truck deliveries of merchandise and foodstuffs, and accelerated parking restrictions. According to the International Council of Shopping Centers, landlords will likely also face increased insurance costs and more restrictive terms and conditions in the wake of the September 11, 2001, terrorist incidents.

VII Energy

Oil prices surged by 13%, or $3.60, in the hours following the World Trade Center and Pentagon attacks, reaching $31.05 a barrel (for Brent crude with an October 2001 delivery). By September 26, 2001, oil prices fell nearly 30% to $21 per barrel. Reductions in air travel and decreased tourism nationwide caused oil demand to decline in September 2001.

Between the date of the attacks through November 12, 2001, the price of oil had declined by about $12 a barrel, to below $17.00 on November 19, 2001. According to economists, such a decline is the equivalent of a $250 billion tax cut for major industrial powers.

According to the Energy Information Administration, the members of the Organization of Petroleum Exporting Countries (OPEC)—Saudi Arabia, Venezuela, United Arab Emirates, Iraq, Kuwait, Nigeria, Libya, Algeria, Qatar, and Indonesia—supply 61% of net exports of oil daily. Non-OPEC oil exports—principally Russia, Norway, Mexico, and Great Britain—account for

39% of global totals.

In late October 2001, OPEC and non-OPEC representatives failed to agree on output production cuts or on how any prospective oil production reductions would occur among distinct countries. While OPEC was supposed to reduce its production by 1 million barrels per day in September 2001, the organization members produced about 800,000 barrels per day above that figure. During fall 2001, world supply was outstripping demand by 1.5 million barrels a day.

Following an OPEC meeting in mid-November 2001, the oil cartel announced that from January 2002, they would reduce oil production by 1.5 million barrels per day, or 6.5%, if non-OPEC members, such as Russia and Mexico, agreed to reduce prohibition by 500,000 barrels of oil a day. In November 2001, Russia announced that it would reduce 30,000 barrels of oil per day; in October 2001, Russia cut oil production by 40,000 barrels a day. In mid-November 2001, Russia pumped about 7 million barrels daily.

During Christmas 2001 it is expected that many consumers will drive to visit relatives rather than fly due to nagging concerns about aviation security and positive factors such as lower gasoline prices. For 2001, Dan Pickering of Simmons & Co. predicted oil demand will fall 0.2%, the first reduction in demand since 1983. Similarly, natural gas prices fell since the attacks. Besides U.S. consumers who benefit from lower oil prices, so, too, do the transportation sector and tire manufacturers.

In October 2001, oil giants Exxon Mobil and Phillips Petroleum announced that 2001 third-quarter profits declined by 29% and 15%, respectively. The decline in oil prices has dimmed down the outlook for oil companies in the short term.

The United States, with 5% of the world population, uses 19 million barrels of oil a day, of which about 11.5 million barrels are imported. U.S. oil consumption is approximately 25% of the world total of 76 million barrels. The leading suppliers of oil to the United States are Canada (9.4%), Saudi Arabia (9%), Venezuela (8.1%), and Mexico (6.3%). OPEC countries sold the United States 28% of its consumption in June 2001. The Persian Gulf region holds nearly two thirds of the world's known oil reserves.

According to oil analysts, maintaining the uninterrupted flow of oil from the Persian Gulf region costs the United States billions of dollars per year. The GAO estimates that the cost of U.S. military and foreign aid programs in the Gulf area from 1980 to 1990 was as high as $365 billion. When military and energy security factors are taken into consideration, the true cost of oil may be as high as $100 per barrel, or $5 a gallon. Good news relating to reduced reliance on Middle Eastern oil arose in October 2001 when ChevronTexaco announced the initial shipment of oil produced in its consortium-led Tengiz oil fields in Kazakhstan. Tengiz, the sixth-largest oil reserve worldwide, is projected to produce 700,000 barrels of oil a day.

The Strategic Petroleum Reserve, a stockpile established in 1975 for use in case of emergencies, could cover oil shortages for a limited time. The oil reserves, stored in underground caverns in Texas and Louisiana, can hold up to 700 million barrels. In October 2001, the reserve had nearly 545 million barrels, sufficient to last the United States 53 days. On November 13, 2001, President Bush ordered that the reserve be filled to capacity by adding 100,000 barrels a day. The decision caused crude oil for December 2001 delivery to rise by 2.1%, or $0.44, to $21.67 a barrel (in New York trading).

The prospect of the United States-Afghan Taliban conflict spreading beyond Afghanistan, particularly into Pakistan, will accelerate instability in oil prices. The energy sector would likely be adversely affected by a major terrorist attack against oil-sensitive installations and locations, particularly in the Middle East. For instance, a shock to oil prices would result, for example, if al-Qaida (or another terrorist group) sinks oil tankers in the Strait of Hormuz, the channel that funnels 14 million barrels of oil a day from the Persian Gulf to the rest of the world.

Also, terrorists could launch attacks on oil loading docks along the Persian Gulf, or on the Red Sea to the west, from which 500,000 to 6 million barrels a day are shipped. Terrorist attacks against U.S. oil interests in the Gulf of Mexico and Alaska would also have serious ramifications. The U.S. Energy Department predicted that world oil prices will likely increase between $3 and $5 per barrel of oil if one million barrels per day were removed from the world supply.

VIII Technology

The information technology industry witnessed declines prior to the September 11 attacks. Subsequently, International Data Corp. predicted that spending on information technology would rise by only 3% in 2001, modified from 6.7% prior to the terrorist incidents. In post-September 11, 2001, First Call suggested that earnings for the technology sector would drop 56% in the fourth quarter of 2001.

According to some estimates, the information technology costs of recovery and relocation after the September 11, 2001, incidents will be at least

$15.8 billion over three years. Yet, those added sales of hardware, software, and services will not compensate for the negative impact of the attacks as a whole.

After the incidents, Morgan Stanley ordered over 25,000 new personal computers from Dell Computer. Dow Jones reported that over $2 million in information technology hardware and office equipment required replacement. It was estimated that Cisco Systems will obtain some $60 million in orders for replacements of damaged equipment.

In nearly 30 days after September 11, almost $75 billion in market value was eliminated from chip makers and equipment makers, which comprise the S&P 500 index. From January-September 2001, the largest U.S. personal computer makers cut, or announced plans to eliminate, nearly 46,000 employees worldwide due to reduced sales.

Advanced Micro Devices Inc. announced in late September 2001 that it was eliminating 15% of its work force and closing two plants. A number of technology companies suffered job cuts in September-October 2001. On October 11, 2001, the fourth biggest software company, Computer Associates International of Islandia, New York, terminated 900 positions, or 5% of its labor force, including 700 in the United States and Canada. In January 2001, Computer Associates had laid off 240 employees. Also, in October 2001, Sun Microsystems reported that 3,900 workers would be fired.

In early October 2001, Yahoo announced that during the third quarter of 2001, it lost $24.1 million on sales of $166.1 million. The figures marked a stark decline from the $295.6 million in sales and profits of $47.7 million during the third quarter of 2000. Yahoo estimated that the terrorist attacks caused advertising cancellations of between $2 million to $3 million.

The September 11, 2001, attacks hurt other U.S. Internet companies as well, including: Expedia (where business fell 55% after the disasters), Travelocity.com (which relies mainly on airline commissions, so lower volumes hit home), Homestore.com (where conditions could deteriorate if real estate worsens), and Priceline.com (where consumers were especially weary about travel).

An October 2001 Gartner Inc. and Soundview Technology Group Inc. survey of corporate technology officers found that technology spending will reach an increase of only 2.5% in 2001 and a growth of merely 1.5% in 2002. With consumer confidence weakened, an upsurge in personal computer sales is unlikely until 2003, foresees Rob Enderle of Giga Information Group.

The implications for the information technology sector will depend on economic conditions, military successes, and consumer confidence. However, some shifts in resources and buying trends may arise. For instance, larger proportions of funds will be backup storage, recovery services, decentralized operations, computer security, and encryption software. Also, knowledge management, which combines tools such as e-mail search programs, collaboration software, and data mining, will become increasingly important.

IX Media and Entertainment

Media

The leading television outlets (the four major broadcast networks, their affiliates and the cable news networks) lost about $500 million in advertising revenue as a result of the September 11, 2001, disaster. Various broadcasters logged 90 hours of nonstop news from the day of the attack through September 14, 2001, at midnight.

CBS announced that the television network lost $85 million in advertising revenue during its commercial-free airing of the terrorist events. Additional CBS news costs relating to covering the event were $7 million. Fox stated that it lost $100 million in advertising revenue and heightened newsgathering costs as a result of the attacks. Likewise, Knight Ridder announced in November 2001 that it lost $9 million in advertising revenue because of the World Trade Center and Pentagon attacks and spent $2 million to cover the story.

Following September 11, traffic at news web sites, such as CNN.com, MSNBC.com, and Time.com, increased dramatically. Also, during this period, cable news ratings for CNN, Fox News, and MSNBC rose sharply as did viewership of broadcast news, including NBC, ABC, and CBS. Higher audiences for these media sources should ultimately result in greater attractiveness to advertisers than existed earlier.

Despite the fragility of the media market following the World Trade Center and Pentagon terrorist incidents, in October 2001 NBC bought the second biggest Spanish-language broadcaster, Telemundo, in a $1.98 billion deal.

It is worth highlighting that during the anthrax attacks occurring in the United States in fall 2001, newsprint and news broadcasting companies— ABC, NBC, CBS, American Media, *New York Post*, and *New York Times*—

were principal targets. The Committee to Protect Journalists has long chronicled attacks against media interests and journalists globally, including incidents of harassment, physical attacks, and murder. During the autumn 2001 conflict in Afghanistan, a number of journalists and photographers were killed.

Entertainment

Walt Disney Company, which is heavily invested in theme parks, hotels, broadcast television, and cable television, may suffer in the aftermath of the September 11, 2001, attack. Due to public anxiety about further attacks and military reprisals, people could travel and shop less than in normal times. In addition, "Big Trouble," a movie that Disney foresaw as a big hit, is in storage because the plot involves a bomb on a plane. Another movie, "Collateral Damage," which involves terrorists and firefighters, was also put in abeyance given possible audience sensitivities in fall 2001.

The U.S. campaign against Afghanistan commenced the same day as the rescheduled Emmy Awards ceremony was expected to take place, October 7, 2001. Instead, the Emmy Awards was postponed for a second time in three weeks. CBS, which planned to air the show, lost millions in advertising as a result of the cancellations. The Emmy Awards ceremony ultimately took place on November 4, 2001, and was broadcast by CBS.

Security at the Super Bowl in February 2002 in New Orleans, Louisiana, is expected to be unusually tight due to fears of a possible terrorist attack. In February 2002, Salt Lake City, Utah, will host the Winter Olympics. The games may be hindered by a number of factors, including: possible future terrorist attacks in a post-September 11 climate; anxiety over air travel; and the background of terrorist attacks during the 1996 Summer Olympics in Atlanta, Georgia, and the 1972 Summer Olympics in Munich, Germany. These issues may negatively interfere with the financial success of the Salt Lake City Olympics.

In October 2001, the U.S. government approved $24.5 million for additional security measures at Salt Lake City, although a further $15.5 million is expected before the games begin. Yet, organizers of the event predict that they need more than 7 times the projected federal government allocation in order to ensure the safety of participants and fans. How well the war on terrorism succeeds domestically and abroad in the coming months will determine, in part, whether the games attract their projected 1.5 million fans.

X Transportation

The transportation system needs to accelerate security measures across all systems: general transportation, aviation, surface transportation, and sea-port/maritime. Railroad operators, such as Burlington Northern Santa Fe, are paying great attention to potential terrorist attacks. Railroad operators are adding more security officers and expanding their roles.

According to the American Trucking Association, the freight transportation market share in 2000 by tonnage was: truck (67.6%), rail (13.6%), pipeline (9.4%), water (8.2%), rail intermodal (1%), and air (0.1%). Declining industrial production, reduced investment, and less consumer demand aggravated by the terrorist attacks in September and October 2001 have resulted in disappointing figures for trucking companies in fall 2001.

On a daily basis, about 76,000 tanker trucks transport millions of pounds of hazardous waste materials nationwide. There is a fear that terrorists will use such materials as part of a possible terrorist attack. Sensitivities were raised in mid-October 2001, following reports by the FBI and the American Chemical Association that 18 suspects with Arabic names in Pittsburgh, Pennsylvania, acquired licenses to transport hazardous materials. Chemical companies, such as Ethyl Corp. of Richmond, Virginia, are among firms that are responding to growing threats with increased vigilance.

As such, state police and the Department of Transportation collaborated on increasing inspection of commercial trucks transporting hazardous waste. State police raised their activities in this regard as random truck checks have increased and truck-weighing stations are open 24 hours a day.

Increased attention to security at ports was advocated in October 2001 by the American Association of Port Authorities (AAPA), which represents more than 150 public port authorities in the United States, Canada, Latin America, and the Caribbean.

Among some of the safeguards advocated by the AAPA were:

- Increase the use of port police and security personnel.

- Port employees should become more security conscious and focus on potential problems (suspicious vehicles or packages, malfunctioning security alarms or locks, damaged perimeter fences, and the presence of strangers on port property).

- Prevent access to port facilities and offices by unauthorized vehicles and persons.

- Take special precautions when handling or storing fuels, chemicals, and other hazardous materials.

- Arrange for an initial security survey of port facilities by competent specialists from a law enforcement agency (such as local Coast Guard, state police, or local police).

- Ensure that the captain of the port possesses up-to-date plans and other pertinent operational information on file.

XI Additional Sectors

Retailers

During September 2001, discount retailers fared well while specialty stores, department stores, and sellers of luxury items had declining sales compared to the same period in the previous year. The Lehman Brothers index of 22 retailers increased just 1.4% in September 2001, the worst monthly sales performance in 20 years.

Among the discount retailers that experienced sales growth during September 2001 were Wal-Mart, Target, Costco, J.C. Penny, and Kohl's. The department stores suffering sales reductions included Neiman Marcus, Gap Inc., Federated Department Stores (Macy's and Bloomingdale's), Dillard's, Sears, and Saks. Specialty stores, including the Gap, Limited, Talbots, Ann Taylor, Pier 1 Imports, Spiegel, Abercrombie & Fitch, and American Eagle Outfitters, also witnessed reduced sales.

It is expected that the Christmas 2001 sales season may face declines as some shoppers will be concerned about rising unemployment, a roller-coaster stock market, an uncertain economy, instability overseas, and the specter of further terrorist attacks in the United States. Some full-price chains began the Christmas price wars a holiday earlier, in Thanksgiving.

With the success of online sales, retailers and other marketers of products have another outlet to sell their products should some shoppers be concerned with buying merchandise in stores, particularly at shopping malls— deemed a possible soft target of terrorists. The percentage of Internet users who made purchases online has risen steadily from 31% in 1999 to 40% in 2000. It is projected that those figures should reach 47% and 52% in 2001 and 2002, respectively. BizRate.com predicted that during the fourth quarter of 2001 revenues from online shopping should rise by 25%. Vividence Corp.'s survey found that 37% of respondents indicated that they will do more online shopping due to the September 11, 2001, attacks.

According to *Business 2.0*, during 2001 online merchants in 9 key categories—travel services, clothing, auctions, computer hardware, books, health and beauty, computer software, electronics, and music—should generate over $40 billion in sales. Online travel services are expected to experience some fallout from the decline in air travel even though sales during 2001 should reach $20.2 billion.

Financial Services

The Bank of America announced on September 28, 2001, that the September 11, 2001, terrorist incidents cost the bank $125 million during the third quarter of 2001. About $40 million of this amount represented foregone revenue, including lost interest on money the bank had but could not invest. The Bank of America had many offices in lower Manhattan, while its main data center was on 101 Barclay Street, a block away from the World Trade Center.

Also, Citigroup lost $100 million to $200 million in business from New York City branches that were closed and for the four days in which the stock markets did not trade. Morgan Stanley, the largest commercial tenant in the World Trade Center, determined the cost of property damage and relocating its employees would be $150 million. For most of these firms, insurance will cover the loss of property, cost of relocation, and foregone revenue.

Merrill Lynch, which had to evacuate its headquarters in the World Financial Center, sent many of its debt and equity traders to offices in Jersey City, New Jersey. The New York Board of Trade had to relocate to backup offices elsewhere in New York.

Public/Private Mail Carriers and Direct Marketers

During fall 2001, a number of anthrax-tainted letters were sent by unknown assailant(s) that resulted in 5 deaths (through November 22, 2001), infected over a dozen people, temporarily closed government and private offices, and injected panic for some segments of the American public relative to the safety of the U.S. mail system. Gene DelPolito of the Association for Postal Commerce remarked that the anthrax threat is "undermining the sense of security, trust, and confidence consumers had when using the mail."

In response, in late October 2001, the U.S. Postal Service acquired 8 electron beam systems (machines to irradiate mail) from SureBeam for $40 million. The U.S. government plans to purchase a few hundred of these devices, totaling additional government outlays to over $1 billion.

John Nolan, Deputy Postmaster General, set out the importance to the nation of the mail system. More specifically, Nolan said, "The mailing industry is a $900 billion market employing 9 million people, representing nearly 8% of the domestic gross national product." The U.S. Postal Service processes over 210 billion pieces of mail annually. Person-to-person mail and consumer-to-business mail make up 20% of mail. It is projected that in Fiscal Year 2002, the U.S. Postal Service's deficit will reach $5 billion.

Some companies, as individuals, have rationalized that given the apparent threats to the U.S. Postal Service system, private carriers—Federal Express and United Parcel Services, for instance—may reduce the possibility of potential harm by terrorists. However, it would likely take only 1 reported case of anthrax delivered through private carriers to modify the public's perception. Yet, as use of private carriers often requires payment by check or credit card, and more built-in potential protections against its use by terrorists (including some store video surveillance), the use of private carriers by a calculating terrorist seems to be less likely.

The significance of the mail system is partially evident in the publishing business where nearly 90% of magazines are forwarded by mail, reported the Magazine Publishers of America. Corporate America, which spends about $800 billion annually on sending mail and packages, is taking the possibility of tainted mail seriously. In light of the threat, U.S. companies have instituted measures such as purchasing x-ray machines to irradiate mail, acquiring bomb detection equipment, testing equipment and kits for detecting biological weapons, calling on advisers on mailroom facilities and equipment, issuing warnings and training to mailroom employees, and enlisting the services of environmental remediation companies to clean suspect offices.

In mid-October 2001, the Direct Marketing Association (DMA) issued guidelines to its 5,000 members that collectively sell $528 billion worth of goods and services annually. Among the suggestions of the DMA were: Do not use envelopes without listing return addresses; and include Internet addresses so that a letter's authenticity can be verified. Some paper catalog retailers are improving their web sites and implementing greater use of e-mail in the wake of anthrax concerns.

Companies such as Pitney Bowes, which rents out postage meters, directs corporate mailrooms, and provides online payment systems, has viewed the impact of anthrax on the mail system with extreme scrutiny. Should the anthrax scare lead to declining demand for its mail services, the company's non-mail revenues should rise from about 25% in 2001 to 35% in 2002.

The U.S. government is highly dependent on the mail system. For instance, nine million Americans receive Social Security payments by mail. With the rising use of the Internet for various functions, including Internal Revenue Service (IRS) tax filings, electronic government—E-Government, as it is known—may not only become a convenient and economical resource, but also an important supplement to the mail system.

Due to the anthrax scare, it is likely that companies will have a higher incentive to use e-mail rather than snail mail. Some consumers are simply tossing away junk mail without opening it.

Automotive

In mid-September 2001, consumers were nervous about the economy, their jobs, and additional terrorist attacks. Therefore, it was envisioned that consumers would delay outlays on large-ticket items such as automobiles. Immediately after the attacks, analysts predicted that car sales would slump and that the ramifications on the automobile sector will be severe.

In order to avoid such negative outcomes, Ford Motor Co. announced it would spend a further $300 million in marketing to entice hesitant buyers. Moreover, to stimulate automotive sales in the post-September 11, 2001, environment, Ford, General Motors, and Daimler-Chrysler offered interest-free (zero rate) financing on 2001 and 2001 models during fall 2001. These measures resulted in substantial attention by consumers. During October 2001 automotive sales in the United States, Canada, and Mexico were the highest, on an annualized basis, since 1986.

Health Services, Pharmaceuticals, and Biotechnology

In 2001, the health care industry comprised about 13% of U.S. economic output; in 2010, that figure is supposed to reach 20%. Increased government spending on bio-terrorism measures, acquisition of antibiotics in response to the anthrax scare, and military and civilian biotechnology and pharmaceutical products aimed at countering biological and chemical agents, calls to improve medical responses to terrorism, an aging populace, and other factors should contribute to growth of the health care industry in the near future.

A survey of the National Association of County and City Health Officers showed that only 20% of local public health entities established a complete bio-terrorism response strategy. A higher figure, 24%, acknowledged that they had no agenda at all for such circumstances while 56% claimed to be generating bio-terrorism response plans.

According to a fall 2001 report of the American Hospital Association (AHA), whose members include 5,000 hospitals, U.S. hospital systems require nearly $10 billion to adequately react to a massive biological, chemical, or nuclear terrorist attack. The AHA report envisioned that hospitals currently lack adequate equipment, supplies, facilities, training, and staff to respond to such incidents.

The pharmaceuticals industry projected that about $50 billion will be required to respond to biological terrorist attacks. During 2001, it is estimated that spending on health care research and development will reach about $43 billion. It is expected that the federal government will spend about $18 billion of this amount and drug companies expending the remaining share.

Against this backdrop, it is evident that the health, pharmaceutical, and biotechnology sectors play a critical role in the fight against the threats of low-technology and super terrorism—biological, chemical, and nuclear—as well as cyber-terrorism. In Chapter 4 there is an extensive discussion of the role that pharmaceutical and biotechnology companies play in the war on terrorism. Also, part of Chapter 6 highlights U.S. government responses with regard to the threat of bio-terrorism.

Chapter 4

War on Terrorism:
The Role of Industry

I   Introduction

Products and services of companies in selected industries (or niches within a specific sector) may experience additional demand as the business community is further mobilized in the fight against terrorism. It is important to underscore, however, that inclusion or omission of any company herein neither implies any endorsement nor judgment on the products, services, capabilities, and financial attributes of any firm.

Below is an illustrative list of some corporations and sectors that appear to necessitate further examination. The goods and services that are covered include: defense; security equipment, technology, and related services; diverse technology products and services; pharmaceuticals, biotechnology, and forensics; germ detection and remediation; transportation; and "survivalist" and miscellaneous merchandise.

II   Defense

Given the current conflict in Afghanistan, possible U.S. incursions elsewhere against other state sponsors of terrorism, and the expanding war against terrorism domestically, the defense industry is likely to experience additional growth in specific sub-sectors. A discussion of the U.S. defense arsenal and developing technologies follows.

It is helpful to provide an overview of the Department of Defense prior to addressing elements of the U.S. defense industry. The four armed services—Army, Navy, Air Force, and Marines—are subordinate to their military departments. The military departments are responsible for recruiting, training, and equipping their forces, but operational control of those forces is designated to specific unified combatant commands. The 9 unified combatant commands include the U.S., European, Pacific, Joint Forces, Southern, Central, Space, Special Operations, Transportation, and Strategic. As of April 2001, the military had 1.37 million people on active military duty, 1.28 million persons on ready and stand-by reserves, and 669,000 civilian employees.

The Department of Defense's authorized budget during Fiscal Year 2001 is $292 billion. The Department of Defense's top defense contractors in Fiscal Year 2000 (in terms of total net value of prime contract awards) were: Lockheed Martin Corp. ($15.125 billion), Boeing Co. ($12.041 billion), Raytheon Co. ($6.33 billion), General Dynamics Corp. ($4.195 billion), Northrop Grumman Corp. ($3.079 billion), Litton Industries, Inc. ($2.737 billion), United Technologies Corp. ($2.071 billion), TRW Inc. ($2.004 billion), General Electric Co. ($1.609 billion), and Science Applications International Corp. ($1.522 billion).

An overview of selected aircraft in the U.S. arsenal as well as the purpose and cost of the aircraft are highlighted below to underscore expenses involved in conducting war: B-1 Bomber (long-range heavy bomber, $200+ million), B-2 Bomber (multi-role, stealth, heavy bomber, $700+ million), B-52 Bomber (long-range, high-altitude heavy bomber, $30 million), C-17 Globemaster (cargo and troop transport, $237 million), EA-6B Prowler (jams hostile radars and communications, $52 million), E-3 AWACS (airborne warning and control systems providing surveillance, command, control, and communications, $270 million), F-14 (multi-role fighter, $38 million), F-15/F-15E (multi-role fighter, $15 million), F-16 (multi-role fighter, $9.5 million), FA-117 (stealth fighter/attack aircraft, $45 million), FA-18 (fighter/attack aircraft, $39.5 million), and KC-10 Tanker (aerial tanker and transport, $88.4 million).

On October 26, 2001, U.S. Air Force Secretary James G. Roche, in an approximately $200 billion award, chose Lockheed Martin Corp. of Bethesda, Maryland, over Boeing Co. of Chicago, Illinois, to design and construct more than 3,000 Joint Strike Fighters (JSF) for the U.S. Air Force, Navy, and Marines and Great Britain's Air Force and British Royal Navy. The JSF is a stealthy (radar-evading), supersonic, multi-role fighter with cutting-edge avionics designed to replace the A-10, AV-8 Harrier, F-16, and F/A-18. The JSF should require less maintenance and support than fighters presently in service, ultimately reducing long-term ownership costs by half. It is envisioned that the JSF will become a cornerstone of future defense capability of the United States and its allies.

Northrop Grumman of Los Angeles, California, and BAE Systems of London, Great Britain, are expected to benefit as principal members of the

Lockheed Martin JSF team. The Lockheed Martin team will fly the first test aircraft in 2005 and deliver the first operational JSF in 2008. In the initial $25 billion system development and demonstration phase, 22 aircraft will be produced. Final assembly will be at Lockheed Martin's Fort Worth, Texas, plant. Major sub-assemblies will take place at Northrop Grumman's El Segundo, California, plant and BAE Systems' facility in Samlesbury, England. The JSF will involve suppliers and thousands of workers in more than 27 U.S. states and in Great Britain.

The JSF will appear in three versions. A conventional takeoff and landing variant (CTOL) will be built and designed for the U.S. Air Force. The U.S. Navy's carrier variant (CV) will feature larger wing and control surfaces, additional wingtip ailerons, and a special structure to absorb catapult launches and arrested landings associated with aircraft carrier operations than exist today. The short takeoff/vertical landing (STOVL) version will be equipped with a unique shaft-driven lift fan propulsion system that enables the aircraft to take off from a very short runway or small aircraft carrier and land vertically. The U.S. Marine Corps will employ the STOVL JSF, which will be the first operational STOVL aircraft capable of sustained supersonic flight. Great Britain is assessing both the STOVL and CV variants.

Northrop Grumman Corp., the manufacturer of the B-2 Bomber, proposed to sell to the Pentagon 40 additional bombers for about $28 billion, or $700 million per aircraft. B-2 Bombers, which are based in Whiteman Air Force base in Missouri, have been used in the U.S. campaign against Afghanistan. Interestingly enough, in October 2001, Air Force Secretary Roche opposed the acquisition of additional B-2 Bombers, suggesting, inter alia, the limited capabilities of the aircraft against potential terrorist targets. Instead, Secretary Roche proposed to upgrade Lockheed Martin's F-15E fighters with improved telecommunications capabilities. Such modifications would enable pilots to obtain critical information from U.S. spy planes or ground forces. Vice President Richard Cheney and Defense Secretary Donald Rumsfeld have been strong supporters of the B-2 Bomber.

Boeing Co.'s C-17 transport plane, designed to operate from short, undeveloped fields, can carry up to 102 paratroopers and their gear although it is also used to transport humanitarian relief supplies. The plane's high wings and other capabilities enable the plane to make short, low-speed approaches and very steep takeoffs, critical features when used in hostile environments. Up to now, Boeing has provided 75 C-17s to the Pentagon, with funds earmarked to acquire an additional 59 during the next few years. Even prior to September 11, 2001, the office of Defense Secretary Donald Rumsfeld advocated spending $15 billion to acquire more C-17s through 2007. Great Britain's Royal Air Force has also leased 4 of these aircraft.

Northrop Grumman's Global Hawk is one of several Unmanned Aerial Vehicles (UAVs) that are used to gather intelligence on enemy forces. UAVs use various sensors and can send data to commanders, undertaking missions too dangerous for manned aircraft. The Global Hawk flies a maximum speed of 397 miles per hour, at up to 67,300 feet, with a maximum range of 3,000 nautical miles. Also, the Global Hawk can fly 42 hours without refueling, and, with synthetic aperture radar, gathers and sends photo-quality images of moving targets (including images of objects as small as a truck) via satellite to other aircraft and commanders on the ground.

General Dynamics of Fairfax, Virginia, produces Predator RQ-1, a $3 million UAV that flies at nearly 15,000 feet with a maximum range of 500 nautical miles. While vulnerable to antiaircraft fire, the Air Force's 75 Predators use ground-penetrating radar that can spot buried land mines, including plastic versions, as well as gather other sensitive information. Also, the Predator RQ-1 was outfitted with Hellfire missiles during part of the U.S. campaign against Afghanistan.

Other UAVs in the U.S. arsenal that may be called upon in Afghanistan or in the future include: (1) the Hunter, which provides near real-time imagery of ground forces in both day and night and has a maximum range of 144 nautical miles with a top speed and altitude of 122 miles per hour and 15,000 feet, respectively; and (2) the Black Widow, a short-distance micro-air vehicle (six inches in length and wingspan), has a maximum altitude of 769 feet, and range of less than one nautical mile. It is still in testing.

Smart weapons guided by Global Positioning System (GPS) signals, cruise missiles, and bombs such as Joint Direct Attack Munition (JDAM) can locate targets in any weather, and distinguish between a tank and a tractor to destroy the chosen target. JDAM, made by Boeing Co., is a precision-guided bomb, and costs $15,000. A Tomahawk Cruise Missile and an AGM-65 Maverick air-to-ground guided missile, produced by Raytheon, each costs $1 million, and $117,000, respectively. Advanced ground-penetrating bombs can pierce deep, multi-story bunkers and explode at precisely the correct level.

Among missiles and bombs in the U.S. arsenal are AGM-86 Cruise Missiles (air-to-ground strategic cruise missiles), AGM-154 JSQW, and SLAM-ER (Standoff Land Attack Missile Expanded Response). The leading six Defense Department missile contractors in 2000, as listed below, will allow us to gain a better perspective on the concentration of market share in this sub-sector of the U.S. defense industry: Lockheed Martin ($1.752 billion, 48.34% market share), Raytheon ($1.317 billion, 36.33% market share), Northrop Grumman ($150 million, 4.13% market share), General Dynamics ($81 million, 2.23% market share), Motorola ($48 million, 1.31% market share), and Boeing ($41 million, 1.14% market share). Lockheed Martin and Raytheon are dominant in this sub-sector.

An aircraft carrier has a crew of about 3,200 sailors plus pilots for 75 or more aircraft. Among some of the aircraft carriers in the U.S. arsenal are: USS *Enterprise*, USS *Nimitz*, USS *Kitty Hawk*, and USS *John F. Kennedy*. On October 23, 2001, the Department of Defense announced its approval of Northrop Grumman Corp.'s proposal to acquire Newport News Building Inc., which builds nuclear submarines and nuclear-powered aircraft carriers. Newport News has 17,800 workers and expects 2001 sales to reach $2.1 billion. Also in 2001, Northrop Grumman acquired Litton Industries Inc., the U.S. Navy's largest builder of conventionally powered surface ships. In conjunction with the announcement on Northrop Grumman, the Department of Justice filed an antitrust lawsuit opposing General Dynamics' April 2001 offer to purchase Newport News for $2.6 billion, fearing the deal would eliminate competition in the market for nuclear submarines.

Ground combat systems that are available to U.S. forces include: M1 Abrams Battle Tank, M2A3 and M3A3 Bradley Infantry Fighting Vehicles, and M270 MLRS self-propelled loader/launcher.

Military-focused technology is also improving the Pentagon's capacity to locate and attack an elusive enemy. Among the key areas that may grow in prominence is covert surveillance capability. Covert surveillance includes sophisticated radar-equipped planes, satellites, and UAVs that aid in mapping terrain, locating and following enemy targets, listening in on communications, and gathering intelligence on terrorists and their sponsors. Ground troops, issued with GPS receivers and satellite equipment, can upload to base camp what each team member sees. A laser viewing system and advanced night vision gear are crucial for identifying buildings, cars, and people during military incursions.

In September 2001, U.S. forces in the Persian Gulf included the aircraft carrier USS *Carl Vinson*, other ships, 70 aircraft, 1 submarine, several cruisers and destroyers, and 400 cruise missiles. U.S. capabilities in the Indian Ocean are comprised of the aircraft carrier USS *Enterprise*, 4 fighter squadrons, 14 ships, and 500 cruise missiles. The Pentagon mobilized military commando units for possible use in Afghanistan, including: Green Berets, Rangers, and Delta Force. Additional soldiers as well as military and support equipment are being advanced at the time of this writing.

The threat of war and subsequent initiation of military activities in Afghanistan generally gave defense stocks a boost in September-October 2001. Raytheon Co., which manufactures Tomahawk cruise missiles as well as sensors and radars for UAVs, saw its stock rise by 37% during the September 17, 2001, trading week. Also, during that period, the stocks of L-3 Communications and Lockheed Martin accelerated 35.8% and 10.1%, respectively.

In early October 2001, Northrop Grumman Corp., which produces UAVs, electronic jamming devices, and surveillance equipment, reached a 3-year high stock price of $107.60. At the same time, the stock of General Dynamics of Falls Church, Virginia, reached a record level, $94.99.

CACI International of Arlington, Virginia, a government information technology company with Federal Aviation Administration (FAA), Justice Department, and Department of Defense contracts, has viewed its stock reach near all-time highs since the World Trade Center and Pentagon attacks, closing at $52.67 on October 18, 2001.

Not as fortunate were the stocks of Honeywell International and United Technologies, which witnessed their stocks drop by 30.5% and 36.2%, respectively, during the September 17, 2001, trading week.

Of note, too, is Specialty Bags Corp. of Carrollton, Texas. The company has played a role in both military and humanitarian efforts in America's role in Afghanistan. Specialty Bags, which produces bags that protect sensitive products from external elements, makes aluminum foil and polyethylene wrappings for "meals ready to eat" (better known as MREs) as well as bomb bags.

Against the backdrop of September 11, 2001, the Pentagon is increasingly interested in anti-terrorism and counter-terrorism capabilities. According to Defense Department officials, the Pentagon is soliciting new initiatives in this vein. After only several days, the department's web site on this matter—www.bids.tswg.gov—received over 5,000 registrations and almost 50 submissions.

Government procurement in information technology, a growing portion of which will be allocated on anti-terrorism and counter-terrorism activities, will reach $45 billion in products and services in fiscal year 2001. According to Lockheed Martin, that figure is projected to reach $60 billion in 2006.

III Security Equipment, Technology, and Related Services

The terrorist attacks have brought to the forefront high technology security equipment and diverse services that will enable the government and businesses to better monitor and safeguard locations, including airports and office buildings, as well as pick terrorists out of a crowd than the public and private sectors have been able to do before. These products include: facial recognition software that can match an image against a database of criminals and terrorists; iris-scanning cameras that authenticate that a particular individual is the person he or she claims to be; small high-resolution digital cameras; technology that can "smell" tiny traces of explosives; motion sensors; smart identification cards; and other gadgets. Demand for traditional security and investigative services as well as firearms may possibly rise in the post-September 11, 2001, environment.

This section covers such developments and subjects in the following order: biometric devices; trace detection and identification instruments; video cameras and video-chip technology; document authentication machines; aviation software and other aviation aids; security, protection, and investigation services; and firearms.

Biometric Devices

For several years, cutting-edge identification and detection technologies have helped specialists in the battle against terrorism instruments. But, the September 11, 2001, terrorist attacks could transform these once exotic technologies into everyday tools used in airports and elsewhere. This is particularly so as the Bush administration plans to invest billions of dollars to enhance airport security by adopting measures ranging from reinforcing aircraft cockpit doors to stationing National Guard members at airport inspection stations.

Airport security seeks to accomplish 2 tasks: identify potential hijackers or criminals; and find and confiscate explosives or weapons before they get onboard a plane. Using biometrics (unique physical characteristics, such as a fingerprint or eye iris used to identify individuals) to search for terrorists among incoming passengers could ultimately prove crucial to keeping some terrorists out of the country or at least identifying and, subsequently, following them.

Biometric systems that scan people's features will prove helpful when matched against law enforcement and other databases, particularly when they contain current profiles of dangerous suspects. The biometric equipment will complement basic x-ray machines and metal detectors airlines currently use.

Iridian Technologies Inc. of Moorestown, New Jersey, manufactures an instrument that verifies the identity of a person by imaging the iris of a person's eye. Iristech of San Jose, California, produces iris-scanning products that also have the capacity to detect recent drug use. On the consumer side, Panasonic of Japan is marketing a personal computer camera, Authenticam, that uses iris identification.

Another line of defense against terrorists is facial-recognition software. The software of Visionics Corp. of Jersey City, New Jersey, and Viisage Technology, Inc. of Littleton, Massachusetts, captures human faces, locates key features, and calculates the dimensions of a person's skull. Subsequently, the software matches "face prints" against a database of persons. Viisage's FaceFinder has been used at the Fresno Yosemite International Airport since October 2001, and plans to be tested at Boston's Logan International Airport in December 2001.

Face recognition systems had only $10 million in sales in 2000, but recent installations by private industry, including casinos trying to spot card-counters, suggest that the technology and respective products will readily find new customers. Also, police in Tampa, Florida, have installed 36 Visionics surveillance cameras in a shopping mall to help identify wanted criminals.

In fall 2001, the U.S. government will be testing face recognition technology as part of a $50 million project called Human-ID-at-a-Distance project funded by the Defense Advanced Research Projects Agency (DARPA). The objective is to identify people at up to 500 feet and determine whether or not they are carrying weapons.

Against a sufficiently current and accurate database, coupled with alert and well-trained personnel operating various facial recognition systems, American borders—whether at airports or cross-points along U.S. borders with Mexico and Canada—could become much more secure than at present. Of course, the utility of facial recognition systems is limited when prospective terrorists are not already in the database due to faulty intelligence or they have not committed acts that would warrant suspicion.

Identix Inc. of Los Gatos, California, sells a device that digitizes fingerprints, which are checked against the Federal Bureau of Investigation (FBI) databases to see if the subject is wanted for crimes. Recognition Systems Inc. of Campbell, California, produces HandReader, a device that matches a person's handprint against information stored in the system so as to limit access to restricted areas. About 180 of Recognition's handprint recognition panels are in use at San Francisco International Airport. Also, Evive Corp. of Rockville, Maryland, offers systems that use finger scanners to enable companies to restrict access to their offices. Vocent of Mountain View, California, sells a voice identification system that may have capabilities at facilities such as airports.

Trace Detection and Identification Instruments

Trace detection machines now operate alongside metal detectors at security checkpoints. In all, several thousand machines are in airports, embassies, police stations, prisons, nuclear power plants, and other tight security environments worldwide. The machines complement bomb-sniffing dogs and devices that search for bombs inside luggage by using CT scanners similar to the ones found in hospitals.

L-3 Communications of New York, and InVision Technologies Inc. of Newark, California, are the only two companies that are currently certified by the FAA to produce explosive-scanning machines. In the case of InVision's CTX5500 model, almost 400 pieces of luggage can be screened in an hour. In September 2001, InVision's explosive scanners were used in 47 U.S. airports. L-3 has sold 26 of its machines worldwide. InVision and L-3 expect to accelerate production of their units to 50 and 40 per month, respectively. Due to the passage of federal aviation security legislation on November 16, 2001— President Bush signed it into law several days later—there is a requirement that by the end of 2002 all 450 airports in the United States will need to screen luggage for bombs by machine. To meet this mandate, about 2,000 additional bomb-detection machines will be required.

Barringer Instruments of Warren, New Jersey, produces several trace and detection devices capable of identifying explosives, narcotics, and chemical weapons agents. Among the products offered by Barringer are: a desktop unit, Ionscan Model 400B; a hand-held unit, Ionscan Sabre 2000; and a non-contact, walk-through unit, Ionscan Sentinel.

American Science and Engineering of Billerica, Massachusetts, produces a device that uses x-rays to penetrate clothing and scan the contours of a person's body. Also, California-based Rapiscan markets Secure 1000, a non-intrusive scanner designed to detect metal and non-metal objects—plastic and wooden weapons, narcotics, and bundled currency—that may be hidden under a person's clothing.

CyTerra Corp. of Waltham, Massachusetts, is developing a handheld device that detects non-metal objects, such as plastic knives, wood, rubber, or explosives. Sandia National Laboratories in Albuquerque, New Mexico, operated by Lockheed Martin for the U.S. Department of Energy, is producing Hound, a 6-inch miniature sniffer that weighs eight pounds and can be produced for $5,000 apiece. Hound will aid in making fast chemical identifications that may be time-sensitive, as in the aftermath of a terrorist attack.

Thermo Electron of Chelmsford, Massachusetts, is a multifaceted manufacturing company with an explosive detection gear division generating about $800 million in 2000. Thermo's EGIS II Explosives Detection System can detect a variety of commercial and military explosives, such as Semtex, dynamite, C4, and TNT.

The EGIS II chemiluminescent detector will only react to nitrogen-based compounds (all nitrogen-based high explosives contain nitro groups), thereby making the machine more selective than other detectors that may display false positives. Also, a hand-held analyzer unit can detect explosives via collecting vapors from volatile explosives, including nitroglycerin and TNT, in addition to trace particles from non-volatile explosives, such as RDX and PETN.

Video Cameras and Video-Chip Technology

A new video-processing chip of Pyramid Vision Technology of Princeton, New Jersey, enables cameras to identify moving objects and keeps them in sharp focus. Creative Labs, a digital camera maker, combines motion-detection features into its software. These attributes enable computers to control multiple cameras and zoom in on an individual's face. EarthCam of Hackensack, New Jersey, markets ConstructionCam, that has a heater, defroster, fan, and windshield wiper for the lens, enabling guards to monitor from afar construction sites and corporate entrances in all weather.

Surveillance cameras and closed circuit television (CCTV) are already in use at airports, government buildings, military facilities, factories, shopping malls, and increasingly throughout other U.S. locations. It is interesting to note that several hijackers involved in the World Trade Center and Pentagon attacks were caught on surveillance cameras at ATM machines, stores, and airports, facilitating the investigation of the terrorist incidents. With better timing, more accurate databases, and a little luck for law enforcement, perhaps some of the attacks of September 11, 2001, could have been prevented.

Document Authentication Machines

Logix Co. of Longmont, Colorado, produces hand-held scanners that enable the operator to authenticate passports and other identification cards (IDs) as well as physical characteristics—hair, color, and height—so officials can make instant comparisons. Since the September 11, 2001, terrorist attacks, Logix has received inquiries from airports and government agencies, such as the U.S. Secret Service.

Aviation Software and Other Aviation Aids

While some companies are focusing on physical security measures on commercial flights—steel-reinforced cockpit doors and arming pilots with stun guns—other firms are developing aircraft technology that would allow ground controllers (or the planes' own navigation systems) to prevent control by hijackers. The envisioned goal is to disable the cockpit controls of a suspiciously deviating aircraft and enable the plane to descend to a safe landing through a capability called autoflight. With autoflight, a jet can be guided safely from a cruising altitude to landing without interference by anyone in the cockpit.

Some problems still remain in achieving a complete autoflight capability. Presently, pilots must enter the destination airport, manually engage the autolander when the aircraft nears the airport, and dial the frequency of the radio signal that guides the plane to the runway.

Most commercial aircraft could modify autoflight to remote-control systems to be triggered in case of a hijacking. However, it is more complex to craft a "kill switch" that would altogether disable cockpit controls. In most planes rudder pedals and throttle levers are linked mechanically through hydraulics, and a strong pilot (or terrorist) at the controls could physically overpower the autopilot.

In contrast, triggering a kill switch would be simple with the new fly-by-wire controls introduced in a growing number of commercial jets. Once initiated, the kill switch would disconnect the cockpit controls and leave everything in the hands of the autoflight system. Two new jetliners, the Airbus A320 and the Boeing 777, are already rigged for fly-by-wire operation. Given the specter of the 4 hijackings on September 11, 2001, it is expected that more commercial jets will be similarly equipped.

Shortly after President Bush promised to set aside $500 million to assist airlines with aviation security, various airlines commenced bolstering security on their aircraft. American Airlines announced it received FAA approval to install reinforcing bars of its own design on the cockpit doors of all its planes.

AIM Group LLC of Great Britain markets a crossbar lock that fits on the doors of MD-80, MD-90, DC-9, and 737 aircraft. The device can be modified to fit on other aircraft types.

Qualcomm, Inc. of San Diego, California, and Globstar Telecommunications LP of San Jose, California, are developing a satellite-based system with a capability to broadcast live commercial airline conversations, flight information, and passenger movements onboard to air controllers. If and when implemented, the system could provide advanced warning to aviation officials on the ground of an impending emergency, including a terrorist attack. Against the backdrop of the 4 hijackings on September 11, 2001, which were clearly terrorist incidents, and the crash of American Airlines Flight 587, which at the time of this writing appears to be due to mechanical failure, technology that Qualcomm and Globstar proposes could be useful to law enforcement, intelligence, and transportation officials in case of future airport disasters.

In November 2001, Taser International announced that United Airlines would purchase about $700,000 worth of stun guns that shoot electrical charges capable of disabling a person for between 30 seconds to 30 minutes. The stun guns would possibly be issued to pilots. During fall 2001, there was also discussion by aviation and security officials as well as aviation employees whether pilots should be issued firearms.

Security, Protection, and Investigation Services

In 2001, the average corporate security budget was $667,000, up about 5% from 2000, according to *Security Magazine*. Following the September 11, 2001, terrorist incidents business is paying greater attention to corporate security than they did before that date. As General Motors chief executive officer (CEO) Rick Wagoner commented, "At all of our sites and at our corporate headquarters, we are revving up security."

The large number of employees required to staff security checkpoints at transportation facilities, businesses, shopping malls, universities, and government installations worldwide should result in a windfall for security service companies. The demand for bodyguards, armored cars, sentries, background checks, and identification screening rose significantly since the World Trade Center and Pentagon incidents.

A company that may benefit is Wackenhut Corporation of Palm Beach Gardens, Florida, one of the largest security companies in the United States. Wackenhut is a leading provider of private security overseas, domestic aviation security, and a major operator of privatized prisons. Wackenhut provides several hundred security screeners at 5 U.S. airports. The company employs about 75,000 people and has operations in over 50 countries.

Guardsmark of New York is another large security services firm with 17,000 employees and 135 offices in the United States. Kroll Inc. of New York also provides corporate security consulting services. Due to increasing demand for its services, Kroll, with already 1,500 workers worldwide, plans to hire about 100 people from the date of the World Trade Center and Pentagon attacks through February 2002. Kroll's stock rose 84% only four weeks following the September eleven attacks.

With regard to security products, Southwest Microwave, Inc. of Tempe, Arizona, sells Intrepid—a new generation perimeter security system containing software-controlled zones with remote diagnostics. ADT Security Services, a supplier of home and business security systems, has received calls from customers seeking additional layers of security.

Companies in the smart card business include Cubic and ActivCard. Cubic is exploring how to adapt its smart card technology, already implemented in mass transit cards, to limit access into secure areas. Pitney Bowes offers secure mail technology products and services. Following the anthrax mail attacks during fall 2001, the company made available its publication, "Mail and Document Security: A Pitney Bowes Executive Advisor," free of charge.

In October 2001, Noel Pearman of St. Paul, Minnesota, obtained a patent for a "method and apparatus," related to safeguarding workers in a building in the event of biological or chemical attacks. Also, Pearman and collaborators at Honeywell Corp. were awarded another patent for a "method and apparatus," focusing on plugging up an edifice's ductwork should a biological or chemical attack occur.

Argenbright Security Inc. provided security at two airports (Dulles International, and Logan International) from where terrorists boarded and hijacked planes on September 11, 2001. Since then, the company has pledged to improve its services and hiring practices. Subsequently, Argenbright announced that it would improve employee training, raise wages for workers, and increase the number of employees assigned to x-ray machines.

In October 2001, Argenbright settled Justice Department claims—stemming from an earlier case—that the firm failed to comply with a court order by continuing to employ security checkpoint screeners with criminal records. In mid-November 2001, Massachusetts officials initiated steps to remove Argenbright's state security license.

Argenbright has 10,000 security screeners working at 38 U.S. airports. In fall 2001, several well-publicized security breaches involved Argenbright, including two incidents at O'Hare International Airport when passengers carrying knives, a stun gun, and other weapons passed company screeners.

Globe Aviation Services was one of four security companies that screened passengers at Logan International Airport, the location of 2 hijacked planes on September 11, 2001. Globe has 3,133 security screeners at 39 U.S. airports. Other leading airport security firms include: Huntleight USA, which has 8,000 security screeners at 35 U.S. airports; and International Total Services of Cleveland, Ohio, which has 5,315 security screeners at 113 U.S. airports.

The passage of November 2001 aviation security legislation, with its mandate for the introduction of 28,000 federal workers to serve as baggage screeners and security workers, in conjunction with additional federal sky marshals, was good news for the airline and tourism industries. Not surprisingly, the development was not embraced by companies offering aviation security personnel at U.S. airports as they hoped that the 28,000 positions would be filled by private contractors. The law does allow for airports to opt out of the federal worker system after three years. Analysts suggested that once adopted, federalization of aviation security will be difficult to modify.

Also, the September 11 attacks caused some employers to accelerate the use of background checks on employees, contractors, and potential hires. As a result, background-screening companies have experienced increased business by employers nationwide. For instance, Choicepoint Inc. of Alpharetta, Georgia; HireCheck Inc. of St. Petersburg, Florida; and Background Check International of Temecula, California, witnessed a dramatic rise in inquiries regarding their services. Potential clients' requests range from standard hiring procedure services to increasing surveillance of employees. Background checks will likely become increasingly important in the highly security-conscious environment that America will find itself.

Companies are legally bound to undertake criminal background checks for airport employees with access to secure areas. The aviation security law mandates additional background checks for other workers as well.

Finally, the possibility exists that international and domestic terrorist groups may kidnap prominent business leaders based in the United States in order to obtain cash to fund their organizations' activities. Such threats are not inconceivable if one observes kidnappings of businessmen by terrorists and criminals in Colombia and Brazil. An historical precedent of terrorists attacking leading business figures includes the murder of the chairman of Deutsche Bank, Alfred Herrhausen, by the German terrorist group, Red Army Faction, in 1989. Due to such threats, some business leaders may also seek counter-terrorism training for executives, bodyguards, and other protection products and services, including, at the extreme, armored cars with specially trained and armed drivers.

Firearms

Psychologists explain that the September 11, 2001, terrorist attacks and anthrax outbreaks had magnified effects on people because the incidents got them to think about becoming a victim of terrorism. People are especially nervous about the catastrophic terrorist incident of autumn 2001 and the complexity of capturing and prosecuting domestic and international terrorists. As such, some Americans are seeking various forms of protection, including purchasing firearms.

A surge in gun sales arose in the days after September 11, 2001, according to gun dealers and law enforcement statistics. Nationally, the FBI, which conducts instant background checks on firearm sales in 25 states, stated that the number of applications to buy handguns rose by 15% above normal during September 11-13, 2001. Applications to buy handguns in Maryland more than doubled during the week of the World Trade Center and Pentagon incidents. Virginia State Police announced that background checks on those who seek to buy handguns, rifles, and shotguns were up 32% during the same period. Many of the buyers were purchasing firearms for the first time.

At the fall 2001 Wanenmacher's Tulsa Arms Show, a leading gun show with about 3,800 vendors and thousands of attendees, heightened interest in self-defense was prevalent. The National Rifle Association reported that during autumn 2001, the organization's firearm training sessions have been packed.

IV Diverse Technology Products and Services

Assorted technology products and services will be called up in the future to counter domestic and international terrorism. Among the instruments that will be available to the private and public sectors are: military-oriented telecommunications and software; security software; data mining; data storage, recovery services, and emergency-management software; national identification cards; videoconferencing, teleconferencing, and the Internet; wireless technology and other telephony; and personal digital assistants and hand-held computers.

Military-Oriented Telecommunications and Software

The U.S. government's interception, exploitation, and jamming of electronic communications—radiated through the atmosphere, sea, or fixed lines—cost billions of dollars. These military telecommunications systems were forged, in part, to eavesdrop on conversations and data traffic of U.S. adversaries. The listening posts in this worldwide surveillance network extend from simple radio antennas wired into sophisticated receivers to undersea fiber-optic cables.

The network is comprised of spy satellites that can catch radio and other waves emanating from earth, beam the captured data to receivers on various continents, and then relay the data to the headquarters of the National Security Agency in Fort Meade, Maryland. Also, some of the above listening points feed data into the computers of a Cold War-inspired intelligence cooperative called Echelon, maintained by the United States, Canada, Great Britain, Australia, and New Zealand. Manufacturers, installers, and contractors for the aforementioned equipment will likely experience additional business as the role of defense and intelligence gathering, both human and electronic, in the war against terrorism should last many years.

Initial investigation of the perpetrators of the September 11, 2001, attacks and other al-Qaida members indicate that they employed everyday technologies (i.e., voice mail, cellular phones, and e-mail) to communicate, though often using codes, encryption, and other methodologies when exchanging operations-sensitive information. These steps were used, in part, to elude intelligence and law enforcement authorities. In some cases, terrorists have used multiple cellular phones to evade interception: some phones only receive incoming calls; others make outgoing calls.

Of particular importance is data encryption technology as the software makes it difficult for government officials to follow terrorists' communication exchanges. In response, law enforcement agents use several means, including a series of devices called Intermediate Frequency (IF)-to-tape converters and cyber-surveillance to investigate suspected terrorists.

Shortly following the September 11 attacks, Solipsys Corp. of Laurel, Maryland, was approached by the U.S. Air Force about providing specialty software at five air defense sites to permit the military to improve detection of a wayward aircraft in the nation's air traffic control system. The project, costing between $1-$2 million, will involve equipping the air defense sites of the North American Air Defense Command (NORAD)—a U.S.-Canadian military organization that detects attacks against North America by aircraft or missiles—with Solipsys's Tactical Component Network (TCN). TCN is a data-fusing system that acquires data from various sources and then garners them into a comprehensive picture. The systems will allow NORAD to incorporate air traffic control data into its monitoring systems to rapidly identify a plane that has swayed off course.

Presently, the FAA alerts NORAD if a plane has veered off course. NORAD then sends out fighter jets from the Air National Guard group closest to the incident to track the plane. Solipsys's software is particularly relevant in light of President Bush's mandate in September 2001 to allow two generals in NORAD emergency authority to shoot down planes that threaten America.

Security Software

In light of cyber-terrorism threats, security software firms, offering anti-virus software, fire walls, and intrusion detection, may experience further inquiries by prospective clients: businesses, governments, and individuals. Among leading and cutting-edge companies offering such services are:

- Check Point Software Technology: a principal supplier of fire walls to cable and DSL Internet service providers

- Cigital: a company offering solutions to firms that experience their wire data networks hacked from wireless networks

- CyberGuard Corp.: markets network firewalls such as KnightStar, a $21,000-$24,000 product, with the highest level of certified security— Common Criteria Evaluation Assurance Level 4

- EDS Corp.: a multi-faceted technology firm that also markets leading-edge data security services

- Entrust: a provider of multiple Internet security solutions

- Internet Security Systems: a provider of multiple Internet security services to the private and public sectors

- Network Associates: a firm that sells critical anti-virus software

- RSA Security: a seller of SecurID technology that permits only authorized users remote access to corporate networks

- Symantec: a company that provides anti-virus software, fire walls (the VelociRaptor product costs about $15,000), and intrusion detection software

Following the World Trade Center and Pentagon terrorism attacks, the FBI's InfraGard website, www.infragard.net, (a private-public organization established in January 2001 that aids in the fight on cyber-terrorism) cautioned companies, including data centers, of possible cyber terrorist attacks. In October 2001, President Bush strengthened American resolve against fighting cyber terrorism with the appointment of Dick Clarke as Special Advisor for Cyber Security.

Another entity assisting in the war on cyber-terrorism is the Internet Security Alliance: a joint venture between the Electronics Industry Alliance and Carnegie Mellon University. Also, Applied Systems Intelligence of Roswell, Georgia, is developing software termed Karnac—for Knowledge Aided Retrieval Activity Context—that would allow for the gathering and synthesizing information from government and private sources for use in criminal investigations.

On October 1, 2001, the FBI and the SANS Institute released a list of the top 20 vulnerabilities in computer systems to help system administrators determine which problems most urgently need fixing and giving them step-by-step guides for correcting the problem. The list and guide can be found at: www.sans.org/top20.htm. Moreover, in a November 2001 report of the House Government Reform Subcommittee on Government Efficiency, the federal government was awarded an overall letter grade of F for computer security, as about 66% of federal agencies' computer security measures were deemed highly deficient.

Despite these negative developments, the FBI is utilizing cutting-edge software technologies to fight against domestic and international terrorist groups. For instance, the FBI uses the system DCS1000—formerly known as Carnivore—that can be placed on an Internet Service Provider's (ISP) server. Once in place, the FBI can monitor the ISP's Internet traffic. In doing so, the FBI can read, analyze, and plan tactical responses to potential terrorist threats uncovered as a result of using DCS1000.

Data Mining

Data mining software enables the government to comb through hundreds of millions of intercepted e-mail messages, faxes, and phone calls in minutes, and thereby aid in tracking down the location of a suspected terrorist. Data mining systems are even capable of distinguishing a single voice out of thousands of cell phone conversations.

Data mining technologies is invaluable, as government entities investigate terrorists by extracting valuable information quickly from raw commercial, scientific, and intelligence information. Companies, such as IBM, Computer Associates International Inc., Oracle Corp., Teradata Corp., and ClearCross Inc., have the capacity to further aid government agencies in the fight against terrorism. Industry analysts suggest that technology for gathering, integrating, and processing information has been underutilized in the past in the war on terrorism.

Data Storage, Recovery Services, and Emergency-Management Software

A September 2001 survey of 5,700 companies by the Society of Human Resource Management found that nearly 33% of such entities do not have any disaster contingency plans. Other industry estimates suggest that less than 25% of companies and government agencies use dedicated software to run disaster-recovery functions. Following the September 11, 2001, terrorist incidents, in conjunction with billions of losses due to cyber-terrorism as well as national disasters, more companies are seeking advanced data storage, recovery services, and emergency management software.

Storage services provide different options. They can furnish limited options, such as the manual downloading of data on magnetic tapes followed by the routine forwarding of the tapes to companies specializing in off-site storage services. Storage services also provide broad options in which companies may purchase software and services that allow for data to be duplicated and transmitted to a remote location through secure, high-speed communications.

Potential customers have increasingly approached data storage leaders Veritas Software Corp. and EMC Corp. Other data storage services worth profiling include Iron Mountain Inc. of Boston, Massachusetts, which stores both paper records and computer tapes at 650 locations around the world. Iron Mountain made regular pickups of data tapes from customers on Wall Street. Following the September 11, 2001, attacks, numerous Iron Mountain clients requested backup tapes from the company.

Recall Corp. of Fort Lee, New Jersey, also stores millions of computer tapes backing up the systems of hundreds of companies. At its New York sites, the company holds 2 million tapes with 160 petabytes (160 million gigabytes) of data, including confidential client information, transaction records, account traffic, and legal briefs. Recall responded to clients who had been based near the World Trade Center. Other companies, such as TLM, SkyDesk, and NovaStor, store crucial data off-site and, in fact, online.

IBM's disaster recovery and contingency-planning business, which generates about $600 million annually, saw additional inquiries from potential customers since September 11. EDS Corp. acknowledged a 200% increase from prospective clients in its business continuity planning and disaster recovery services. EAI Corp. of Abingdon, Maryland, advises U.S. government agencies on emergency preparedness.

Emergency management software firms, such as Essential Technologies Inc., Alert Technologies, and E Team Inc., obtained additional exposure since the September 11, 2001, terrorist incidents. E Team sold its software system, which enables numerous agencies and thousands of workers to coordinate distinct emergency activities, to the New York City Mayor's office months prior to the attacks.

In the aftermath of the September 11, 2001, terrorist incidents, the Bank of New York suffered an 8-day outage in its network of automated teller machines (ATMs). Yet, customers were able to get their money from branches or from ATMs owned by other banks. Also, some companies with offices in the World Trade Center acknowledged that they did not copy all of their important documents in another location, such as at a document storage facility.

Nationally, terrorist incidents prompted leaders of small and large companies to rethink disaster planning. In particular, such planning has raised the question of whether every company needs some form of "off-site" computer backup to supplement in-house support. A post-September 11 mantra in this sector is that centralized activities may engender greater susceptibility of harm during a catastrophic terrorist attack.

It should be noted, however, that some Wall Street firms would be inoperative after the September 11, 2001, had they not been prompted to establish contingency plans. Such developments were spurred, in part, by the 1987 stock market crash and the 1993 bombing of the World Trade Center. Financial firms used various services that enabled them to gear up shortly after the disaster. In light of the importance of a second line of defense against a terrorist attack on the principal operations, Morgan Stanley announced in October 2001 that it would build a fully functioning, backup trading floor within 35 miles of its Manhattan headquarters.

Government entities also realize the importance of being prepared for emergencies. For example, the Office of Personnel Management (OPM) has had a comprehensive disaster plan in place for nearly two years. At OPM's Washington, D.C., headquarters, which houses 2,500 workers and contractors, about 200 people have been assigned to act as an emergency response team.

In case of an attack against telecommunication systems, the Telecommunications Service Priority System (TSPS) is triggered. The TSPS is a U.S. government agency that was created to ensure the efficacy of government communications—for military, law enforcement, fire and rescue, and other government agencies—even under severe shocks to telecommunications systems.

Professor Ron LaPorte of the University of Pittsburgh and other public health experts are proposing expanded use of the Global Health Network (GHN), which links doctors and scientists worldwide for news on infectious disease outbreaks. The GHN system and possibly others could be helpful in using the Internet to distribute information on health crises, such as those prompted by bio-terrorism attacks.

National Identification Cards

In another measure to fight terrorism, the U.S. government may require citizens, resident aliens, and others to obtain and carry a National ID. The card could be a relatively unsophisticated paper card with little information, such as a name, a national identity number, and perhaps, an address. Such a card would be of little value as it could easily be forged. Without a photo of an individual's face, it would not be helpful for purposes of identification.

Alternatively, the National ID could be made similar to a smart card and could be imbedded with computer chips. Such a smart card would be difficult to alter or forge. Also, the smart card National ID could store more information than an anachronistic paper card and could be easily scanned by U.S. government authorities.

The U.S. government may seek to include data on National ID, such as: a digital photograph and thumbprint; designation of height, weight, race, blood type, eye and hair color; citizenship or immigration status; home address, and telephone number; voter registration data; and driving and criminal records.

According to some estimates, a simple data-storage National ID would cost between $10 to $35 apiece to produce and implement. With the U.S. population soon approaching 300 million, establishment of such a system would involve significant financial and bureaucratic resources, however necessary. It is worth noting that more than 100 nations use National IDs, although the technological complexity of National IDs and the information contained therein vary widely.

The National ID may counter some of the threats of the multi-billion dollar global counterfeit and stolen document racket. On the black market, for example, the selling price for a phony state driver's license is $25; for a U.S. immigration card it is $500; and for an authentic diplomatic passport is about $25,000. At San Ysidro, an entry point on the U.S.-Mexican border, the U.S. Immigration and Naturalization Service (INS) apprehended 52,000 people using false identification cards in the year 2000. It is important to remember that a number of the terrorists involved in the September 11, 2001, attacks used valid state driver's licenses, fraudulently obtained driver's licenses, and forged passports. Manufacturers and firms specializing in smart identification cards and related peripherals may get a windfall of business if the United States undertakes procurement of these items.

Videoconferencing, Teleconferencing, and the Internet

In their post-September 11 mindset, many business travelers may avoid travel. Several companies providing videoconferencing, teleconferencing, and Internet-based collaboration tools, including Picturetel, Polycom, Tandberg, and Webex, are expected to see a surge in business. The stocks of such firms accelerated in the aftermath of the terrorist incidents, with Polycom and Picturetel shares rising by 34% and 43%, respectively, less than 2 weeks after the events.

Communications technologies are available to those executives who are reluctant or unable to travel. These technologies include e-mail, teleconferencing, data collaboration, and satellite broadcasting.

While all face-to-face business meetings and events cannot be replaced by videocameras and Internet chats, executives across many industries are cognizant of the factors weighing against frequent business travel: time, expense, and with the specter of terrorism, safety. Fortunately, technological advances will enable individuals worldwide to meet regularly and inexpensively. Moreover, the growing need and use of such technologies will raise their acceptability.

The U.S. Postal Service delivers nearly 680 million pieces of mail daily, amounting to 208 billion items distributed each year. Due to confirmed and suspected cases of anthrax in autumn 2001, there was some disruption to mail distribution in parts of Florida, New Jersey, New York, and Washington, D.C. Some individuals and entities have chosen to only open mail from established customers, people they know, and regular bills, while immediately discarding junk mail.

Consequently, greater use of e-mail as a form of rapid, relatively safe (aside from computer viruses), and secure (besides possible hacking) communication for personal and business purposes has taken hold in fall 2001. In fact, Neal MacDonald of the Gartner Group predicted that the anthrax scare and postal system interruptions will accelerate yearly e-mail use by an additional 5%, over and above recent 40% annual rises. Nielsen/NetRatings announced that in October 2001, 115.2 million people in the United States used the Internet.

Companies specializing in e-mail management services are expected to benefit from augmented use of e-mail for personal, business, and government correspondence. One such firm is EchoMail Inc. of Cambridge, Massachusetts. The firm defines and develops E-Mail Relationship Management (ERM) solutions. The company's EchoMail Suite powers large volumes of inbound and outbound e-mail by automatically receiving, processing, responding, storing, and tracing e-mail correspondence.

While accelerated use of e-mail is expected to occur, the use of "snail mail" seems to be entrenched for many years for various reasons. Also, only 70% of U.S. households have computers, and of those, Internet penetration, while growing, still lags under 60%. Furthermore, specific data, files, photos, awkwardly shaped documents, or highly sensitive papers would have to go through a scanner—another computer peripheral not all households own—and be forwarded to it by e-mail. Also, products and other items that must be forwarded from one geographical location to another cannot be e-mailed. In some cases, neither the sender nor the recipient wants the document forwarded over the Internet.

The majority of U.S. companies have not established systems that would enable them to send bills and receive payment online. Still, nearly 40 million consumer bills are expected to be received and paid for online. This level of online interaction is still less than 1% of the almost 15.9 billion consumer bills that are sent by mail annually.

Nevertheless, as corporations make further use of e-mail for billing, coupled with consumers being more at ease with the Internet, online payment systems, and online currency—already in use for several years with varying levels of success—the use of e-mail for such transactions should accelerate. It is noteworthy that business-to-business (B2B) Internet commerce established itself following initial difficulties.

Wireless Technology and Other Telephony

Wireless technology, exemplified in free-space optics and broadband wireless, showed its utility following the World Trade Center incidents on September 11, 2001, when some traditional fiber-optic cables were damaged or destroyed. During the attacks in New York City about 300,000 voice lines and over 3 million data lines were obliterated. Broadband wireless service transfers data via radio waves. As fixed line telecommunications providers struggled to restore telecom service in lower Manhattan in early fall 2001, wireless technologies have received renewed interest.

Iridium Satellite and Globestar Telecommunications, sellers of handheld satellite phones, received additional business as a result of the effectiveness of those phones during the attacks, when cell phone systems in the Washington, D.C., and New York City areas were overloaded. Due to their transmission through rapidly orbiting satellites, satellite handsets can be used in any location, including office basements and remote areas (as in the mountains of Afghanistan). During the week of the incidents, Iridium reported that system utilization rose 25% and new activations increased 4-fold over previous weeks. A satellite phone reseller, Stratos Global, revealed a 400% rise in sales for the week following the attacks.

In light of the terrorist attacks of September 11 the use of cell phones as a tool of public safety rose to prominence. Cell phones were used to make 911 calls following the terrorism incidents as well as to communicate among family, coworkers, and friends. Analogously, the Federal Communications Commission required cellular phone companies to have the technology in place by October 1, 2001, to aid emergency workers in tracking down the location (within 100 meters, two-thirds of the time) of a 911 call made from a wireless phone.

Personal Digital Assistants and Hand-held Computers

Easily accessible, portable, and small gadgets, such as hand-held computers and personal digital assistants (PDAs), probably will gain immense application throughout U.S. military forces. As Commander Terry Sutherland of the U.S. Atlantic Fleet explained, the military needs "devices that make it easier to transfer information and to communicate."

PDAs produced by Palm Inc. and Handspring Inc. are principally used for data collection and information dissemination. From 2000 through June 2001, Palm sold about 70,000 Palm units to the Navy and Army. A Palm or Handspring PDA costs from $150 to $500.

Hand-held computers, essentially modified and upgraded PDAs, are adapted for military ruggedness, including special waterproofing. Paramount Computer Systems Inc. of Palm Bay, Florida, and Symbol Technologies Inc. of Holtsville, New York, produce a variety of such models. These companies offer instruments that are multi-dimensional and ultimately could map enemy locations, track personnel, and conduct heat-stress surveys. Symbol Technologies, under a $248 million contract with the Defense Department, has supplied industrialized, hand-held computers, such as Symbol PDT 2700 for $1,250.

V   Pharmaceuticals, Biotechnology, and Forensics

Pharmaceuticals and Biotechnology

Because of multiple anthrax attacks in the United States during September-November 2001, coupled with the prospects of further bio-terrorism, manufacturers of antibiotics and vaccines have experienced additional sales as governmental and consumer demand for these products accelerated. Regular immunization against pathogens, such as anthrax and smallpox may become the norm in years to come. Also, companies providing forensics investigative services may be called upon again as governmental medical and investigative teams respond in the aftermath of terrorist attacks.

Treatment for anthrax includes antibiotics, such as ciprofloxacin (Cipro), doxycycline, and penicillin. Alternate drugs include gentamicin, erthromycin, and chloramphenicol. The rule for treatment is the sooner the better. Untreated, inhalation anthrax is believed to be more than 90% fatal. Doctors fear that pervasive, prolonged use of the antibiotics could lead to spreading resistant bacteria, further undermining the efficacy of antibiotics.

Cipro is manufactured by Bayer of Leverkusen, Germany. Cipro is Bayer's best-selling drug, generating annual revenues of $1.6 billion. Cipro has rare side effects, including severe diarrhea, gastrointestinal bleeding, rashes, and sensitivity to light.

Sales of Cipro accelerated dramatically in New York City during the last two weeks of September 2001. More specifically, during the week ending September 28, 2001, 14,800 new prescriptions for Cipro were filled there, a 27% rise over a similar 2-week period a year earlier. Nationally, retail purchases of Cipro were level during the last week of September 2001. A month's supply of Cipro in the United States costs about $350.

Some individuals initially treated with Cipro in the U.S. Congress and in postal facilities in Washington, D.C., New Jersey, Florida, New York, and elsewhere received the antibiotic for free from public and private health care workers. During October 2001, about 32,000 Americans were given Cipro and other antibiotics in response to the anthrax scare.

Yet, by mid-October 2001, over 60 web sites, including the web site of VirtualMedicine Group of Morrisville, North Carolina, were selling Cipro. Nearly half of these web sites appeared since the World Trade Center and Pentagon attacks. Maryland and Virginia health officials warned against online purchases of Cipro as some Web sites do not ship products. Also, due to the hoarding of Cipro and the growing anthrax-related hysteria, the American Medical Association warned its members against prescribing Cipro to patients who do not exhibit any evidence of anthrax exposure.

Also, in mid-October 2001 Secretary of Health and Human Services (HHS) Tommy Thompson announced that the U.S. government would obtain sufficient supplies of Cipro from Bayer at a discount price of $0.95 a pill to treat 12 million people. Bayer tripled its production of Cipro with the intention of delivering 200 million tablets in 3 months. Under HHS Program 340B, Bayer will also supply Cipro at $0.43 a tablet. As of September 2001, the U.S. government is reported to have sufficient antibiotics against anthrax to treat 2 million people for 2 months.

In seeking alternatives to Cipro, in October 2001, the U.S. government began discussions with manufacturers of other antibiotics, such as doxycycline, that are effective against biological agents such as anthrax. That same month, Bayer announced it would supply more antibiotics, including doxycycline. The U.S. drug manufacturer, Pfizer, produces a generic form of doxycycline, Vibramycin.

Other medicines reportedly deemed effective against the inhalation form of anthrax include: Levaquin, made by Johnson & Johnson; Tequin, produced by Bristol-Myers Squibb; and Pencillin, manufactured by Pfizer and others.

In October 2001, the Canadian Health Ministry ordered 1 million tablets of the generic version of Cipro from Apotex Inc. of Toronto, Canada, a leading national generic drug maker. While Bayer charges C$2.00 per 500 milligram tablet of Cipro, Apotex sells its generic version for C$1.50 per pill. A month's supply of Indian generic versions of Cipro costs about $10.00.

With regard to preventing harm from anthrax, BioPort Corp. of Lansing, Michigan, produces a vaccine given in 6-shot series. However, the vaccine has thus far been available only to military personnel. The company has not manufactured the product since 1998, as the Food and Drug Administration (FDA) was examining BioPort's operations. Yet, it is expected that following expansions and renovations that are underway, the plant should receive FDA approval by the end of November 2001.

In October 2001, Acambis PLC, a British biotechnology company, entered into an agreement with the HHS to produce and deliver 40 million doses of a new smallpox vaccine in 2004. This amount was later raised to 54 million doses under a modified, accelerated schedule. The HHS also announced its plan to ultimately stockpile 300 million smallpox vaccine doses for civilian use, nearly 15 million more than the current U.S. population. It was revealed that in October 2001, HHS accepted bids to produce additional smallpox vaccines from 10 companies, including Baxter International Inc. of Deerfield, Illinois, and GlaxoSmithKline of Research Triangle, North Carolina.

BioReliance Corp. of Rockville, Maryland, is a principal subcontractor to Acambis on the smallpox vaccine. BioReliance, which is also a subcontractor of DynPort Vaccine Co. (a partnership between DynPort Corp. of Reston, Virginia, and Porton International Inc. of Washington, D.C.), has an agreement with the Department of Defense to supply the smallpox vaccine. On October 24, 2001, BioReliance announced third-quarter income for 2001 in the amount of $2.2 million on revenues of $18.6 million. This disclosure, coupled with the company's relationship with Acambis and the growing fear of bio-terrorism nationwide, helped to triple BioReliance's stock since September 10, 2001, closing at $30.31 on October 24.

Avant Immunotherapeutics, Inc. of Needham, Massachusetts, is developing various infectious disease vaccines, including oral vaccines against pathogens, such as cholera and typhoid, that may be used by terrorists. The company is reported to be testing oral anti-cholera vaccines on U.S. Army volunteers. Avant's prospects were positively received by investors, raising the stock's price by 90% from $2.71 on September 17, 2001, to $5.15 on October 12, 2001.

Noteworthy, too, is the October 2001 award of a 3-year, $800,000 grant to Advanced Biosystems Inc. of Alexandria, Virginia, to analyze medical defenses against anthrax. Also, Meridian Medical Technology of Columbia, Maryland, provides auto-injectors and drug-injection that deliver antidotes to nerve gas to the U.S. government. Meridian has seen its stock price nearly double to $19.46, in the five weeks after the World Trade Center and Pentagon attacks.

Also, GeneSoft Inc. of San Francisco, California, obtained an $8 million DARPA grant for support of novel research to counter natural and bio-engineered infections.

Forensics

Celera Genomics Corp. of Rockville, Maryland; Myriad Genetics Inc. of Salt Lake City, Utah; and Bode Technologies of Springfield, Virginia, are assisting government authorities in the largest forensics investigation ever: the September 11, 2001, terrorist attacks.

These firms are undertaking the difficult task of confirming the dead. Identifying the victims will aid grieving families, assist in securing insurance claims and death certificates, and provide remains for burial. Medical examiners usually identify victims of crime and disaster through fingerprints, dental records, wallets, tattoos, or other distinguishing body attributes. Hundreds of World Trade Center victims have been identified this way. But, as few bodies remain intact, investigators are also using DNA testing. The medical examiner's office sends DNA from samples and forwards them to Celera, Myriad, and Bode for examination.

VI Germ Detection and Remediation Services

In concert with the growing anthrax threat of September-November 2001 and the possibility of additional bio-terrorism attacks, germ detection and remediation services could play a larger role in the future.

The Ruggedized Advanced Pathogen Identification Device (R.A.P.I.D., as it is marketed) of Idaho Technology Inc. is a portable, 50 pound, pathogen detection device. This specialty instrument is optimal for use in military field hospitals, sites for first responders, and other rough environments. R.A.P.I.D. integrates proprietary technology into a portable, impact-resistant package. Distinctive software enables simple pushing of the R.A.P.I.D. Systems by field personnel with limited training. This procedure facilitates field identification of possibly dangerous pathogens in a rapid, safe, and accurate manner. R.A.P.I.D. is capable of analyzing 32 test samples simultaneously for the presence of any DNA sequence in less than 30 minutes.

In December 2000, R.A.P.I.D. was used to test patient samples of U.S. personnel based in the Prince Sultan Air Base, Saudi Arabia. The samples were rapidly identified as salmonella, a bacterial agent often associated with foodborne illness. This prompt response enabled medical and services personnel to limit the foodborne outbreak to about 3% of the base. The U.S. Air Force played a critical role in the development of R.A.P.I.D. The device is now the primary diagnostic test platform of the U.S. Air Force's Biological Augmentation Team.

Bruker Daltonics Inc. of Billerica, Massachusetts, develops and provides various tools based on mass spectrometry that allow for the detection of atomic, biological, and chemical weapons as well as chemical, drug, environmental, and explosive detection. Bruker's Neutron Induced Gamma Spectrometer can detect explosives and chemical warfare agents in ammunitions. Also, the Chemical Biological Mass Spectrometer is a rugged, U.S. Army-tested device with a fully automated operation "button" user-interface via a touch-screen computer.

Igen International Inc. of Gaithersburg, Maryland, develops and markets biological detection and measurement systems using its proprietary Origen technology. The company's Origen-based systems are used by hospitals and clinical reference laboratories to conduct 50 tests in fields including infectious diseases. Igen also markets tests for foodborne pathogens while it is developing tests for waterborne pathogens. On October 12, 2001, Igen announced that in conjunction with the U.S. Army Medical Research Institute of Infectious Diseases, it will accelerate efforts to detect food, water, and airborne pathogens. The U.S. Army and the Centers for Disease Control and Prevention (CDC) are already using Origen technology for research and assay development for identifying pathogens.

In late October 2001, the U.S. Postal Service announced that it would use the electron beam systems, x-ray products, and systems integration services of SureBeam Corporation of San Diego, California, to reduce the threat of anthrax in the U.S. mail system. SureBeam is a subsidiary of Titan Corporation of San Diego, California. Titan is the prime contractor with the U.S.

Postal Service in a deal of about $26 million for 8 SureBeam systems. As background, SureBeam is a provider of electron beam and x-ray food safety systems and services for the food industry.

Also, in light of the growing anthrax scare nationwide, including in locales and facilities previously thought to be "immune" to bio-terrorism, a number of corporations are seeking quick approval from the FDA for instruments that can test for anthrax on surfaces and in the air.

OraSure Technologies Inc. of Bethlehem, Pennsylvania, offers a fluorescent labeling anthrax test, which still awaits FDA approval. Under this test, a human or environmental sample is collected and attached to an anthrax antibody. If anthrax is present, the sample will emit phosphors that develop a signature fluorescent glow under infrared light.

Cepheid Inc. of Sunnydale, California, develops small devices that allow for the rapid and accurate detection of infectious disease agents, human genes, and industrial and environmental contaminants. The products offered by the company include: Smart Cycler System (a highly versatile and efficient thermal cycler with real-time optical detection) and Smart Cycler TD System (the aforementioned product with a laptop computer and a durable wheeled case). Also, Cepheid is developing GeneXpert Platform, which will feature full integration of sample preparation with rapid analysis and detection.

In August 2001, Cepheid announced it was collaborating with Environmental Technologies Group Inc. of Baltimore, Maryland, to design biological agent detection systems for military and other domestic preparedness applications. In fall 2001, Cepheid is producing an anthrax test based on analyzing DNA samples with the objective of finding anthrax's DNA signature in samples. Cepheid is trying to improve the test so that results appear within an hour.

Tetracore Inc. of Gaithersburg, Maryland, sells Bio-Threat Alert test strips that can detect anthrax, botulism, plague, and other contaminants. A set of 25 strips sells for $495. MesoSystems Technologies of Kennewick, Washington, manufactures a $9,600 hand-held, detection device that can take air samples that will enable the user to determine whether deadly biological agents such as anthrax and bubonic plague exist.

A number of entities—the Mayo Clinic, Roche Diagnostics Corp., Georgia Institute of Technology, and Emory University—are developing quick tests (under 1 hour) that will identify the presence of anthrax.

Cyrano Sciences Inc. of Pasadena, California, makes a hand-held device, Cyranose 320, that "digitizes smell." In other words, the machine has the sensitivity and detection capability to "smell" pure solvents (butanol, tolune, DMSO), complex mixtures (commercially available perfumes), naturally-occurring compounds, and other substances. The company is conducting tests to verify the Cyranose 320's capacity to detect warfare agents and anthrax.

Versar Inc. of Springfield, Virginia, is offering a mailroom bio-terrorism service during which the company analyzes suspicious letters and packages, decontaminates workplaces, and formulates revised mail-handling procedures. The company charges between $13,000 and $20,000 for such services. Versar saw its stock price double to $4.20 about a month after the World Trade Center and Pentagon attacks. Environmental services company Clean Harbors Environmental Services Inc. of Braintree, Massachussetts, performs anthrax testing of offices and remediation.

The traditional method to respond to anthrax contamination, advocated up to now by the CDC, is to use a bleach-based solution. Alternate methods to respond to contaminated buildings include a formulation for mitigation and decontamination of chemical and biological warfare agents licensed by Sandia National Laboratories Decon Formulation Technology. Two companies, Modec, Inc. of Denver, Colorado, and EnviroFoam Technologies, Inc. of Huntsville, Alabama, are the only 2 companies licensed by Sandia to market the formula.

With the proliferation of positive identification of anthrax at various U.S. postal facilities, coupled with the death of two postal workers as a result of anthrax exposure, the U.S. Postal Service is planning to acquire hundreds of thousands of N-95 masks and synthetic gloves for those employees who handle mail. Such masks, which cover the nose and mouth and contain a filter, as well as gloves have already been distributed in the Washington, D.C.; Trenton, New Jersey; and New York metropolitan areas.

The anthrax incidents of September-November 2001 also raised concerns in mailrooms at private companies and government offices nationwide. Mailroom employees were instructed to handle mail with great care as well as to use appropriate masks and synthetic gloves. Due to rising demand, Memphis Glove Co., which makes industrial and other types of gloves, stated that sales of disposable gloves during October 2001 were nearly double the figures for October 2000.

National, state, and local officials face significant expenses in the growing war of countering bio-terrorism. For instance, a truck and a full complement of gear cost $1.2 million. The costs of emergency personnel gear are immense: an Air Boss PSS-100 self-contained respirator costs $3,770; and a Tychem 10,000 encapsulated Level-A vapor-proof suit costs $780.

VII Transportation

The significant downturn in the use of commercial airlines by the public, including business travelers, since September 11, 2001, has spawned great interest in the use of business aviation and chartering planes as well as use of trains and buses as alternative modes of transportation.

Business Aviation

The September 11, 2001, hijackings significantly damaged the commercial airline industry, at least in the short term. Concurrently, the incidents energized the world of business aviation. As such, Corporate America may place a higher reliance on acquiring, fractionally owning, or leasing a jet than it did in the past.

More than 9,317 companies already own at least one jet, a 40% increase in the past 10 years. The number of planes used for business aviation has increased by two-thirds in that period, to 14,079.

Corporate jets are used by senior and middle managers 86% of the time. Until September 11, 2001, companies most often cited convenience as a reason for purchasing jets. Proponents of business aviation now also compliment its safety and security attributes. There is a benefit of knowing who is on board the aircraft.

For companies that do not want to purchase planes outright, an increasingly popular option is fractional ownership of aircraft. Under such a scheme, the provider offers companies a share of a plane and provides pilots and crews. Less than a month after the attacks, the U.S. fractional jet business industry received about 10,000 inquiries.

Executive Jet Inc. of Woodbridge, New Jersey, had 3,694 fractional owners of business aircraft in 2000. The least expensive contract offered by Executive Jet on 12 types of planes begins at $375,000 per year. Under this service level, the customer purchases one-sixteenth of a Citation V plane, which seats 8, for 50 hours of actual flying time (the equivalent of 25 round-trip tickets for 8 people from Boston to Washington, D.C.). The total annual cost for the base service is around $500,000.

Other companies offering similar services include: FlexJet, a company founded by Canadian aircraft maker Bombadier, with a fleet of 100 planes; and Raytheon with a fleet of 100 planes. UAL Corporation, parent of United Airlines, intends to enter the fractional-ownership corporate jet business in June 2002 with the launching of United BizJet Holdings.

Charter Planes

The aftermath of the September 11 attacks has spurred growth in plane rentals at more than 200 U.S. charter companies. Growth in the charter business is not a new phenomenon, as demonstrated by charter revenues growing more than 25% from 1995 to $2 billion in 2000.

By renting planes and a pilot's services, families, friends, and businesspeople can avoid inconvenient commercial flight schedules and long delays at airports due to fewer flights and increased security at major airports than was the case in the past. The customers also know the other passengers on the plane, which often seats 6 to 10 people.

At Universal Jet Aviation in Florida, business is up 50% from September 11, 2001, until early October 2001. Avbase Aviation in Cleveland, Ohio, experienced a traffic rise by 25% during the same period. Due to major airlines reducing their routes, particularly flights to Los Angeles, California, Executive Aircraft Services of Scottsdale, Arizona, has witnessed its traffic rise by 35%.

While this increased traffic helped charter companies, the extremely lax (and sometimes nonexistent) security at the nation's 5,000 general aviation airports has alarmed air safety experts. As such, since September 11, 2001, the FAA has banned some small planes from flying close to major airports—with broader restrictions near New York City and Washington, D.C. The FAA has also requested general aviation airports to report suspicious activities and may take over security responsibility at smaller airports.

Trains

For the five days following the September 11, 2001, attacks ridership at Amtrak rose by an estimated 80,000 passengers. Nearly all of Amtrak's long-distance trains were sold out for over a week after the attacks. Amtrak added trains along the Northeast corridor from Washington, D.C., to Boston, Massachusetts. Also, the company added cars to regularly scheduled trains throughout the rest of the country.

Amtrak serves 45 states and more than 500 communities. While 22.5 million people rode Amtrak in 2000, there is potential for greater activity as passenger capacity is about 45 million passengers annually. Additional train passengers will become a reality if increased security at U.S. airports forces long lines and delays at ticket counters and security checkpoints.

Buses

During the week following the attacks, Greyhound Lines Inc. saw a 50% increase in ridership, with a 45% rise in passengers in Washington, D.C. In cities such as Las Vegas, Nevada, six times the number of regularly scheduled buses were used to transport visitors home. Yet, following the incipient rise in business, bus ridership experienced cancellations and postponements of trips, as other modes of passenger transportation had experienced. In fact, the American Bus Association requested the U.S. government to provide a $1 billion bailout for the industry.

The attack on a Greyhound driver in Tennessee in September 2001, leading to an accident resulting in 6 deaths, by a man with a history of mental illness (not deemed a terrorist by initial reports) did not reduce ridership levels although it has prompted improved security on buses.

VIII "Survivalist" and Miscellaneous Merchandise

After the most horrific terrorist act on U.S. soil, some Americans have taken steps to fortify their homes and acquire food and medicines in anticipation of possible mass destruction violence caused by biological, chemical, or nuclear terrorism. Among the products that these persons have been purchasing since mid-September 2001 are: duct tape, gas masks, dust masks, antibiotics, emergency kits, electric generators, propane tanks, water filters, radios, flashlights, bottled water, and canned food. At the same time, a number of companies and entrepreneurs are marketing contraptions that claim to be helpful in the aftermath of a terrorist attack.

For those who believe that gas masks are a necessity, experts suggest that consumers receive guidance on purchasing the right mask that fits along with its filters, and maintains the equipment. The leading military masks are difficult to acquire and harder to use than civilian brands, but include the U.S. M40 and MCU/2-P. Micronel's M95 ($230), MSA's Advantage 1000 ($230), and MSA's Millenium Mask ($266) are the dominant civilian masks. Among gas mask manufacturers are Geomet Technologies of Germantown, Maryland, and Mine Safety Appliances of Pittsburgh, Pennsylvania.

According to specialists in emergency readiness and civil defense, two types of disaster kits should be prepared. Smaller provisions, enough to sustain oneself for three days, would include, for instance: storm-proof matches, a short-wave radio, a Swiss Army knife, a lantern-style flashlight, high-calorie foods that do not need refrigeration nor heating, and a gallon of water per person per day. For circumstances arising in a long-term crisis, 55-gallon drums of water, portable hand-pumps, huge amounts of canned and dried foods, ample toiletries and disinfectants, and large quantities of prescription and other medications may alleviate some of the strains associated with widespread epidemic or national crises.

A number of products that may also appeal to "survivalists," or persons overly anxious about the threats of terrorism are: Utah Shelter Systems' $16,000 bomb shelters; Executivechute Corp.'s $795 powered parachute; BioSafe Mail and MailSafe Containment Chambers—both aquarium-like apparatuses purported to be helpful when opening potentially anthrax-laden mail; and a newly developed anthrax-testing kit of Vital Living Products Inc.

Against this backdrop, public officials have cautioned citizens against these types of "what-if preparations," particularly with regard to people who stockpile antibiotics for self-medication and who acquire gas masks. For civilians, gas masks are ineffective, stated Dr. Luciana Borio of Johns Hopkins University's Center for Civilian Biodefense Studies. After all, she and others assert that people would need to wear them all day or carry them around at all times in order to have any chance at mitigating the danger. Even then, people would not realize that they have been exposed to biological or chemical attacks until after several hours or days. Some chemical weapons are odorless and invisible. In this regard, nerve gas and sarin are absorbed by the skin, making a mask ineffective.

The battle against terrorism continues at home and abroad. Under such circumstances, plus the threats of future catastrophic terrorist incidents, some segments of the American public may partially assuage their fears by stockpiling "survivalist" merchandise.

Chapter 5

Terrorism and the Impact on U.S. Labor

I   Introduction

The massacre of nearly 3,000 people during the ghastly terrorist attacks of September 11, 2001, was followed up with the killings of 4 U.S. workers and a 94 year-old woman from anthrax exposure in October 2001 and November 2001, respectively. Additional threats of anthrax exposure and government warnings of major terrorist attacks continued during fall 2001. Unfortunately, in the future, other segments of the U.S. workforce and society may become victims of different types of terrorist attacks in the United States.

This chapter covers some of the multi-dimensional issues that are relevant when assessing the impact of terrorism on U.S. labor in a post-September 11, 2001, environment. First, the physical consequences of terrorism on the U.S. workforce are examined. Second, the emotional ramifications of terrorism on U.S. labor are addressed. Third, diverse employer, governmental, and non-governmental assistance offered to U.S. workers victimized by terrorism are probed. Fourth, the responses of the victims' families are assessed. Fifth, the effect of terrorism on the National Guard, military reserves, and prospective recruits is evaluated. Sixth, the new paradigm for U.S. workers in the post-September 11, 2001, era is appraised. Seventh, the impact on employers in this New Age of Terrorism is highlighted.

II   Physical Consequences of Terrorism on U.S. Labor

September 11, 2001, Terrorist Attacks

The nearly 3,300 persons murdered during the September 11, 2001, incidents included: 246 persons (excluding the 19 hijackers) on the 4 hijacked planes; 125 persons at the Pentagon (excluding those on the plane that crashed into the building); and the remaining at the World Trade Center. The ages of the victims ranged from the age of two, Christine Hanson, to 82, Dorothy Dearaujo and Robert Norton.

Many of the World Trade Center victims worked at domestic and international companies from all sectors of the economy as well as governmental and nongovermental organizations. The fatalities represented over 80 nationalities, all races, and numerous religious faiths. The list of foreign casualties includes persons from Australia, Bangladesh, Canada, China, Dominican Republic, France, Germany, Ghana, Great Britain, Indonesia, Ireland, Israel, Japan, Lebanon, Malaysia, Mexico, Nigeria, South Africa, South Korea, and Sweden.

Among international institutions located at the World Trade Center were: the Bank of Taiwan (Taiwan), Shenzhen Trade Promotion Association (China), Deutsche Bank (Germany), the Government of Thailand Trade Promotion Office (Thailand), Hyundai Securities (South Korea), Fuji Bank (Japan), Union Bank of Switzerland (Switzerland), and Zim American Israeli Shipping (Israel).

About 2,000 people who worked in the financial industry died as a result of the attacks on the World Trade Center. The brutality at the World Trade Center decimated particular companies and organizations especially hard, including: Cantor Fitzgerald/eSpeed, which lost almost 700 employees; the New York City Fire Department, which lost 343 members; Marsh & McLennan Co., which lost 292 workers; Aon Corp., which lost 171 employees; Fiduciary Trust, which lost 87 members; and Carr Futures, which lost 70 workers.

Besides the businesses and concerns set out above, other firms suffered devastating harm due to the assault on the Twin Towers. Keefe, Bruyette & Woods Inc. lost 67 of the firm's 172 New York-based employees, including 5 board members. At Fred Alger Management, a money management firm controlling $15 billion in assets, the chief executive and brother of the founder, as well as 24 of the firm's 32 fund managers and research analysts, were killed in the World Trade Center incidents. Due to the loss of leadership, the founder, Fred Alger, 66, will return as chief executive of his firm.

The discount clothing retailer TJX, which owns several chains, including TJ Maxx and Marshall's, lost 7 executives and buyers on September 11, 2001. They were traveling from Boston, Massachusetts, to Los Angeles, California, on American Airlines Flight 11 that slammed into the North Tower of the World Trade Center.

Twenty-three buildings in and around the World Trade Center—the World Trade Center complex was comprised of 7 buildings—were destroyed or damaged during the September 11, 2001, attacks. The law firm of Sidley

Austin Brown & Wood had 600 lawyers, paralegals, and secretaries on four floors at the North Tower at One World Trade Center, and one employee perished. Garban Intercapital, an interdealer broker, had 675 employees at both towers, and all but one was saved. Sun Microsystems, a computer firm, had 346 employees in the South Tower, and all survived; but one employee perished on one of the planes. The 618 employees of Lehman Brothers based at the North Tower survived the attacks. All of the 360 employees of Deutsche Bank were evacuated from the South Tower (Two World Trade Center).

At American Express, eleven of 3,200 employees at the North Tower, Three World Financial Center, and Seven World Trade Center were killed during the attacks. Morgan Stanley had 3,700 employees at the South Tower and at Five World Trade Center; six perished. All 800 workers at Dow Jones, based at One World Financial Center, survived the attacks.

Generally, the companies and employees that had offices near or above where the hijacked planes smashed into the North and South Towers of the World Trade Center had little chance to escape or often suffered severe injuries. At the North Tower, the hijacked plane hit between the 96th and 103rd floors. At the South Tower, the hijacked airline smashed through the 87th and 93rd floors.

The victims at the Pentagon included military personnel, contractors, and civilian employees. Lt. Col. Dennis Johnson, 48, who worked at the Office of the Deputy Chief of Staff of Personnel, perished. Sgt. Maj. Lacey B. Ivory, 42, based at the Office of the Assistant Secretary of the Army for Manpower and Reserve Affairs, and Sgt. Tamara Thurman, 25, an administrative assistant in the Office of the Deputy Chief of Staff for Personnel, also were killed. Booz, Allen & Hamilton consultant Gerald P. Fisher, 57, with a 30-year career in government, academia, and private industry, lost his life.

The Air Line Pilots Association (ALPA) provided the toll in human life aboard the four hijacked jets:

- American Airlines Flight 11 carried 2 pilots, 9 flight attendants, and 81 passengers (including the hijackers).

- United Airlines Flight 175 flew with 2 pilots, 7 flight attendants, and 56 passengers (including the hijackers).

- American Flight 77 carried 2 pilots, 4 flight attendants, and 58 passengers (including the hijackers).

- United Flight 93 flew with 2 pilots, 5 flight attendants, and 38 passengers (including the hijackers).

The dead and missing from the four strikes included thousands whose significant contributions will be remembered by families, friends, survivors, employers, and many others. Among the leaders of U.S. and foreign business, military, media, religious, and civic communities who lost their lives during the horrific events were:

- Dr. Paul Ambrose, 32, Fellow, Association of Teachers of Preventive Medicine

- Garnet "Ace" Bailey, 53, Director of Pro Scouting, Los Angeles Kings

- Betty Berenson, 53, Los Angeles actress and photographer

- Barbara Edwards, 58, Foreign Language Teacher in Las Vegas

- Jason Dahl, 43, Pilot, United Flight 93

- Peter J. Ganci Jr., 54, Chief, New York City Fire Department

- Edmund Glazer, 41, Chief Financial Officer, MRV Communications

- Michele Heidenberger, 57, Flight Attendant, American Airlines Flight 77

- Karen Kincaid, 40, Partner, Wiley Rein & Fielding

- Steven "Jake" Jacoby, 43, Chief Operating Officer, Metrocall

- Father Mychael Judge, 68, Chaplain, New York City Fire Department

- Daniel Lewin, 31, co-founder and Chief Technical Officer, Akamai Technologies Inc.

- Timothy J. Maude, 53, Lieutenant General, U.S. Army

- John P. O'Neill, 49, Head of Security, World Trade Center

- Barbara K. Olson, 45, Conservative Legal Analyst

- Darin H. Pontell, 26, Lieutenant j.g., U.S. Navy

- Lisa Raines, 42, Senior Vice President of Government Relations, Genzyme

- Joseph P. Shea, 47, Executive Managing Director, Cantor Fitzgerald Inc.

- Ernest M. Willcher, 62, Consultant, Booz, Allen & Hamilton

The American Federation of Labor-Congress of Industrial Organizations (AFL-CIO) reported that hundreds of union workers were killed (or are missing) during the September 11, 2001, terrorist incidents, including:

- Firefighters: More than 350 New York City firefighters are missing.

- American Federation of State, County and Municipal Employees (AFSCME): Two employees from the AFSCME District Council 37 emergency services are missing.

- American Federation of Teachers (AFT): Three District of Columbia teachers were onboard the hijacked plane that crashed into the Pentagon. As of September 14, 2001, more than 40 members of the AFT-affiliated New York State Public Employees Federation (PEF) who worked in the World Trade Center were missing.

- Air Line Pilots: The 4 United Airlines pilots killed were members of ALPA, an AFL-CIO affiliate. The other pilots who worked at American Airlines belonged to another union.

- Carpenters: Fifteen members are missing.

- Civil Service Employees Association: There are 5 missing from this group.

- Communications Workers of America: There are hundreds that are thought to be missing.

- Electrical Workers: Twenty persons are missing.

- Flight Attendants: Twenty-five flight attendants were on board the 4 hijacked flights.

- Hotel Employees and Restaurant Employees International Union: Forty-seven are missing.

- Machinists: The union lost 2 members that were on board United Airlines Flight 175.

- Office and Professional Employees: One union member is missing from the World Trade Center.

- International Union of Operating Engineers: Two union members are dead, and several others are unaccounted for.

- Painters and Allied Trades: Two union members are dead and 3 are missing at the World Trade Center.

- Plumbers and Pipe Fitters: Four union members lost their lives at the World Trade Center.

- Police: Sixty-three police officers are missing.

- Public Employees Federation: Fifty union members are missing.

- Service Employees International Union: An estimated 62 union members are missing.

It would be an oversight not to mention the survivors of the World Trade Center and Pentagon attacks. They were left with physical injuries that ranged from slight abrasions and bruises, broken bones that will heal, scars from burns that will instill agony and imprints for a lifetime, and severely crippling ailments that will lead to permanent disability. Also, firefighters, police officers, and rescue workers involved in the search, rescue, and cleanup of the World Trade Center area, or Ground Zero, have experienced some respiratory problems that may continue to afflict them. These walking wounded signify that the damage of terrorism lasts long after the event concludes.

September-November 2001, Anthrax Cases in the United States

During September and November 2001 a number of anthrax-tainted letters and subsequent anthrax exposures occurred throughout the United States. By November 21, 2001, 4 U.S. workers—two U.S. Postal Services employees in Washington, D.C.; an employee of American Media of Boca Raton, Florida; and a worker at the Manhattan Eye, Ear, and Throat Hospital—and one retiree died as a result of complications stemming from separate anthrax attacks, which are still under investigation. By that date, too, at least 13 people were infected with anthrax in Florida, New York, and Washington, D.C. By mid-November 2001, anthrax spores were found in locations in Florida, Indiana, Maryland, Missouri, New Jersey, New York, Virginia, and Washington, D.C.

On October 5, 2001, Bob Stephens, 63, an employee of American Media, died from complications stemming from inhalation anthrax. On October 21, 2001, Thomas L. Morris, Jr., 55, a postal employee at the Brentwood mail center in Washington, D.C., perished, succumbing to inhalation anthrax. The next day, a co-worker of Morris, Joseph Curseen, Jr., 47, died from the same ailment. On October 31, 2001, Kathy Nguyen, 61, an employee at the Manhattan Eye, Ear, and Throat Hospital, died of inhalation anthrax. Ottilie Lundgren, 94, from Oxford, Connecticut, died on November 21, 2001, from exposure to anthrax.

Among direct targets of anthrax-contaminated letters were New York City-based Dan Rather of CBS News and Tom Brokaw of NBC News. Both of the assistants of the news anchors (Claire Fletcher, 27, of CBS and Erin O'Connor, 38, of NBC) developed the cutaneous (skin) form of the disease after they opened respective letters addressed to the anchors. A 7-month old boy of an ABC News employee in New York City also suffered exposure to anthrax while visiting the company's offices. At this writing, all 3 are reported to be recuperating. Another anthrax-contaminated letter was sent to the editor of the *New York Post*, and was examined by investigators.

In October 2001, Senate Majority Leader Tom Daschle (Democrat–South Dakota) was mailed an anthrax-tainted letter that was later opened by a member of his staff. This congressional staff member was also infected with the skin form of anthrax, though he is convalescing. The letter, referred to as the Daschle Letter, spawned avid interest in the Congress about additional tainted mail in and around Capitol Hill. Ultimately, the Capitol Building and various congressional office buildings were closed for a period.

As of October 30, 2001, the Ford, Hart, and Longworth buildings were closed although the Rayburn and Cannon buildings reopened. These events displaced thousands of workers, impeded productivity as some Members of Congress and employees worked from home or at make-shift offices, and resulted in many people taking tests for anthrax and using antibiotics when prescribed.

Following the Federal Bureau of Investigation (FBI) review of 280 barrels of congressional mail quarantined during October 2001, only one barrel was found to have a high concentration of anthrax spores. The suspect barrel contained a letter to Sen. Patrick J. Leahy (Democrat–Vermont), which contained fine anthrax spores similar to those found on the Daschle Letter.

Other confirmed anthrax cases as of November 18, 2001, included: 2 additional postal employees from the Brentwood mail center in Washington, D.C., who received inhalation anthrax; a person working at the State Department mail facility; six postal workers in New Jersey—four suffered cutaneous anthrax, two inhalation anthrax—and a non-postal worker in New Jersey who had cutaneous anthrax.

In addition, a number of federal office buildings in the Washington, D.C., area, mostly mail rooms and ancillary offices, tested positive for the presence of anthrax spores, including: Congress, the Central Intelligence Agency, State Department, Justice Department, Supreme Court, Food and Drug Administration, Voice of America, Veterans Administration, and Walter Reed Army Institute of Research.

In turn, during October 2001, 32,000 employees in the private and public sectors were administered antibiotics, such as Cipro and doxycycline, as a safety precaution against anthrax. Others underwent anthrax testing in order to determine whether antibiotics were necessary.

It was reported that former President Bill Clinton was sent a package containing the bacteria salmonella at his office in Harlem. The incident is being investigated by government authorities.

III Emotional Ramifications of Terrorism on U.S. Labor

The initial mental symptoms with which terrorist victims, their families, and co-workers may cope include depression, anxiety, excessive stress, and other ailments. While some levels of mourning are typical, with each individual responding to the traumatic events in his or her own way, some workers may have after-effects that do not readily dissipate.

The baleful emotional consequences of terrorism range from denial of the event; mild forms of confusion, stress, and anxiety; to profound manifestations of depression, schizophrenia, and post-traumatic stress disorder (PTSD). The time, mental anguish, physical illness, and large strains on personnel departments and health advisers weigh adversely on business in terms of productivity and human capital development.

The experience of workers in Oklahoma City, Oklahoma, home of the 1995 terrorist bombing that resulted in 168 deaths, may shed light on the possible impact of employee behavior following terrorist incidents. The behaviors and actions exhibited by employees in Oklahoma City after the attack included: high absenteeism and leave-taking, large turnover, impulsive and reckless behavior, and low productivity accompanied by, for some, excessive drinking and smoking. The hurtful emotional behavior experienced by some workers in Oklahoma City lasted from several months to more than a year.

In terrorist incidents on the scale of the World Trade Center and Pentagon attacks, some employees may find it challenging to get back to work and pick up uncompleted projects when familiar environments, such as their offices, have been destroyed. Employees' new surroundings are often sterile, containing different environments in variant locales. Also, damaged personal items, missing business records, and destroyed telecommunications, computers, and furniture only aggravate the unpleasantness that some victims may feel upon returning to work.

While some workers may permit the shock of the attacks to undermine their capabilities, others respond to a crisis with resilience and a fighting spirit. At J.P. Morgan in New York, software and systems employees worked nearly 24 hours after the attack to get computer equipment running. They switched to 12-hour shifts the second day after the attack. Millions of workers in lower Manhattan, the Pentagon, and across the United States returned to work on September 12, 2001, with renewed vigor to show the world that neither they nor the United States would be stopped by terrorism.

What might prove helpful to some employees facing emotional challenges dealing with the September 11, 2001, terrorist attacks is the American Psychological Association's (APA) web site. The Association gives workers helpful hints in managing traumatic stress, such as a terrorist incident. For our purposes, the most relevant portions of that information are cited below:

- Shock and denial are typical responses to terrorism, disasters, and other kinds of trauma, especially shortly after the event. Both shock and denial are normal protective reactions.

- Shock is a sudden and often intense disturbance of an emotional state that may leave a person feeling stunned or dazed. Denial involves not acknowledging that something very stressful has happened, or not experiencing fully the intensity of the event. One may temporarily feel numb or disconnected from life. As the initial shock subsides, reactions vary from one person to another. The following, however, are normal responses to a traumatic event:

  - Feelings become intense and sometimes are unpredictable.

  - Thoughts and behavior patterns are affected by the trauma. A person might have repeated and vivid memories of the event.

  - Recurring emotional reactions are common.

  - Interpersonal relationships often become strained.

  - Physical symptoms may accompany the extreme stress.

The APA further instructs that there are a number of steps one can take to help restore emotional well-being and a sense of control following a terrorist act, disaster, or other traumatic experience, including the following:

- Give time to heal.

- Ask for support from caring people who will listen and empathize with a situation.

- Communicate experiences in whatever ways feel comfortable, such as by talking with family or close friends, or keeping a diary.

- Find out about local support groups that often are available.

- Try to find groups led by appropriately trained and experienced professionals.

- Engage in healthy behaviors to enhance ability to cope with excessive stress.

- Eat well-balanced meals and get plenty of rest. If a person experiences ongoing difficulties with sleep, he may be able to find some relief through relaxation techniques. Avoid alcohol and drugs.

- Establish or reestablish routines, such as eating meals at regular times and following an exercise program.

- Avoid major life decisions, such as switching careers or jobs, if possible, because these activities tend to be highly stressful.

IV Employer, Governmental, and Non-Governmental Support in Times of Crisis

During the nearly three months following the World Trade Center and Pentagon terrorist attacks, numerous employer, governmental, and non-governmental activities and initiatives were undertaken to help the incidents' victims and their families. The forms of assistance have included financial, psychological, and spiritual support. The calling up of military reserves as well as anthrax attacks during fall 2001 have further tested employer, governmental, and non-governmental capabilities with regard to U.S. labor.

Employer Responses

American employers nationwide have experienced a huge demand for emergency mental health services in the wake of the September 11, 2001, terrorist incidents. American employees, including many based geographically distant from the attacks, have identified with the "direct" victims of the attacks. Companies have witnessed significant requests from employees for therapy and crisis counseling. Previously such services were viewed with suspicion.

Many employers are depending on employee assistance program (EAP) counselors to address workplace fears after the attacks. The terrorist attacks hurt morale as well as productivity at some companies. Past studies have demonstrated that EAPs aid in containing costs for workers' compensation. EAPs also help workers and their families to struggle with substance abuse and marital, family, and workplace issues. The programs are available to about 62 million Americans through internal departments or outside consultants on contract.

All employees at the offices of ESPN, the U.S. television sports cable network, in the New York City area were given contact numbers for counselors for group or individual sessions shortly after the World Trade Center and Pentagon attacks. By September 12, 2001, PricewaterhouseCoopers received 17 requests from client companies about what their EAP should be doing to assist. Counselors at TJX will coach nearly 625 employees who must travel despite their newfound fear of flying.

Because small companies are unlikely to have EAPs, management at such firms has an additional obligation to play an active role in assuaging the fears that workers may have in a post-September 11, 2001, environment. Among the steps that management may undertake to soothe employees' fears and readjustment are: stimulate workers to openly discuss their concerns; modify established, routine procedures, such as who should open mail and how mail should be opened; attempt to keep workers focused on their daily duties; underscore that the threat of terrorism is manageable and limited; emphasize that living in fear is not a solution and only plays into the hands of terrorists; and stipulate that workers' financial future and the economic success of the United States depends on small companies to contribute their share to the U.S. economy.

Among the various therapies that victims have undergone for PTSD developing out of incidents of terrorism is the controversial therapy termed Eye Movement Desensitization and Reprocessing (EMDR). EMDR involves free association-based treatment as opposed to traditional therapies in which patients concentrate on things for extended periods. The EMDR Humanitarian Assistance Program has already been contacted by victims of the World Trade Center and Pentagon attacks.

An illustration of some financial support given by employers is the response of Cantor Fitzgerald. The bond trading firm that lost nearly 700 employees in the World Trade Center terrorist attacks pledged to provide each victim's family up to $100,000 from its partnership profits as well as 10 years of health insurance.

A number of employers at companies miles away from the sites of the attacks allowed workers to watch the unfolding events on television and leave work early. Due to some security fears, banks, office buildings, and other institutions in Virginia, Maryland, and Washington, D.C., closed early on September 11.

Governmental Assistance

Governmental aid and guidance to the survivors and victims' families of the World Trade Center and Pentagon terrorist incidents are discussed below. Also, there may be some applicability to this section for victims of anthrax attacks, particularly if they are federal workers, as in the case of U.S. postal employees.

The web site of the U.S. government's human resource agency, the U.S. Office of Personnel Management (OPM), offered aid and advice regarding the September 11, 2001, attacks and their aftermath, including:

- Relocation site information for New York City federal employees impacted by loss of offices

- Pay and leave guidance for federal employees affected by the attacks at the World Trade Center and the Pentagon

- Rights and benefits of reservists called to active duty

- Emergency situation hiring flexibilities and information

- Frequently asked questions about federal benefits payable to victims of the terrorist attacks of September 11, 2001, and their families

- Benefits for victims of the World Trade Center and Pentagon tragedies

- Excused absence and assistance to federal employees affected by the attacks at the World Trade Center and the Pentagon

- Relief effort for victims of the terrorist actions

- List of organizations assisting in disaster relief efforts

- Handling traumatic events: a manager's handbook

- Call for blood donation

- Emergency dismissal and closure procedures

According to the OPM, survivors of federal civilian employees who are killed in the line of duty may be entitled to:

- Worker's compensation benefits administered by the Department of Labor's Office of Workers' Compensation Programs (OWCP)

- Payments under the Civil Service Retirement Systems (CSRS) or the Federal Employees Retirement System (FERS)

- Federal Employees' Group Life Insurance (FEGLI) proceeds

- Thrift Savings Plan (TSP) account proceeds

- Social Security survivor benefits administered by the Social Security Administration (SSA)

- Lump sum final salary payments

- A death gratuity payment

- Public Safety Officer's benefits

Federal civilian employees who are injured in the line of duty may be eligible for:

- Worker's compensation benefits administered by OWCP

- Disability payments under the CSRS or the FERS

- FEGLI proceeds

- Social Security disability benefits administered by the SSA

Families of Department of Defense military employees may receive: up to $250,000 in life insurance, a portion of the employee's salary, and a death gratuity of $6,000. Relations of Pentagon military employees may also expect to obtain: funds for covering immediate expenses from the Army Emergency Relief/Navy-Marine Corps Relief Society as well as children's college tuition.

The families of other victims killed in the September 11, 2001, terrorist attacks may receive varying amounts of life insurance, other benefits, and compensation over and above funds distributed through various charities. Some reports suggest that families of New York police officers killed in the September terrorist attacks are expected to receive: $196,635 from city, federal, and union compensation; 12 months salary; an annuity of 6 months salary; and basic health insurance. The Justice Department reports that families of firefighters, police, and emergency members killed at the World Trade Center are entitled to a U.S. government death benefit of $150,000.

Over 150,000 layoffs were announced within 10 weeks following the September 11, 2001, terrorist incidents, including some job losses that were a direct result of the attacks. To help ensure that Americans are able to continue to support themselves and their families, the Bush administration proposed a new temporary Emergency Extended Unemployment Compensation Program. This program proposal included the following provisions:

- Provides 13 additional weeks of unemployment compensation for individuals who become unemployed after September 11, 2001, in states where the state's total unemployment rate increases by 30% over what it was prior to that date

- Provides these same extended benefits automatically to states in which President Bush issued an emergency or major disaster declaration due to the direct effects of the terrorist attacks on September 11, 2001

- Provides additional weeks of compensation at the same level as the prior weeks of unemployment compensation

- Pays for the additional compensation entirely with federal dollars

- Maintains this program for 18 months

With this temporary expansion of the program, grants may be used by states to help ensure that dislocated workers: (1) maintain health insurance coverage, (2) receive some form of income support during the recovery period, and (3) return to the workforce as quickly as possible with the help of job training and job search assistance.

More specifically, under the program, states experiencing a major plant closure, mass layoff or multiple layoffs, or dislocations are eligible for special National Emergency Grants (NEG) if the governor of a state certifies that the events of September 11, 2001, contributed significantly to the closure, layoffs, or dislocations. Grants could be used by the states to:

- Pay up to 75% of health care premiums covered by the Consolidated Omnibus Budget Reconciliation Act (COBRA) for up to 10 months for laid off or dislocated workers. COBRA is a federal law that enables many workers the option of continuing their employer-provided health insurance, at the employee's costs, when the employees are laid off.

- Provide additional weeks of income support for individuals who have used up their unemployment compensation and are not in a state eligible for the Emergency Extended Unemployment Compensation program (as long as those individuals are enrolled in training).

- Provide income support payments for individuals who are ineligible for unemployment compensation but are able to demonstrate a sufficient attachment to employment (as long as those individuals are enrolled in training).

- Provide additional dollars to furnish a full array of job search and training services, including customized training, placement assistance, and relocation expenses.

Also, the Bush administration is attempting to convince workers to take advantage of existing services that can assist labor. The Department of Labor, in cooperation with the states, currently administers and funds several programs to assist Americans financially during times of unemployment and help them improve their skills and return to work quickly. The Bush administration's Fiscal Year 2002 budget proposal includes over $6 billion for these programs. Available services include:

- Job training

- Vocational, careers and personal counseling, including grief counseling

- Comprehensive assessment of employability, development of a re-employment plan, workshops on interviewing and resume preparation

- Job search and job placement assistance and useful labor market information

- Needs-related payments

- Supportive services to help the individual to return to the workforce and/or complete training, including transportation assistance, child care, dependent care, and relocation expenses

According to the White House, states can apply for expedited review of proposals to expand the health insurance coverage they offer through

Medicaid and the State Children's Health Insurance Program (SCHIP). The U.S. Department of Health and Human Services (HHS) is announcing that states have $11 billion in unspent SCHIP match funds available immediately to support these expansions (in addition to the $3.1 billion in SCHIP allocations for Fiscal Year 2002).

Other labor-related HHS activities worth noting are:

- Since January 2001, HHS has approved state plan amendments and waivers that are projected to expand health insurance coverage to 1.5 million Americans and enhance benefits for another 3.5 million Americans.

- To speed further expansion of coverage, especially to cover the majority of uninsured Americans who have low incomes, an expedited review process is available through the Health Insurance Flexibility and Accountability (HIFA) Initiative.

- HHS will also provide expedited review for health insurance coverage expansions that assist workers who have lost their jobs.

- With substantial funding and a rapid, flexible review process, states have an unprecedented opportunity to implement health insurance coverage expansions best suited to the needs of their citizens.

Non-Governmental Support

Professional organizations are also offering help to U.S. labor harmed during fall 2001 terrorist attacks. The American Management Association held free workshops for managers and human resource professionals to address emotional reactions. The Association of Flight Attendants commenced a hot line on which EAP representatives provide information for members, families, and friends regarding mental health professionals in their areas.

The Association of Trial Lawyers of America offered to provide free representation to all victims and surviving family members who seek damages from the Victim Compensation Fund. The organization planned to establish an office in Manhattan in fall 2001 with between 1,000 to 2,000 association members to assist the victims.

Various unions pledged to contribute to existing disaster relief funds or to establish their own disaster funds. In September 2001, the United Auto Workers authorized a contribution of $250,000 to the American Red Cross Disaster Relief Fund. The September 11th Relief Fund of the Service Employees International Union garnered over $1 million by early October 2001. Also, the International Brotherhood of Teamsters encouraged its members to donate blood as well as contribute to the Teamsters Disaster Relief Fund, local relief agencies, and the Red Cross.

Other aid that may be available to families of New York City Police Officers comprises: $10,000 from Police and Fire Widows' and Children's Fund plus $5,000 per family and $2,000 per child from the New York City Police Foundation Heroes Fund.

On September 25, 2001, the American Red Cross began providing $100 million in cash assistance to about 7,000 families of those killed or missing in the attacks on the World Trade Center and Pentagon. The tax-free distributions, averaging $18,000 per family, are aimed at meeting short-term needs. The amounts will include up to $5,000 a month for rent or mortgage costs and other money for funeral, food, and utility expenses. Initially, the grants will not be allocated to the passengers who died on the hijacked planes because the airlines will be assisting them.

By late September 2001, the American Red Cross raised $200 million for the September 11 relief efforts. Other remarkable demonstrations of charity and support for those victimized during the tragedy include: the September 11 Fund's $215 million and the estimated $150 million raised during a telethon on September 21, 2001. The total donations made or pledged by the end of September 2001 reached more than $675 million.

By mid-October, 2001, $1.4 billion had been raised by charities benefiting the direct and indirect victims of the September 11, 2001, terrorist attack. Among the principal charity funds are: American Red Cross ($452 million), September 11th Fund ($320 million), Twin Towers Fund ($50.3 million), New York Times 9/11 Neediest ($36 million), Salvation Army ($35 million), Families of Freedom ($25.5 million), New York City Fighters 9-11 Disaster Relief Fund ($25 million), New York State World Trade Center Relief Fund ($20.5 million), Robin Hood Relief Fund ($16.8 million), and World Vision and Concerts of Prayer ($8.4 million).

By mid-November 2001, Red Cross collections rose to $564 million For a period, there was a debate over whether the Red Cross might use a portion of the funds collected for September 11 relief efforts for other purposes. Following complaints by some donors and others, the Red Cross announced that the September 11 funds would be used solely for those intended relief efforts.

Numerous organizations, some already highlighted, that are working to assist the victims of the World Trade Center and Pentagon terrorist attacks include:

- American Bar Association created a hot line with the Federal Emergency Management Agency (FEMA) to help survivors of the attacks and families of the victims with questions about housing, insurance, lost documents, public benefits, unemployment, probate matters, and guardianship.

- American Red Cross established a fund for the victims as well as solicited blood donations.

- American-Arab Anti-Discrimination Committee is collecting funds for the American Red Cross to help families of those killed in the attacks.

- B'nai B'rith International created a fund to aid victims and their families.

- Elks National Foundation established a fund to assist rescue workers and victims.

- FEMA has a hot line with information on how to donate money to the World Trade Center Relief Fund and how to serve as a volunteer.

- Independent Insurance Agents of America and the Independent Insurance Agents Association of New York are raising money for victims' families.

- National Association of Realtors established a fund to help the mortgage and rental costs of victims. By the end of September 2001, it raised $4 million.

- National Burglar and Fire Alarm Association established a scholarship fund for children of police officers and firefighters who were killed in New York.

- Salvation Army is providing emergency food and counseling for victims.

- United Services Organization (USO) of Metropolitan Washington, D.C., is providing housing, food, and other items for the families of active-duty military touched by the attack at the Pentagon, and for housing and support for 600 active-duty personnel replacing rescue and recovery teams at the Pentagon.

- Washington Redskins established a fund to benefit the families of Pentagon victims.

V Victims' Families Responses

Despite the generosity of the public and these organizations, some victims' families have not pursued various levels of aid, or have been frustrated, to some degree, by organizations' bureaucracies and multiple relief-related application forms—with various requirements and eligibility standards—that they must file. Due to the breaches in security at the airports from which the 4 hijacked planes originated, victims' families may choose—with varying levels of merit and success—to initiate claims against institutions and companies, such as airport authorities, airlines, and airport security companies. Also, the landlords and property management companies at the World Trade Center complex and neighboring buildings may face claims that insufficient measures were in place and improper guidance to tenants was given following the attacks. In addition, employers who lost employees during the World Trade Center attacks may encounter claims that the company should have instituted better measures to deal with disasters.

Some of these potential lawsuits may be stymied or pre-empted by fall 2001 laws that were enacted to insulate some companies and organizations that otherwise might have been subject to various levels of financial liability. For example, the September 2001, aviation bailout law included language that limited damages American Airlines and United Airlines—hosts of the four hijacked planes—could suffer due to suits arising under the September 11, 2001, incidents. The November 2001, aviation security law contains provisions protecting the City of New York, New York and New Jersey Port Authority (owners of the World Trade Center complex), the owners of the lease on the World Trade Center complex, Logan International Airport (where two of the hijacked flights originated), and plane and aircraft equipment manufacturers. Also, drafts of pending insurance and bio-terrorism legislation contain language that would restrict lawsuits and prevent punitive damages from suits based on claims arising from terrorist events.

With reference to lawsuits connected to the anthrax attacks, the families of postal workers victimized may be estopped from suing the U.S. Postal Service as the law already provides for some measures to compensate victims in such circumstances. Nevertheless, plaintiffs may pursue other suits as in the case of the son of a Washington, D.C., postal worker who died following exposure to inhalation anthrax. More specifically, in November 2001, Thomas L. Morris III filed a $37 million wrongful-death action against Kaiser Permanente in Maryland, claiming that a Kaiser physician did not recognize and treat the anthrax symptoms of his father—Thomas L. Morris Jr.—but rather directed him to take Tylenol for his symptoms.

It is also worth highlighting that there is precedent for families of victims killed during a terrorist attack to file a civil action in U.S. courts against the perpetrators, the terrorist groups, and their state sponsors. For instance, the family of Leon Klinghoffer—an elderly, disabled American who was killed during the October 1985 Palestine Liberation Front attack on the cruise ship, Achille Lauro—filed suit against the Palestine Liberation Organization (PLO), based on several grounds, including a tort claim of assault based on the PLO's intentional acts. Also, the relatives of those killed during the bombing of Pan Am 103 in December 1989, filed suit against the government of Libya for its role in that terrorist attack. In addition, victims' families have been successful in suing U.S.-based, hate groups for crimes carried out by their members.

Criminal cases involving terrorists have been successfully prosecuted in the United States, as in prosecutions stemming from the 1995 Oklahoma and 1993 World Trade Center attacks.

VI   The Effect of Terrorism on the National Guard, Military Reserves, and Prospective Recruits

As background information, it is worth noting that the Secretary of Defense, with the advice of the military service secretaries and Joint Chiefs of Staff, recommends to the president and Congress the level of military mobilization. There are four levels of mobilization: presidential selected reserve call-up (the president has the authority to call up 200,000 members of the selected reserve for up to 270 days to meet mission requirements); partial mobilization (mobilization by the president of not more than 1,000,000 ready reservists for 24 months or less); full mobilization (call-up of all forces in the current force structure and the resources required for their support for the duration of the emergency plus six months. Congress must declare that a state of national emergency exists.); and total mobilization (an extension of full mobilization by activating and organizing additional units beyond the current approved force structure).

Since September 11, 2001, companies and employees throughout the United States have been anticipating the challenging personal and economic implications of U.S. reserve forces being called for military duty. In September 2001, it was anticipated that only about 50,000 reserve members would carry out their service domestically and internationally.

As of October 17, 2001, 30,087 military reserve and National Guard members from 237 units, 44 states, Washington, D.C., and Puerto Rico were called to active duty. This total included forces from: the Army National Guard and Army Reserve, 11,304 individuals; Navy Reserve, 3,100; Air National Guard and Air Force Reserve, 12,722; Marine Corps Reserve, 333; and the Coast Guard Reserve, 2,628. This mobilization has decreased the ranks of some government offices and businesses where military reserves and National Guard members work.

By the end of October 2001, it was reported that more than 50,000 would likely be called for duty in fall 2001, including a growing portion on homeland defense. The 1.3 million people in the military reserves make up about half of the U.S. armed forces. During the Persian Gulf War, the Defense Department relied on more than 265,000 reserve troops.

Employers are required to permit national guardsmen and military reservists to leave their jobs in order to fulfill military duties. Once the employee returns, the employer is obligated to reinstate the worker at the same salary, level, status, and retirement benefits as prior to the call-up. The 1994 Uniformed Services Employment and Re-employment Rights Act guards military personnel and reservists from retaliatory or discriminatory actions by employers arising from the employees' fulfillment of military duties.

The financial strain that such employees may face includes reduced income (the difference between military and civilian compensation) during their military reserve duty. Under present legislation, an employer needs only to provide unpaid leave during a "temporary" soldier's absence, although some employers do give complete or partial pay to these individuals. According to a September 2001, Watson Wyatt survey of 51 companies about military reservists' compensation: 6% provide full pay for a set time (average of half a year), 12% offer differential pay indefinitely, 48% give differential pay for a set period (average of half a year), 10% provide no compensation, and 24% were other/undecided.

In a fall 2001, survey conducted by Challenger, Gray & Christmas, 30% of 200 companies surveyed stated that they were enhancing their military leave policies. As American patriotism, spurred by the September 11, 2001, terrorist attacks and the mobilization of armed forces, grows in the coming months and years, undoubtedly additional companies will augment benefits to civilian-soldiers.

With reference to university members of the National Guard or reserves, they are not guaranteed refunds of tuition or fees. Nevertheless, the

U.S. Department of Education directed lenders and colleges to postpone student loan payments for reassigned or activated guardsmen and reservists. Also, the USO Worldwide Operations solicited donations for the USO Fund for Freedom's Finest to support U.S. armed forces in the United States and abroad.

VII The New Paradigm for U.S. Workers

Introduction

As a result of the attacks of September 11, 2001, and further anthrax terrorist attacks in fall 2001, some employees are reassessing their priorities, including taking more vacations, working fewer hours, volunteering less for complex and high-profile assignments, and spending more time with friends and family. The anthrax scare hit U.S. Postal Service's 800,000 workers particularly hard as anthrax spores were identified in a variety of postal distribution facilities in seven states and Washington, D.C. Moreover, as two postal service workers died following exposure to anthrax, with others falling ill, the sensitivity and concern of postal workers and others to future terrorist incidents are clearly understandable.

The effects of the September 11 attacks on U.S. labor can be seen as well through the disruption to basic worker routines previously scheduled to take place that fateful day. For example, within hours of the attacks, the federal government sent home 260,000 workers in the Washington, D.C., area. Subsequently, many local governments and businesses closed for the day and numerous events were cancelled.

Manhattan and other New York City workers were severely impacted: Wall Street suspended trading, numerous buildings throughout the city— including structures of the United Nations—were evacuated, and subway lines and Grand Central and Penn Stations were closed. Nationwide, airplanes were grounded and thousands of airline business travelers were stuck at airports.

A number of generalities can be proffered about the possible impact of terrorism on the psyche of selected U.S. workers. For instance, the attractiveness of a specific role or the compatibility of a particular employer may have changed. Whereas formerly, some sought to get the most prominent, high-profile job at the finest, well-respected institution—whether in industry or in government—workers may now consciously choose less prominent and risky opportunities in the name of safety.

The concern or fright that may be felt by other segments of the labor force may ultimately result in their seeking employment in small cities or towns they may consider to be less of a target to terrorists. Also, employees may try to develop additional skills outside their respective job profile or industry just in case a terrorist attack would severely undermine an industry, such as the airline sector, and concurrently adversely affect their job security.

Positions that at this time may seem to be high risk—postal worker, congressional staffer, media employee, flight attendant, and pilot—may show a decrease in attractiveness in the short period. Other front-line jobs in the war on terrorism—firefighter, police officer, emergency medical technician, hazardous waste disposal personnel, security guard, and member of the military reserves—already entailed various degrees of risk. Should terrorists attack other targets in the United States, as has occurred elsewhere in the world during the past 4 decades, few segments of workers will be immune.

It is probable that once U.S. labor has a better understanding of the small chance of becoming victimized by terrorism (aside from a massive chemical, biological, and nuclear terrorist attack), workers will continue their important roles in society and the economy while being more vigilant of possible threats. Despite some hesitation about personal safety, workers in post-September 11 high-risk positions, as other employees, are ignoring potential risks or putting them in proper perspective, and going on with their duties.

Due to the terrorist attacks during fall 2001, labor may expect employers to serve roles in addition to providing a job and wage. In fact, labor may view the employer as playing a semi-paternalistic/quasi-government role: provide physical security, emotional assistance, and guidance in times of catastrophe. Whether such new demands by some segments of the labor force are warranted—or even could be properly filled by employers—only time will tell.

Another negative effect of the September 11, 2001, attacks is the nearly 200 hate crimes against Arab Americans (or persons mistaken to be of Middle Eastern or Asian—Afghani or Pakistani—descent) currently investigated by the FBI. Among the incidents are: about 110 personal threats or attacks; and over 80 attacks or threats against institutions and other property.

While the majority of the 19 hijackers involved in the September 11 incidents were Arabs, and the current leadership of al-Qaida consists of this group as well, millions of innocent Arab Americans—as well as millions of others, including U.S. citizens of Sikh, Pakistani, and Afghani ancestry—have unjustly been painted by racists with the same broad brush as the perpetrators of the terrorist attacks. The relevance to U.S. labor arises when innocent individuals of a particular ethnic group attempt to enter the job market and face employment discrimination. Also, those already in the workforce may encounter bias based on ethnicity.

U.S. workers may end up facing reduced competition from foreign workers (documented and illegal) in the wake of the September 11 attacks, given greater concern of foreign workers' political and military affiliations and weak economic conditions. In the year ending September 30, 2001, the Immigration and Naturalization Service (INS) issued 163,200 business visas (the figure does not include about 60,000 applications that are still pending), mostly for the high technology industry.

Employment Opportunities

Due to the November 2001 congressional passage and presidential signature of aviation security legislation, 28,000 federal workers will be given the duty to screen passengers and their luggage. As a result, there will be many opportunities for Americans to pursue such positions, as only U.S. citizens are eligible to serve in these federal worker roles. (In fall 2001 about 25% of private security workers are foreign nationals.) These newly created, federal jobs will likely offer higher pay and better benefits than security workers with private contractors received.

A number of U.S. government units, including the Department of Defense, Central Intelligence Agency (CIA), and the FBI are increasingly seeking to recruit native speakers of Arabic, Farsi, Dari, Pashto, Hindi, Urdu, and Uzbek. The U.S. government is avidly contacting translation companies with language capabilities in those and other languages. This trend is spurred by the fact that investigators are focusing on documents and evidence left by the 19 Arabic-speaking hijackers involved in the September 11, 2001, terrorist attacks. Also, many members of Usama bin Laden's al-Qaida group, as well as some funders of their terrorist operations, communicate among themselves in various languages, including Arabic.

Enhanced language capabilities in the native tongues and dialects of Afghanistan, Pakistan, India, and Iran are important for U.S. military and anti-terrorism efforts. U.S. citizens and other U.S.-based individuals with excellent oral and written skills in such languages will be in further demand in the coming years. Also, given U.S. activities in Afghanistan and launching points in Pakistan and the Caucasus, and possible future anti-terrorism actions elsewhere—Iraq, Sudan, Somalia, and Yemen—access to diverse language skills is essential.

The current scarcity of people with non-Western language skills working in the U.S. translation business is evidenced by the fact that only 120

Arabic-, 21 Farsi-, 6 Dari-, 6 Azeri-, and 1 Pashto-speaking professional translators are members of the American Translators Association. Due to the demand for people with such language skills, there could be an upsurge in college students who train to become specialists in these languages. Analogously, the FBI's call in September 2001 for applicants with Middle Eastern and Asian language skills and cultural understanding was received enthusiastically by thousands of job seekers.

Also, growing appeal among recent university graduates has been demonstrated for government services roles. This premise is supported by a post-September 11, 2001, poll in which 32% of university students nationwide expressed an interest in public service. Interest by university students in possible public service in the aftermath of the World Trade Center and Pentagon attacks was profiled by *Newsweek*. The magazine referred to these students as Generation 9-11. Among the desired agencies by college students and older workers are the CIA, FBI, INS, State Department, Congress, U.S. Customs Services, U.S. Border Patrol, and Federal Air Marshals.

Other government agencies, including the Health and Human Service and Food and Drug Administration, are increasingly appealing as the importance of emergency medical preparedness, health issues, medicines, and vaccines in the fight against terrorism is widely appreciated.

Following the World Trade Center and Pentagon terrorist incidents, military recruiters saw a significant rise in interest by prospective soldiers. However, some applicants fail to make the initial cut into the military services due to minimal educational background and the lack of physical fitness. With the military successes in mid-November 2001 in Afghanistan, it is likely that interest in joining the military will not wane.

Likewise, with greater attention and funding earmarked for corporate, facility, and other security management, seasoned security executives are expected to be very much in demand. Recruiting firm Korn/Ferry International reported a significant increase in requests for candidates with security expertise. Likewise, Security Management Resources Inc. cited strong demand for security executives since the World Trade Center and Pentagon attacks. The unpleasant reality that domestic terrorism may threaten the United States for several years to come should only prolong the need for persons with significant military and security experience.

As highlighted in Chapter 4, a number of industries—defense, security equipment and services, germ detection, technology, and pharmaceuticals—may experience a rise in business activity, boding well for future employment with companies in those sectors.

Interestingly enough, despite the threats associated with employment in the U.S. mail system since the anthrax outbreak in fall 2001, the U.S. Postal Service has received sufficient applications from students, retirees, homemakers and others to fill the up to 40,000 temporary positions available during fall 2001 and winter 2001.

During the week ending November 11, 2001, new jobless claims were 444,000—an 8,000 decline from the previous week. Yet, for the week ending November 3, 2001, the number of laid-off workers receiving jobless benefits increased to 3.83 million—the highest point in nearly 9 years.

According to Manpower Inc.'s quarterly survey of thousands of U.S. companies, released in mid-November 2001, 16% planned to add more jobs, and 16% expected to reduce the number of workers during January-March 2002. In January-March 2001, 27% of companies predicted they would add jobs, while 10% of companies planned cuts.

VIII Ramifications to Employers in Post-September II Era

Due to the perception of growing terrorist threats, employers are undertaking additional security efforts, such as: to heighten security awareness at office buildings and manufacturing facilities, erect barriers near building entrances, and install fences; acquire security and other equipment (metal detectors, mail irradiation, and germ detection); contract with security personnel services for general duties and specific assignments, such as body guards for senior management; enlist corporate security and disaster specialist consultants; and issue mailroom employees gloves and masks as well as acquire special ventilation equipment. Also, Corporate America comprehends the need for better emergency and safety preparedness training for its employees—for moral, morale, and potential liability purposes.

At the same time, employers are increasingly using internal reviews to monitor employees' use of the Internet, telephone, and fax communications to ensure that their workers are not involved in any illegal activities, anti-employer actions (e.g., destroying files), nor in corporate espionage. Furthermore, companies are undertaking more background checks prior to hiring new employees to reduce the possibility of hiring a criminal or person with unsavory associates.

Employers are very interested in their potential liability should a worker be injured or killed during a terrorist incident that occurs while the employee is at the office or carrying out functions on behalf of the employer outside of the office. Depending on the circumstances, of course, workers generally would only obtain workers' compensation payments, rather than the capacity to obtain punitive damages in a civil suit.

Among other issues that in this environment may lead to litigation are: employees who refuse to return to offices that are damaged during terrorist attacks; employees who decline to relocate to a new office that is much further away than the original office; workers refusing to return to an office because they claim that the work environment is not safe, as in the case of postal workers who contend that some mail distribution facilities are unsafe; and chronic absenteeism, poor performance at work, and strange behavior as a real or false manifestation of PTSD.

The negative implications of terrorism on U.S. labor may be compounded by inappropriate actions by management. For instance, without sufficient training in being able to distinguish among dilatory tactics blamed on terrorism, reasonable anxiety, and mental illness, an executive could make small matters much worse—perhaps leading to litigation. In truth, not all managers may have the requisite knowledge or interpersonal skills to differentiate between small and large worker behavioral deviancies.

Employers may face escalating mental health expenses. The harmful financial consequences to business are significant because recent studies and mental health experts concluded that depression and high stress topped the list of the leading factors resulting in heightened medical expenses for employers. Workers who had high stress had 46% larger medical costs than employees without such ailments.

In addition to the direct financial costs of mental illness, affected employees may experience reduced levels of productivity, drive, and creativity in conjunction with high incidents of absenteeism. In trying to soothe particularly troubled employees, bosses may defer urgent projects, reassign duties and projects to other employees, or readjust business plans based on the sensitivities and speed of recovery of key employees.

With the specter of terrorism looming over America in the coming years, workers will demand, and employers will provide, improved security at the workplace, such as the use of metal detectors, additional security guards, restricted access to buildings, and improved disaster and emergency responses.

The relevance of safety in the workplace is profoundly evident to airline crew members. Under such realities, the Association of Flight Attendants (AFA) has made various proposals with the goal of improving aviation security, while indirectly helping to create a safer work environment on airplanes. The key suggestions that AFA proposed a week following the September 11, 2001, attacks are outlined below:

- Updated training procedures and certification of flight attendants

- The imposition of a single standard that strictly limits carry-on baggage

- Federalization of airport security screening, with jurisdiction turned over to the Department of Justice

- An increase in the percentage of checked baggage that is screened

- Passengers pre-screening to be expanded for domestic and international passengers

- Positive passenger baggage-match expanded to all flights

- The ban on all remote check-ins

- All current and future commercial aircraft to be retrofitted with fortified doors and new regulations to ensure a secure cockpit with limited access

- A mandate on the use of, and increase in, the number of federal marshals on domestic flights

- Disaster relief for all the families of victims of the September 11, 2001, attacks and for flight attendants whose jobs are affected by cutbacks as a result of the attacks

- Trained and certified personnel to perform searches of aircraft cabins

- K-9 bomb-sniffing dogs made available at all major airports for use in route and aircraft bomb searches

The aviation security legislation enacted in November 2001 addresses some of the concerns raised by AFA. As anthrax attacks severely affected the U.S. Postal Service, mail delivery, and U.S. postal workers, in late October 2001, the U.S. government ordered 4 million masks and 86 million disposable gloves for postal workers to use while on the job. The U.S. government is irradiating some mail, killing potentially harmful biological agents in turn. In addition, the U.S. government has purchased additional irradiating machinery in late 2001 in order to add to the arsenal in reducing the threat of pathogen-laced parcels.

Postal employee unions and postal workers strenuously complained that the response to the slightest chance of exposure to anthrax in the Congress resulted in much more rapid public health and investigative responses than anthrax exposures at postal facilities. In late October 2001, Postmaster General John Potter denied that the U.S. Postal Service ignored postal worker safety at the Brentwood postal facility in Washington, D.C. (Two postal workers who worked there died of anthrax inhalation.) Potter argued that the Postal Service followed the advice of the Centers for Disease Control and Prevention that public health concerns at the Brentwood facility did not warrant its closure. Moreover, he added, the suspect Daschle Letter was sealed and, with conventional wisdom at the time, because it was not opened at Brentwood, its potential exposure to that building was limited. Potter concluded that the Postal Service was providing gloves and masks as well as obtaining additional x-ray machines to irradiate and sanitize the mail.

In any case, the tension between postal workers and senior management may be replicated as employers must balance responding to threats to employee safety while concurrently trying to run a business in an ever-increasingly competitive environment. The employers' calculations on such matters are further complicated by the fact that employers may have limited or faulty investigative and health data critical in making decisions that weigh worker safety with running a profitable business. Miscalculations on either spectrum could lead to death of employees at one extreme, and to financial ruin at the other. As employers and employees gain additional experience and understanding of this tension, it is foreseeable that better decisions will be made by all. Indeed, this dialectic also brings into focus the quagmire of the role of employers when facing the challenges of terrorism.

Due to additional security and training costs, disruptions to business operations, investments in data-storage and emergency-preparedness, lower productivity of employees, and other strains on employers, companies may be forced to find ways to reduce costs elsewhere—through job cuts, less investment in research and development, decreased spending on marketing, less investment in infrastructure and capital goods, and curtailed training of employees—and pass along these costs to their customers in the form of higher prices and additional fees, or both.

Chapter 6

Terrorism and U.S. Government Responses

I Introduction

The September 11, 2001, terrorist attacks had a significant impact on the United States in terms of human, economic, political, social, and military conditions. The U.S. government is instituting multiple responses to that incident, and to current and future terrorist threats. Such an approach is critical in the campaign against terrorism and includes, as Secretary of State Colin L. Powell pronounced, "multiple dimensions to it." The steps include financial, law enforcement, intelligence, military, and social responses.

In September 2001, President George W. Bush delivered a moving speech in which he condemned the four hijackings and subsequent attacks on the World Trade Center and the Pentagon. President Bush also called for: the Taliban leadership in Afghanistan to turn over Usama bin Laden and leaders of his al-Qaida organization; the Taliban to immediately and permanently close all terrorist training camps in Afghanistan and allow U.S. forces to have access to such locations to ensure that they are no longer in operation; and the Taliban to release all "unjustly imprisoned" foreign nationals, including several U.S. citizens. In addition, President Bush proclaimed that the United States would deem any country that harbors or supports terrorists to be a hostile regime. He also announced the creation of the Office of Homeland Security, headed by former Pennsylvania Governor Tom Ridge (Republican), as a cabinet-level post. The new organization's mandate is to coordinate the efforts of numerous government agencies in the war against terrorism.

This chapter discusses the $40 billion emergency funding measures and other government resources that were approved following the September 11, 2001, terrorist incidents and the anthrax attacks during fall 2001. The $15 billion Airline Transportation and Systems Stabilization Act, the multi-billion aviation security law, other aviation security measures, and calls for support by other transportation industry segments are addressed. Government responses to the crisis in the insurance industry in the aftermath of the World Trade Center and Pentagon attacks are discussed. Public health initiatives of the Bush administration and Congress aimed at heightening U.S. capabilities against bio-terrorism are examined.

The chapter then reviews a multitude of security and investigative actions undertaken since the World Trade Center and Pentagon attacks, including: establishment of the Office of Homeland Security; passage of the Uniting and Strengthening America by Providing Appropriate Tools Required to Intercept and Obstruct Terrorism Act of 2001 (USA Patriot Act); selected law enforcement and judicial anti-terrorism actions; steps taken by government authorities in the fight against terrorist funding activities; Securities and Exchange Commission's investigation of terrorists' participation in illegal stock and funding activities; strengthening of Capitol Hill security; and miscellaneous anti-terrorism activities of the departments of State, Treasury, Defense, and Justice, and the intelligence community.

Federal government assistance to state governments economically disadvantaged as a result of the September 11, 2001, attacks is reviewed. A variety of U.S. forms of international and humanitarian aid as well as international cooperation in the war against terrorism are analyzed. Finally, a review of prospective government funding measures, such as the Fiscal Year 2002 Budget, is conducted.

II Emergency Funding and Other Financial Support

Within days of the September 11, 2001, attacks, the U.S. Congress passed, and President Bush signed, a $40 billion emergency funding measure to respond to the enormous damage caused by the tragedy. As a result of this measure, the White House was given free reign in the allocation of the initial $20 billion. The remainder of the $20 billion will be allocated on a line-by-line basis through cooperation between the White House and Congress.

On September 21, 2001, President Bush released $5.1 billion in emergency spending to assist in the humanitarian, recovery, and national security needs related to the attack on the United States. The funds distributed in this first installment will assist victims of the attacks and address other consequences of the attacks, including funding for: debris removal, search and rescue efforts, and victim assistance efforts of the Federal Emergency Management Agency (FEMA); emergency assistance to disaster-affected metropolitan area health providers; investigative expenses of the Federal Bureau of Investigation (FBI); increased airport security and the number of sky marshals; initial repair of the Pentagon; evacuation of high-threat embassies abroad; additional funding for the Small Business Administration (SBA) disaster loan program; and initial crisis and recovery operations of the Department of Defense and other national security operations.

The emergency legislation also established a fund that would enable victims of the September 11 attacks to receive compensation within three months if they waive their right to obtain punitive damages in lawsuits relating to this matter. In October 2001, the Bush administration was examining how to limit the liability of companies to pay above their liability coverage arising from the attacks.

The allocation of the initial portion of the emergency funding and related activities will take place along these lines:

- Department of Defense—Military: $2.548 billion. Of these funds, $1.772 billion will enable the Department of Defense to begin the following activities: upgrading intelligence and security, enhancing force protection, improving command and control, and increasing full readiness. $776 million of these funds is for supporting the initial crisis response, repairing the Pentagon, and providing for other recovery needs.

- Environmental Protection Agency (EPA): EPA is monitoring the disaster sites to ensure that rescue workers and the public are not facing dangerous environmental risks. Over 200 EPA personnel participated in the response to the terrorist attacks in New York, Pennsylvania, and Virginia. Also, EPA was responsible for cleaning and washing down all workers, equipment, and resources employed during the rescue stage. The agency sampled air, water, and asbestos as well as conducted radiological and dust monitoring. EPA vacuumed and cleaned sidewalks, streets, and buildings in the World Trade Center area. The EPA has provided $600,000 to the Association of Metropolitan Water Agencies to secure an existing web site that would serve as a means of communication among the 18,000 water companies in the United States in case of a terrorist incident. Entities dealing with the water supply are requesting $100 million in federal funds to enable the 750 biggest water systems to undertake physical vulnerability tests. The water sector also asked for an additional $55 million to aid the systems in their efforts to enhance their emergency response plans.

- Army Corps of Engineers (Corps): The Corps structural engineering teams surveyed buildings and structures in New York City so that the city can assure the safety of search, rescue, and debris-removal operations in and around the affected areas. The Corps developed a debris operations plan for New York City. In addition, the Corps considered potential improvements to a harbor facility for removing debris by barge.

- Internal Revenue Service (IRS): The IRS and Treasury extended deadlines for all taxpayers affected by the tragedy. The IRS released new information to assist the public in using charitable organizations and sped up the processing of requests for tax-exempt status from new charities formed to assist victims of the September 11, 2001, attacks. Also, the IRS created a special e-mail address that would allow businesses to send their questions to the IRS and receive answers about extensions and other relief stemming from the disasters.

- FEMA: $2 billion. These funds will support overall emergency assistance in New York and other affected jurisdictions. The Bush administration authorized FEMA to pay for 100% of public assistance activities in New York and at the Pentagon (typically, states pay 25% of these costs). Examples of public assistance activities include debris removal, repair, and restoration of public facilities. FEMA called up 10 FEMA Urban Search and Rescue task forces from around the nation to assist in FEMA's efforts in New York and Virginia. Urban Search and Rescue task forces are teams of local emergency responders that have specialized FEMA training and equipment for rescuing people in the wake of disasters, such as earthquakes and terrorist events.

- Department of Transportation (DOT): $141 million. These funds will support increased airport security measures and expenses for additional federal law enforcement officials to perform Sky Marshal functions, conduct New York Harbor patrols, and get involved in the related recall of Coast Guard reservists.

- Department of Health and Human Services (HHS): $126.2 million. These funds will provide assistance for the health-related needs of the disaster-affected areas of the New York metropolitan area, Virginia, Maryland, and the District of Columbia. Activities that will be supported include: emergency grants for health care providers, community health centers, and mental health and substance abuse services; assessments and services related to environmental hazards; enhancements to the physical security of pathogenic agents and toxins in Centers for Disease Control and Prevention (CDC); and social services, including services for the disabled, supplying home-delivered meals, and furnishing transportation for senior citizens in affected areas. CDC deployed personnel to assist the New York City Health Department in patient care and follow-up needs. CDC staff is also testing, analyzing, and comparing powders from anthrax cases from across the United States.

- SBA: $100 million. These funds will support low-interest disaster loans for renters, homeowners, and businesses in designated disaster areas. Along with FEMA and other federal agencies, SBA's Disaster Loan Program set up disaster field offices in New York and Virginia where disaster victims may come for assistance. Also, SBA sent out 5,677 applications for low-interest disaster loans. SBA directly assisted 4,598 individuals and businesses with loan applications and responses to inquiries. In addition, SBA approved disaster loans totaling $6,052,900. SBA is also conducting information workshops at different locations around New York to reach as many disaster victims as possible.

- Department of State: $48.9 million. Approximately half of these funds will be used to provide rewards for information to assist in apprehending terrorists. The State Department will also use funds to improve emergency communications at domestic facilities and embassies abroad. Also, the funding will be available to evacuate personnel at high-threat embassies, should evacuation be required.

- Department of the Treasury: $48.4 million. These funds will support the immediate response and recovery needs of the approximately 1,000 Treasury employees who were located in or near the World Trade Center complex. Most of those offices were destroyed. These funds will also be used to establish a Foreign Terrorist Assets Tracking Center as well as fund Customs Service air support for counter-terrorism activities.

- Department of Justice: $40.8 million. These funds will support the FBI's extraordinary expenses incurred in investigating the attacks and will provide assistance to the U.S. Marshals Service for increased airport and courthouse security, and for other activities. In addition to this amount, the Justice Department will administer $68 million that was previously allocated for death and disability payments for fire, police, and rescue personnel from the Public Safety Officer's Benefits account.

- Department of Labor (DOL): $29 million. These amounts will provide funding for: the DOL's Dislocated Workers program to provide temporary jobs involving clean-up and restoration efforts in New York; immediate information technology and other costs of disaster recovery; unemployment insurance claims; and the Occupational Safety and Health Administration's (OSHA) monitoring of health and safety at the disaster sites. About 180 OSHA agents have been deployed to provide around-the-clock safety and health assistance.

- Department of Education: $9 million. These funds include: $5 million for the Rehabilitation Services Administration to help individuals who suffered disabling physical or mental trauma as a result of the World Trade Center attacks, as well as funds to help previously disabled Americans who lost jobs; rehabilitation or other support structures as a result of the attack; and $4 million to New York City schools and $1.7 million to New York State schools for School Emergency Response to Violence, or Project SERV, grants that support counseling and mental health services for affected children. The Department of Education also established a loan forgiveness program to help those who live or work in New York City by providing temporary relief from student loan payments.

- General Services Administration (GSA): $8.6 million. These funds will support increased security coverage of federal buildings, purchase of security equipment, structural studies of 7 federal locations affected by the New York City disaster, overtime and travel costs for law enforcement personnel, and other security costs.

- District of Columbia: $6 million. These funds will be used for short-term response activities, including personnel and overtime costs of the Metropolitan Police Department, Fire Department, and Public Works Department of the District of Columbia.

- Department of Energy: $5 million. These funds will support heightened security needs at the Department of Energy's national laboratories.

- International Assistance Programs: $5 million. These funds will primarily cover the costs of the evacuation of Peace Corps volunteers in 9 Peace Corps posts, improved overseas emergency communications, and the potential evacuation of high-risk U.S. Agency for International Development (AID) and Peace Corps posts.

- Legislative Branch: $3.3 million. These funds will support increased security measures, including overtime compensation for the U.S. Capitol

Police and for installation of protective window film for the U.S. Capitol.

- Department of the Interior: $3.1 million. These amounts will provide funding for National Park Service (NPS) and U.S. Park Police emergency response costs in New York City and Washington, D.C., as well as increased security patrols in both cities.

- Judicial Branch: $1.3 million. These funds will be used to install protective window film for the U.S. Supreme Court.

- Executive Office of the President (EOP): $500,000. These funds will be used to install protective window film for the EOP.

- Commodity Futures Trading Commission (CFTC): $200,000. The CFTC's New York office, which was located in the World Trade Center, will use these funds to purchase computers and office equipment for its temporary office space.

- National Transportation Safety Board (NTSB): $150,000. The NTSB will use these funds for the recovery of flight recorders for the four planes and for assistance to the plane crash victims' families.

- Department of Commerce (DOC): $100,000. These funds will enable the International Trade Administration (ITA) to relocate 6 employees who worked at 6 World Trade Center, which was damaged beyond repair, and to purchase new equipment and furniture.

- Export-Import Bank of the United States (Ex-Im Bank): $75,000. These funds will be used to relocate the office of the Ex-Im Bank previously located at the World Trade Center.

By mid-October 2001, the Bush administration proposed ways to spend the second half of the $40 billion in emergency funds. More specifically, the Bush administration proposal request that the $20 billion be funded in the following manner: war-related defense needs, $7 billion; FEMA, $6 billion; domestic priorities, $3 billion; grants to dislocated workers, $2 billion; and chemical and biological defense, $2 billion.

In mid-November 2001, the House Appropriations Committee defeated 3 measures that would increase the $20 billion level of emergency funding by $7.1 billion (a Democrat-sponsored proposal), $9.73 billion (sponsored by New York representatives), and $6.5 billion (by a Democrat representative). The committee did approve a $20 billion plan which is similar to the Bush administration's proposal.

III Government and Industry: The Transportation Sector

Aviation Stabilization Legislation

On September 22, 2001, President Bush signed the $15 billion Airline Transportation and Systems Stabilization Act (ATSSA), which provided the tools to improve the safety and immediate stability of the U.S. commercial airline system. The legislation also established a process for compensating victims of the terrorist attacks.

On September 25, 2001, President Bush provided up to $5 billion to the Department of Transportation's Compensation for Air Carriers account. The funds were intended to stabilize the air transportation industry and compensate air carriers for direct and incremental losses resulting from the Secretary of Transportation's order to ground all aircraft immediately for two days following the September 11, 2001, terrorist attacks and their aftereffects. More specifically, the ATSSA covers incremental loss from September 11, 2001, through December 31, 2001.

The airline industry received $5 billion in grants to be allocated based on the size of the airlines. By October 29, 2001, the Department of Transportation had disbursed $2.5 billion. Also, the legislation called for the creation of a 4-member Air Transportation Board (ATB) .The ATB was established to handle the $10 billion in loan guarantees.

On October 5, 2001, the Bush administration issued regulations for the federal loan guarantees Congress authorized to aid U.S. airlines. The regulations will allow each U.S. airline to apply for assistance after submitting a business plan outlining the company's intention. Yet, the government will not guarantee 100% of a loan, and the maximum length of a guarantee would be seven years.

The factors that would be weighed by the ATB include attracting financial assistance from the private sector and from non-federal sources, such as states, counties, or airport authorities. The ATB was also instructed to favor applicants with the best business plans and the strongest likelihood of repaying.

The rules are designed to give preference to applicants that put up the most private collateral, agree to repay the loans in the shortest amount of time, and present a plan in which workers and creditors agree to make concessions. The government's fee will escalate each year of the loan as an incentive for the airlines to repay it and return to the commercial credit markets. Airlines have until June 28, 2002, to apply for loans.

Some large carriers may have difficulty obtaining the loan guarantees, as there is also a requirement to show the airlines cannot obtain loans without them. Bankrupt carriers will also be able to receive a guaranteed loan if their application is accompanied with a court-approved reorganization plan.

Furthermore, the ATSSA limited the liability of American Airlines Inc. and United Airlines Inc. arising from the four hijackings of the two airlines involved in the September 11, 2001, hijackings, to a maximum of $6 billion.

Aviation Security Legislation

The Bush administration took various steps to enhance aviation safety and security. For instance, since the September 11, 2001, terrorist attacks, the U.S. government has been steadily increasing the number of Federal Air Marshals by using law enforcement officers loaned from various federal agencies. During fall 2001, National Guard units in 50 states were called up, at federal government expense, to provide additional security at airports. Also, effective October 1, 2001, a $500 million fund was established to finance aircraft modifications to delay or deny access to the cockpit. The funding, provided through grants or cost-sharing arrangements, will be used for a number of projects, including those to develop and implement means to:

- Restrict opening of the cockpit door during flight

- Fortify cockpit doors to deny access from the cabin to the pilots in the cockpit

- Alert the cockpit crew to activity in the cabin

- Ensure continuous operation of the aircraft transponder in the event that the crew faces an emergency

During autumn 2001, President Bush also pledged to have the federal government play a larger role in airport security and screening services. After several proposals, the Bush administration suggested a new security system that would be operated through a combination of federal and non-federal workers, with federal uniformed personnel managing all operations and maintaining a visible presence at all commercial airports.

The Bush administration's plan additionally sought to:

- Establish new standards for security operations

- Supervise the passenger and baggage security at the 420 commercial passenger airports nationwide

- Perform intensive background checks as well as train and test screeners and security personnel

- Purchase and maintain security equipment

- Oversee patrolling of secure areas and monitoring the quality of the airport's access controls

- Work with other law enforcement authorities at the federal, state, and local levels as well as serve as a key facilitator of coordination regarding homeland security

On October 11, 2001, the Senate approved legislation tightening security at U.S. airports and airlines, ending a long and heated deadlock between Senate Democrats and Republicans. The Senate bill would sharply increase the number of federal marshals on commercial flights and let commercial pilots carry firearms. It would require that federal workers, rather than airline employees or private security firms, screen passengers and baggage at the nation's 142 largest airports. This measure would result in the creation of a federal work force of 28,000 screeners. Screening at the roughly 300 remaining U.S. airports will be overseen by federal supervisors and conducted by a mix of federal, state, and local officials.

The Senate bill would require new anti-hijacking training for airline crews and strengthened cockpit doors. Also, the proposed legislation would levy a $2.50 passenger fee on flights to cover the estimated $1.9 billion cost of the new security measures.

On November 1, 2001, the House of Representatives approved, in a 286-139 vote, a bill that would improve government standards for screening airline passengers, strengthen training for airport security workers, and require federal government control with respect to training and supervising workers. Nevertheless, the House bill allowed for the president to decide if the front-line workers will be federal government or contract workers. Earlier that same day, the House defeated a Senate-passed, Democratic-backed alternative on aviation security by a vote of 218-214. The Democratic-backed House bill would have made the airport screeners and other aviation security personnel federal employees.

The House and Senate aviation security bills were similar in several respects, such as: increasing the number of federal air marshals on commercial flights, fortifying cockpit doors, expanding anti-hijacking training for crews, requiring thorough background checks on all aviation security officials, raising wage scales for security workers, and moving towards inspecting all checked bags and matching passengers with luggage.

Two issues required resolution at the House-Senate conference committee: whether the screeners should be federal or contract employees and whether aviation security should be under the mandate of the Justice Department (as the Senate Democrat bill stipulates) or within a newly created transportation security agency in the Transportation Department (House Republican approach). The federalization of the aviation security issue was particularly thorny as Republicans argued that such a transformation would require over a year to undertake, while Democrats said that it would take only 3 months. Also, Democrats suggested that under the private contractor model, it behooves airlines to choose the lowest bidder, thereby causing poorly trained and underpaid workers to be posted at aviation security locales.

On November 19, 2001, President Bush signed into law aviation security legislation that was crafted following a compromise reached between Senate and House leaders. This legislation creates a new federal agency, the Transportation Security Agency (TSA), whose mandate is to ensure the security of air, ground, and sea security. The TSA will undertake the security responsibilities formerly carried out by the Federal Aviation Administration (FAA) for aviation security. The TSA, once fully staffed, is envisioned to have nearly 45,000 employees. Included among them are 28,000 passenger and baggage screeners and an expansion of the air marshal program. Prior to full federalization of the work force, federal airport security managers will oversee private contractor security operations. Also, criminal background checks for about 750,000 airport employees will take place.

The law mandates that all checked baggage be screened with explosives detection equipment by the end of 2002. Within 60 days of enactment of the law, all checked baggage must be screened by whatever methods available (by hand or otherwise). While in autumn 2001, U.S. airports have less than 150 bomb detection machines at 47 airports, over 2,000 additional machines will be required at another 403 airports. In addition, the aviation security law requires the strengthening of cockpit doors.

The legislation allows for the possibility for airports to reverse the federalization of the workforce within three years and return to private contractors. However, in practice, this is highly unlikely as it would give an additional shock to the system. Moreover, the flying public—at least now—believes a federal workforce is preferable to private contractors.

The cost of implementing this legislation includes about $700 million of annual contributions by airlines and $2.50 airplane security taxes per boarding (a maximum $5 fee for a one-way trip) on passengers. The costs to the U.S. government in recruiting, training, and absorbing the current and new staff, additional equipment, and the requisite mandates will run into the billions of dollars.

Other Aviation Security Measures

On October 17, 2001, the FAA pronounced that it will require criminal background checks on all workers (e.g., airline crew, mechanics, ramp workers, gate agents with access to planes or ramps, catering truck drivers, and baggage workers) with access to secure areas of airports. The background checks, to be conducted by the FBI and the Office of Personnel Management (OPM), would affect more than 1 million people. In addition, the FAA stated that it would require all checked luggage to be screened.

The seriousness that aviation security warrants can be understood by examining several security breaches that occurred in the post-September 11, 2001, setting. For example, in late September 2001, a 63-year-old man who unknowingly carried a handgun, passed through a metal detector post at Atlanta's Hartfield Airport without the alarm going off. Only prior to boarding the airplane did the man claim to remember he had the weapon on him.

Likewise, in October 2001, a Southwest Airline passenger traveling from New Orleans, Louisiana, to Phoenix, Arizona, mistakenly carried onboard a loaded gun in his briefcase. Neither security personnel nor the x-ray machine at Louis Armstrong New Orleans International Airport stopped the 68-year-old man when he passed through airport security. Also, various security breaches during fall 2001 at O'Hare International Airport have given cause for concern. These examples illustrate that much more needs to be done to improve aviation security.

Trains

On October 2, 2001, Amtrak requested $515 million from Congress for new security measures and for safety improvements in its passenger train network. That amount was a portion of the $3.1 billion package that Amtrak requested from the federal government to expand its capacity with more trains, tracks, and upgraded electrical power. Amtrak witnessed a rise of about 15%

in the number of passengers during the first few weeks following the World Trade Center and Pentagon attacks.

The funding for Amtrak security and safety measures would be used for additional police officers, extra lighting and fencing, bomb-detection systems, and surveillance cameras in and around stations, tracks, yards, tunnels, and bridges. In addition, Amtrak seeks to improve escape routes in critical areas.

These upgrades are in stark contrast to the minimal level of security that Amtrak had provided on its trains. Generally, Amtrak has allowed passengers to board without security checks. Also, metal detectors and luggage searches are practically nonexistent. Since the September 11, 2001, terrorist attacks, Amtrak has instituted some changes, including requiring customers to show photo identification when they purchase tickets.

Buses

The American Bus Association stated in autumn 2001 that the industry requires at least $1 billion to: enhance security at the thousands of points it serves nationwide, preserve vital services provided by small business that have become economically devastated, and preserve and enhance the industry's vehicle and terminal infrastructure. Also, the industry requested tax relief as follows:

- An immediate exemption from the 7.4-cent federal fuel tax on diesel for motorcoaches for the forseeable future.

- A 10% tax credit for the purchase of new or used commercial highway passenger transportation vehicles.

- Tax credits amounting to 50% of the cost of purchasing and installing wheelchair lifts.

Ports

Following the World Trade Center and Pentagon terrorist attacks, the Airport and Seaport Terrorism Prevention Act, Senate bill 1429, was proposed. Among its provisions are:

- Grants of up to $250,000 for port security infrastructure improvements for construction, acquisition, or deployment of surveillance equipment and technology.

- Pilot program for tracking cargo will be established and anti-tampering standards will be adopted to ensure that cargo is not opened during shipment within the United States.

IV Government and Industry: The Insurance Sector

Executives from U.S. insurance companies informed Congress in autumn 2001 that terrorism risks will probably not be covered in future insurance policies unless the federal government serves as a backup to the insurance industry. Without the government serving as the insurer of last resort, the onus of hedging against terrorism will rest with insurers. Reinsurers, too, have indicated that they may no longer issue policies covering terrorism.

Insurance executives explained that whether insurance companies can afford to pay future terrorism claims is causing a crisis in the industry. The immediate need of resolving the matter is that about 70% of commercial insurance policies expire January 1, 2002, as do 90% of insurance policies that contain terrorism and war provisions.

In early October 2001, the American Insurance Association (AIA) proposed that the federal government establish an insurance company that would back a fund to insure against future terrorist attacks. More specifically, the government would assist in paying claims if funds pooled by the new Homeland Security Mutual Reinsurance Co. would be insufficient to cover losses from additional terrorist attacks.

Involvement in the federal program, the AIA envisions, would be voluntary with each participating insurance firm keeping 5% of the premiums collected and retaining 5% of the risk. The pool would receive the rest of the premiums, covering the remainder of the risk up to when it was low on money and the federal government stepped in. The pool proposal is similar in nature to a government-backed reinsurance fund established in Great Britain, which suffered severe terrorist attacks in the 1980s. Under the Great Britain system, insurance firms pool funds to create a reinsurance fund, which is backed by the government if any losses go beyond the reserves.

On October 15, 2001, the Bush administration proposed that the federal government would take on the most immediate financial risk of another terrorist attack by paying up to 90% of insurance claims resulting from a future incident. The Bush plan would be based on claims from a single incident that would have to be certified as terrorism by the Treasury Department. The Bush administration initiative parallels the current U.S. approach for insurance on nuclear power plants.

During the first year of the White House plan, the government would pay 80% of the first $20 billion in claims and 90% for damage in excess of $20 billion. In the second year, insurance companies would pay the first $10 billion in claims and then split the cost with government up to $20 billion. The government would pay 90% of losses over $20 billion. By the last year of the program, private insurers would cover the first $20 billion in claims. The government would split the cost of claims between $20 billion and $40 billion while the government would pay 90% of claims over $40 billion. Total liability for both the public and private sectors under the Bush administration plan would be capped at $100 billion.

On October 23, 2001, the Bush administration modified the proposal such that the government would pay 80% of the first $20 billion in claims if any attacks occurred in 2002 and 90% of the next $80 billion. The modified proposal would cap the industry's liability from terrorist claims to $23 billion in 2003 and $36 billion in 2004, the final year of the program. Insurers would pay all of the losses on the first $10 billion in claims in 2003 and in the first $20 billion in 2004.

In late October 2001, the House of Representative drafted its approach to aid the insurance industry in case of further terrorist attacks. According to the House initiative, insurance companies will be required to pay a deductible of less than $10 billion prior to federal aid applying. Also, under the House plan, money will be loaned to insurers, rather than provided to them as a grant. Furthermore, insurers will be forced to include an additional premium on specific terrorist-related policies. By late October 2001, the Bush administration and Senate leaders were concluding a draft of the insurance plan that would expire after 2 years, with an option to extend it for a certain period.

In November 2001, the Air Transport Association (ATA), several large airlines, and the insurance broker Marsh & McLennan proposed a plan under which the air carriers establish and make payments to an insurance pool focused on enabling the airlines with insurance coverage for war and terrorism. The airlines could purchase the insurance from the fund, which would offer $2 billion or more in coverage per terrorist incident. Under the terms of the proposal, the airlines' liability would reach $300 million initially with reinsurance coverage by the FAA. Once the insurance funds reach a sufficient level, FAA reinsurance would no longer be needed, the ATA proposal projects.

Due to sharp rises in insurance rates, airlines may be forced to expend nearly $2 billion additional fees for war and terrorism coverage insurance (if it is still available). The insurance crisis is particularly critical as under the terms of the ATSSA, airlines' availability of FAA $7.50 per flight for war and terrorism will expire January 11, 2002. Some private insurance proposals for war and terrorism coverage cost $3.10 per passenger per flight.

V Public Health Responses

The Bush administration has taken a number of steps to respond to the threat of bio-terrorism. On October 17, 2001, HHS Secretary Tommy G. Thompson outlined the Bush administration's request for $1.5 billion in further bio-terrorism readiness measures and supplies. Of that total, $1.2 billion was called for stockpiling emergency medicines as well as expanding the National Pharmaceutical Stockpile. The aforementioned figures would be in addition to the $345 million that the HHS had initially planned to spend on bio-terrorism initiatives.

Secretary Thompson requested $509 million for stockpiles of 300 million smallpox vaccine dosages to be available by the end of 2002. Presently, the United States has a stockpile of 15 million doses that could be diluted to inoculate up to 77 million persons with 95% effectiveness. Some funds would also be used to raise stockpiles of antibiotics, including Cipro, which is effective against anthrax. In October 2001, the federal government had sufficient antibiotics to treat 2.2 million people for anthrax for 60 days. The objective is to raise the anthrax antibiotic supply to treat 12 million people.

To complement the funds to be allocated for antibiotics and vaccines, Secretary Thompson asked for: $175 million for state and local efforts for counter-terrorism; $61 million for hundreds of food inspectors, labor specialists, and other compliance personnel; and $20 million for federal laboratories. Also, to demonstrate the seriousness of the terrorist threat to the public health system, Thompson declared that HHS was in a war mode, and it thereby established a new 24-hour situation room to confront bio-terrorism and other threats in October 2001.

The Senate's proposal in responding to the specter of bio-terrorism is led by Senators Bill Frist (Republican-Tennessee) and Edward Kennedy (Democrat-Massachusetts), who proposed a $1.4 billion package.

VI Government Investigative, Enforcement, and Security Measures

Homeland Security

President Bush formally appointed Tom Ridge, former Governor of Pennsylvania, as Assistant to the President for Homeland Security on October 8, 2001. The Office of Homeland Security's mission is to develop and coordinate the implementation of a comprehensive national strategy to secure the United States from terrorist threats or attacks. The office will coordinate the executive branch's efforts to detect, prepare for, prevent, protect against, respond to, and recover from terrorist attacks within the United States. On a daily basis since commencing his position, Governor Ridge served as President Bush's point man on domestic terrorism, although, on occasion, he was joined by other senior Bush administration representatives.

On October 29, 2001, President Bush issued his first two homeland security presidential directives: Organization and Operation of the Homeland Security Council (HSC) and Combating Terrorism Through Immigration Policies. The first directive emphasized that securing the American public from terrorist threats or attacks has become a critical national security function. As such, it requires extensive coordination across a broad spectrum of federal, state, and local agencies to reduce the potential for terrorist attacks and to mitigate damage should such attacks arise. The HSC's role will be to ensure coordination of all homeland and security-related activities among executive departments and agencies while promoting the effective development and implementation of all homeland security policies.

To better perform its duties, the HSC will establish a HSC Principals Committee (HSC/PC) that will be the senior inter-agency forum under the HSC for homeland security issues. The HSC/PC will be comprised of the following members: Secretary of Treasury, Secretary of Defense, Attorney General, Secretary of HHS, Secretary of Transportation, Director of the Office of Management and Budget, the Assistant to the President for Homeland Security (who will serve as Chairman), the Assistant to the President and Chief of Staff, the Director of the Central Intelligence Agency (CIA), the Director of the FBI, the Director of FEMA, and the Assistant to the President and Chief of Staff to the Vice President. Also, the Assistant to the President for National Security Affairs will be invited to attend all meetings of the HSC/PC.

A senior sub-cabinet inter-agency forum for consideration of policy issues affecting homeland security will be established in the form of the HSC Deputies Committee. Also, HSC Policy Coordination Committees (HSC/PCCs) will coordinate the development and implementation of homeland security policies by multiple departments and agencies throughout the federal government while concurrently coordinating those policies with state and local governments. The HSC/PCCs shall be the main day-to-day fora for inter-agency coordination of homeland security policy. They shall provide policy analysis for consideration by the more senior committees of the HSC system and ensure timely responses to decisions made by the president.

In order to carry out their mandate, eleven HSC/PCCs will be established for the following functional areas, each to be chaired by a designated senior director from the Office of Homeland Security:

- Detection, Surveillance, and Intelligence (by the Senior Director, Intelligence and Detection)

- Plans, Training, Exercises, and Evaluation (by the Senior Director, Policy and Plans)

- Law Enforcement and Investigation (by the Senior Director, Intelligence and Detection)

- Weapons of Mass Destruction Consequence Management (by the Senior Director, Response and Recovery)

- Key Asset, Border, Territorial Waters, and Airspace Security (by the Senior Director, Protection and Prevention)

- Domestic Transportation Security (by the Senior Director, Protection and Prevention)

- Research and Development (by the Senior Director, Research and Development)

- Protection and Prevention (by the Senior Director, Protection and Prevention)

- Domestic Threat Response and Incident Management (by the Senior Director, Response and Recovery)

- Economic Consequences (by the Senior Director, Responses and Recovery)

- Public Affairs (by the Senior Director, Communications)

With reference to the second Homeland Security Presidential Directive, Combating Terrorism Through Immigration Policies, the Bush administration indicated that the United States would continue to welcome immigrants and visitors, but it would need to aggressively prevent aliens who engage in or support terrorist activity from entering the United States and would detain, prosecute, or deport any such aliens who are already in the United States. Under those guidelines, the Attorney General created in November

2001 a Foreign Terrorist Task Force (Task Force). The aid of the Secretary of State, the Director of the CIA, and other government officials would be called upon as required.

The Task Force ensures that federal agencies coordinate programs that will accomplish the following: deny entry into the United States of aliens associated with, suspected of being engaged in, or supporting terrorist activity; and locate, detain, prosecute, or deport any such aliens already present in the United States. The Task Force's effectiveness will be strengthened by its expert staff from the Department of State, Immigration and Naturalization Service (INS), U.S. Secret Service, Customs Service, intelligence and military communities, and other federal units, as necessary.

The Attorney General and Secretary of the Treasury, in concert with the Director of Central Intelligence, will develop and implement multi-year plans to enhance the investigative and intelligence analysis capabilities of the INS and Customs Service. The aim of such steps is to raise efforts to identify, locate, detain, prosecute, or deport aliens associated with, suspected of being engaged in, or supporting terrorist activity in the United States.

The Bush administration pledged to implement measures to end the abuse of student visas and prohibit certain international students from receiving education and training in sensitive areas, including areas of study with direct application to the development and use of weapons of mass destruction. The Bush administration further seeks to prohibit the education and training of foreign nationals in developing military skills that later could be used to harm the United States and its allies.

The INS, in consultation with the Department of Education, will conduct periodic reviews of all institutions certified to receive non-immigrant students and exchange visitor program students. These reviews shall include checks for compliance with record keeping and reporting requirements. Failure of institutions to comply may result in the termination of the institution's approval to receive such students.

The Secretary of State, in coordination with the Secretary of the Treasury and the Attorney General, will initiate negotiations with Canada and Mexico to assure maximum possible compatibility of immigration, customs, and visa policies. The goal of the negotiations will be to provide all involved nations with the highest possible level of assurance that only individuals seeking entry for legitimate purposes enter any of these countries. At the same time, however, border restrictions that hinder legitimate transnational commerce will be minimized.

Another measure will involve the Director of the Office of Science and Technology Policy, who in conjunction with the Attorney General and the Director of the CIA, will make recommendations about the use of advanced technology to help enforce U.S. immigration laws, implement U.S. immigration programs, facilitate the rapid identification of aliens who are suspected of engaging in or supporting terrorist activity, deny them access to the United States, and recommend ways in which existing government databases can be best utilized to maximize the ability of the government to detect, identify, locate, and apprehend potential terrorists in the United States.

In addition, in November 2001, the Justice Department declared it would restructure the INS into two separate sections. One INS bureau would focus on immigration services (processing visa and other immigration documents), while the other would address immigration enforcement (safeguarding border controls and investigating immigration infractions). Analogously, the Justice Department declared that visa applicants from selected Muslim and Arab nations would undergo more stringent criminal background checks.

The impetus for INS modifications stem, in part, from revelations that, without undergoing an interview, 15 of the 19 hijackers in the September 11 incidents received relatively quickly visas from the U.S. Embassy in Saudi Arabia. Also, affecting these changes was a Justice Department Inspector report showing that the INS had mismanaged monitoring of foreign visitors, as about 40% of the 5 million illegal immigrants in the United States in 2000 overstayed their visas. In October 2001, the Justice Department requested the State Department to add 46 terrorist groups to the list of terrorist organizations that are not permitted to enter the United States.

Another critical issue that U.S. anti-terrorism policies requires is a good understanding of budgetary matters in this vein. Therefore, the Office of Management and Budget will work closely with the Attorney General, the Secretaries of State and of the Treasury, the Assistant to the President for Homeland Security, and all other appropriate agencies to review budgetary matters. In particular, the assessment will recommend appropriate support for a multi-year program to provide the United States with a capability to prevent aliens who engage in or support terrorist activity from entering or remaining in the United States or smuggling implements of terrorism into the United States.

On October 9, 2001, President Bush strengthened the anti-terrorism team with the appointments of Dick Clarke as Special Advisor for Cyber Security and General Wayne Downing as National Director and Deputy National Security Advisor for Combating Terrorism.

In November 2001, it was reported that the U.S. military is discussing whether to create a regional commander in chief for troops involved in homeland (domestic) defense. Yet, the use of U.S. military forces for domestic purposes may face political and legal obstacles.

USA Patriot Act

On October 26, 2001, President Bush signed into law the USA Patriot Act. At that time, he underscored the importance of the legislation in that it "will give intelligence and law enforcement officials important new tools to fight a present danger." He remarked at the time, "Countering and investigating terrorist activity is the number one priority for both law enforcement and intelligence agencies."

The USA Patriot Act enables the U.S. government to be better equipped to identify, investigate, follow, detain, prosecute, and punish suspected terrorists. As today's terrorist increasingly uses sophisticated tools—advanced technology and international money transfers—the government's capabilities must be formidable, as well. In essence, the USA Patriot Act will significantly improve the surveillance of terrorists and increase the rapidity of tracking down and intercepting terrorists.

The main elements of the USA Patriot Act are:

- To allow for federal warrants to be effective nationwide and to no longer be limited to specific districts

- To enable law enforcement to obtain subpoena power for alleged terrorists' communications, including fixed and wireless telephones, e-mail, web surfing, as well as unopened voice mail and e-mail

- To attach roving wiretaps to alleged terrorists and thereby eliminate the need for the government to request wiretaps for specific telephone numbers as previously required

- To improve coordination and cooperation, such as information-gathering between U.S. intelligence and law enforcement investigators, with respect to terrorist investigations

- To allow law enforcement to use new subpoena power to obtain payment information, such as credit card or bank account numbers of suspected terrorists on the Internet

- To create rules to counter terrorists' access to, and use of, illicit funds as well as to prevent or impede other improper terrorist activities, such as counterfeiting and smuggling

- To punish those who aid or harbor terrorists

The broad surveillance powers available in the USA Patriot Act were capped in the sense that a 4-year expiration (or sunset clause) was included in order to allay fears of overextending such expansive police rights if the threat of terrorism wanes in future years.

Law Enforcement and Judicial Anti-Terrorism Measures

On the day of the World Trade Center and Pentagon incidents, the FBI established a web site, www.ifccfbi.gov/complaint/terrorist.asp, that allowed individuals to report information about the attacks. Since then, the FBI's participation in the investigation of the September 11, 2001, attacks has been significant, involving 7,000 workers—1 in 4 of the FBI's personnel. Between the day of the attack through October 24, 2001, the FBI gathered more than 3,700 separate pieces of evidence. Also, through the medium of the FBI's web site and 1-800-CRIME-TV, the American public contributed over 170,000 potential leads and tips that FBI agents and support personnel are pursuing. This figure is 40% of the 420,000 total leads that have been generated in FBI investigations from the fateful day in September through November 2, 2001.

The FBI also established a terrorist prevention task force, which is composed of representatives from different agencies. In addition, the FBI's long-standing 35 task forces on terrorism gather intelligence and pursue leads to identify and apprehend terrorists and their co-conspirators.

On October 5, 2001, Secretary Powell redesignated, as required under U.S. law every two years, 25 groups as Foreign Terrorist Organizations (FTOs). This characterization enables the U.S. government to continue to take measures against these organizations in accordance with the provisions of the Anti-terrorism and Effective Death Penalty Act (AEACT). More specifically, the AEACT makes it illegal for persons in the United States or subject to U.S. jurisdiction to provide material support to these terrorist groups. The law requires U.S. financial institutions to block assets held by them and allows U.S. immigration officials to deny visas to representatives of these groups. The designation of FTO deters donations or contributions to the named organizations as well as heightens public awareness and knowledge of terrorist organizations.

According to Secretary Powell:

Every one of these groups has continued to engage in terrorist activity over the past two years. Most of these groups—such as the Islamic Republic Movement (Hamas), Palestinian Islamic Jihad (PIJ), the Liberation Tigers of Tamil Eelam (LTTE), the Revolutionary Army Forces of Colombia (FARC), Basque Fatherland and Liberty (ETA) and, of course, Usama bin Laden's al-Qaida organization—have carried out murderous attacks on innocent people since their designation in 1999. Others—such as the Abu Nidal Organization (ANO), Aum Shinrikyo, and the Kurdistan Workers' Party (PKK)—have been less active but nonetheless continued to plan and prepare for possible acts of terrorism. Still others—such as the al-Jihad (Egyptian Islamic Jihad) and the Gama'a al-Islamiyya (Islamic Group)—have provided direct support for the terrorist activities of Usama bin Laden's network.

Two previously designated groups in Israel, Kahane Chai and Kach, are listed as one group for purposes of this list. Two groups, the Japanese Red Army and the Tupac Amaru Revolutionary Movement in Peru did not meet the criteria for redesignation. Secretary Powell had designated two new FTOs, the Real Irish Republican Army (Real IRA) and the United Self-Defense Forces of Colombia (AUC) in 2001.

Against this backdrop, as of October 5, 2001, the current list of designated FTOs includes: ANO, Abu Sayyaf Group, Armed Islamic Group (GIA), Aum Shinrikyo, ETA, Islamic Group, Islamic Republic Movement, Harakat ul-Majahidin (HUM), Hizballah (Party of God), Islamic Movement of Uzbekistan (IMU), Egyptian Islamic Jihad, Kahane Chai (Kach), PKK, LTTE, Mujahedin-e Khalq Organization (MEK), National Liberation Army (ELN), PIJ, Palestine Liberation Front (PLF), Popular Front for the Liberation of Palestine (PFLP), PFLP-General Command (PFLP-GC), al-Qaida, Real IRA, FARC, Revolutionary Nuclei (formerly ELA), Revolutionary Organization 17 November, Revolutionary People's Liberation Army/Front (DHKP/C), Shining Path (Sendero Luminoso, SL), and AUC.

On October 10, 2001, President Bush joined Attorney General John Ashcroft, Secretary of State Colin Powell, and FBI Director Robert S. Mueller, III, in announcing a new joint program to heighten global awareness of America's efforts to locate known terrorists and bring them to justice. The new program will be managed jointly by the Department of Justice and the State Department. The FBI portion of the program will be known as the list of "Most Wanted Terrorists." The State Department facet of the program will be managed through the department's Rewards for Justice Program.

On October 10, 2001, the Bush administration put 22 terrorists, including Usama bin Laden, Ayman Al-Zawahiri, and Muhammad Atef (killed in Afghanistan in November 2001), leaders of al-Qaida, on the list of "Most Wanted Terrorists." President Bush explained, "These 22 individuals do not account for all the terrorist activity in the world, but they're among the most dangerous: the leaders and key supporters, the planners and strategists. They must be found; they will be stopped; and they will be punished."

Among the other terrorists listed on the Most Wanted Terrorists list are: Abdelkarim Hussein Mohamed Al-Nasser, Abdullah Ahmed Abdullah, Muhsin Musa Matwalli Atwah, Ali Atwa, Anas Al-Liby, Ahmed Khalfan Ghailani, Hasan Izz-Al-Din, Ahmed Mohammed Hamed Ali, Fazul Abdullah Mohammed, Imad Fayez Mugniyah, Mustafa Mohamed Fadhil, Sheikh Ahmed Salim Swedan, Abdul Rahman Yasin, Fahid Mohammed Ally Msalam, Ahmad Ibrahim Al-Mughassil, Khalid Shaikh Mohammed, Saif Al-Adel, Ali Saed Bin Ali El-Hoorie, and Ibrahim Salih Mohammed Al-Yacoub.

The FBI issued its first national terrorism alert on October 11, 2001, stating: "Certain information, while not specific as to target, gives the government reason to believe that there may be additional terrorist attacks within the United States and against U.S. interests overseas over the next several days. The FBI has again alerted all local law enforcement to be on the highest alert and we call on all people to immediately notify the FBI and local law enforcement of any unusual or suspicious activity."

The anthrax scare that riveted the nation's attention in fall 2001 was exacerbated by numerous hoaxes, pranks, and threats involving chemical or biological agents. During the first 15 days of October 2001, the FBI responded to over 2,300 incidents or suspected incidents involving anthrax or other dangerous substances. The vast majority were false alarms or practical jokes. FBI Director Mueller warned that all incidents "will be investigated thoroughly and vigorously by Special Agents of the FBI, by the postal authorities, and by other law enforcement officials." The negative implications of anthrax hoaxes, Mueller explained, were that they squander "millions of dollars in public health and law enforcement resources, resources that could be better spent in responding to actual terrorist acts. More importantly, they are taking manpower and time away from individuals who could be ensuring that there are no future terrorist acts."

As such, federal and state authorities nationwide are arresting and prosecuting such mischief-makers. In post-September 11, Tennessee, the state government initiated a $10,000 reward system to persons providing tips that lead to convictions for terrorist hoaxes.

In order to respond to the rising concern of Americans about suspicious mail, the FBI issued a press release on October 15, 2001, entitled, "What to Do if You Receive a Suspicious Letter or Package." In the document, the FBI illustrated some of the characteristics that one might find in a suspicious letter or package, including: no return address; restrictive markings; excessive or overseas postage; foreign return address; misspelled words; addressed solely to a job title or incorrect title; badly typed or written; protruding wires; lopsided or uneven, rigid or bulky; strange odor; wrong title with name; oily stains; discolorations; crystallization on wrapper; and excessive tape or string.

Moreover, the advisory suggested that the receiver of suspicious mail should: (1) handle with care; do not shake or bump the object, (2) isolate and look for indicators, (3) don't open, smell or taste, (4) treat it as suspect! Call 911.

Also, if the parcel is opened and/or a threat is identified, then:

- For a Bomb: Evacuate immediately, call 911 (police), and contact the local FBI office.

- For a Radiological Substance: Limit exposure (do not handle), create distance between yourself and the item (evacuate the area), shield yourself from the object, call 911 (police), and contact the local FBI office.

- For a Biological or Chemical Substance: Isolate (do not handle), call 911 (police), wash your hands with soap and warm water, and contact the local FBI office.

On October 29, 2001, Attorney General John Ashcroft issued the Bush administration's second national terrorism alert warning. Ashcroft warned, "Based on information developed, there may be additional terrorist attacks within the United States and against United States interests over the next week. The administration views this information as credible, but unfortunately it does not contain specific information as to the type of attack or specific targets." The next day, Director of Homeland Security Tom Ridge warned governors of possible attacks against nuclear power plants and storage facilities, bridges, and tunnels.

The FBI warned on November 1, 2001, "unspecified groups are targeting suspension bridges on the West Coast" in "6 incidents." Authorities deemed as possible the following major targets in California: San Francisco's Golden Gate Bridge, the San Francisco-Oakland Bay Bridge, the Vincent Thomas Bridge in Los Angeles, and the Coronado Bridge in San Diego. The FBI also contacted law enforcement officials in Arizona, Idaho, Montana, Nevada, Oregon, Utah, and Washington.

In November 2001 the Justice Department issued rules enabling the government to hold for up to six months selected illegal aliens deemed suspected terrorists or persons whose release would severely harm U.S. foreign policy interests. Also announced that month was a new Justice Department rule enabling investigators to monitor written and oral communications between prisoners and their attorneys if the U.S. government perceives that the suspect could use those exchanges to assist potential violent or terrorist acts.

The Justice Department announced another investigative initiative on November 9, 2001. In this matter, the department detailed its interest in questioning over 5,000 men, aged 18-33 and foreign born, who entered the United States since January 2000, for possible links with future terrorist attacks. The list of persons was sent to various federal, state, and local authorities with the view to conducting investigations with the potential witnesses during the subsequent 30 days.

On November 13, 2001, President Bush stated that "an extraordinary emergency exists for national defense purposes," caused him to issue a military order which related to the detention, treatment, and trial of non-citizens suspected of being members of al-Qaida, "engaged in, aided or abetted, or conspired to commit, acts of international terrorism," or harboring them. More specifically, the order allows for the secretary of defense to detain, either in the United States or abroad, such individuals and initiate charges against them in a military tribunal. The military tribunals are mandated to reach decisions following a two-thirds majority vote of the military commission members. The decisions are non-appealable although they are reviewable by the secretary of defense or president, at the latter's designation.

According to White House Counsel Al Gonzales, the military tribunals would provide another avenue, disparate from civilian courts, by which to prosecute alleged terrorists. Critics of the presidential order proffer, inter alia, that the tribunal should include more procedural and substantive safeguards to suspects. It has been suggested that the U.S. action could prompt some foreign countries to charge U.S. citizens abroad with various crimes and prosecute them in their own military tribunals.

Fighting the Funding of Terrorists

The Bush administration has taken a variety of steps to reduce the capabilities of U.S. and foreign terrorist organizations, terrorists, and their sympathizers to raise funds for terrorist activities. For example, President Bush issued an Executive Order on Terrorist Financing (EOTF), effective September 24, 2001, that blocks property and prohibits transactions with persons who commit, threaten to commit, or support terrorism. President Bush stated, "Because of the pervasiveness and expansiveness of the financial foundation of foreign terrorists, financial sanctions may be appropriate for those foreign persons that support or otherwise associate with these foreign terrorists."

Treasury Secretary Paul O'Neill explained the importance of EOTF: "We have the President's explicit directive to block the U.S. assets of any domestic or foreign financial institution that refuses to cooperate with us in blocking assets of terrorist organizations. This order is a notice to financial institutions around the world, if you have any involvement in the financing of the al-Qaida organization, you have two choices: cooperate in this fight, or we will freeze your U.S. assets; we will punish you for providing the resources that make these evil acts possible."

The 27 terrorists, terrorist organizations, foreign businesses, and charities listed in the executive order include al-Qaida/Islamic Army, Usama bin Laden, Ayman al-Zawahiri, Muhammad Atef (aka Subhi Abu Sitta, Abu Hafs Al Masri), Abu Sayyaf Group, GIA, HUM, al-Jihad, IMU, Asbat al-Ansar, Salafist Group for Call and Combat (GSPC), Libyan Islamic Fighting Group, Al-Itihaad al-Islamiya (AIAI), Islamic Army of Aden, Shaykh Sai'id (aka Mustafa Muhammad Ahmad), Abu Hafs the Mauritanian (aka Mahfouz Ould al-Walid, Khalid Al-Shanqiti), Ibn Al-Shaykh al-Libi, Abu Zubaydah (aka Zayn al-Abidin Muhammad Husayn, Tariq), Abd al-Hadi al-Iraqi (aka Abu Abdallah), Thirwat Salah Shihata, Tariq Anwar al-Sayyid Ahmad (aka Fathi, Amr al-Fatih), Muhammad Salah (aka Nasr Fahmi Nasr Hazanayn), Makhtab Al-Khidamat/Al Kifah, Wafa Humanitarian Organization, Al Rashid Trust, and Mamoun Darkazanli Import-Export Company.

On November 1, 2001, the Bush administration added 22 entities as suspected terrorist organizations that would be subject to the provisions of EOTF. It is worthwhile to note that the 22 organizations already appear on the State Department's list of 28 FTOs.

Also, the Bush administration intends to push for various measures that will make it more difficult for terrorists to launder money than is currently the practice. Among the Bush administration's plans are to:

- Make it a crime to launder proceeds of most foreign crimes. Under current law, it only is illegal to launder gains from bank fraud, terrorism, or drug trafficking. Terrorists sometimes make their money through other crimes, and then use it to finance terror operations.

- Control the movement of bulk cash over U.S. borders more stringently than ever.

- Allow the federal government to issue administrative subpoenas to get account records from foreign banks that have correspondent banking arrangements with U.S. institutions.

- Grant the Treasury secretary discretionary authority to impose special controls on suspects' foreign financial institutions or transactions, including prohibiting a foreign bank from having a correspondent relationship with U.S. institutions.

The Treasury Department has approached U.S. financial institutions to provide information that will assist in identifying patterns of terrorist financing. On October 11, 2001, the Treasury Department's Financial Crimes Enforcement Network established a Financial Institutions Hotline (Hotline) for financial institutions to voluntarily report to law enforcement agencies suspicious transactions that may relate to recent terrorist activity against the United States. The purpose of the Hotline, operational 7 days a week, 24 hours a day, will be to facilitate the immediate transmittal of this information to law enforcement.

On October 25, 2001, the Treasury Department announced the creation of the Anti-Terrorist Financing Task Force, Operation Green Quest. The goals of Green Quest are:

- Identify, disrupt, and dismantle the financial operations of charities and non-governmental organizations (NGOs) associated with Usama bin Laden and al-Qaida.

- Identify, disrupt, and dismantle the financial operations of terrorist organizations beyond al-Qaida.

- Identify, infiltrate, and ultimately dismantle hawalas and other underground remittance systems used to provide funds to bin Laden, al-Qaida, and other terrorist groups.

- Develop individual and group targets for analysis by the Foreign Asset Tracking Center.

- Take preventive action by providing interested nations with technical assistance and support to identify accounts linked to terrorist networks.

In order to achieve the goals of Green Quest, the government will undertake a number of measures. The Bush administration will attempt to deny terrorist groups access to the international financial system, impair terrorists' ability to raise funds, and expose, isolate, and incapacitate the financial networks of terrorists.

On October 25, 2001, the Bush administration announced that it established a 100-person inter-agency team, headed by the U.S. Customs Service, that would conduct undercover surveillance operations of terrorist funding sources, including: counterfeit credit cards, corrupt financial institutions, fraud operations, illicit charities, and phony import-export companies.

International cooperation in the fight against terrorists' financial operations was witnessed on October 6, 2001, when the finance ministers of the Group of Seven (G-7) nations pledged to establish functional financial investigative units (FIUs). The FIUs will respond to information-sharing requests by individual governments while facilitating information sharing among the nations.

Multinational collaboration was witnessed later that month when representatives from 29 nations (including the United States), comprising the Financial Action Task Force (FATF), adopted 8 special recommendations to prevent future terrorist financing in their jurisdictions. Some of the proposed changes included: requiring nations to crack down on alternative remittance systems such as hawala, strengthening customer identification measures for wire transfers, and ensuring that charities are not misused to finance terrorism. The FATF also adopted an action plan to call for compliance for the recommendations by June 2002.

Further action on attacking terrorist funding was taken on November 7, 2001, when President Bush ordered the blocking of assets of 62 individuals and organizations connected to two investment and money-transferring networks—Al Barakaat and Al Taqwa—used by terrorists. According to President Bush, the activities of Al Barakaat and Al Taqwa include: raising, investing, and distributing funds for al-Qaida; offering terrorist supporters with Internet service and secure communications; and arranging for the shipment of armaments.

Al Barakaat, established in 1989 by Shaykh Ahme Nur Jimale, operates in 40 nations and provides telecommunications, wire transfer, Internet, and currency exchange services. The conglomerate transfers instructions, intelligence, and funding to terrorist cells worldwide.

Al Taqwa, controlled by a naturalized Italian citizen, Youssef Nada, is based in four countries: Bahamas, Italy, Liechtenstein, and Switzerland. Al Taqwa enables al-Qaida and other terrorist groups to invest funds and transfer cash among its members.

Securities and Exchange Commission

On October 18, 2001, the Securities and Exchange Commission (SEC) requested all securities-related entities (whether or not registered with the SEC) to cooperate voluntarily with law enforcement authorities in their ongoing investigations in the September 11 attacks. Since that date, brokers, dealers, investment advisers, investment companies, transfer agents, exchanges, and other self-regulatory organizations and industry groups have been asked to review their records and work with law enforcement officials to identify any transactions or relationships with certain individuals or entities that have been identified by the FBI and other law enforcement agencies. The SEC and law enforcement agencies undertook to forward a unified list of suspected individuals and entities, the Control List, to various financial institutions. These institutions will voluntarily be requested to check their records to determine if any of the individuals or entities on the Control List have or had any transactions or relationships with these institutions in the United States or overseas.

Following the September 11, 2001, attacks, the SEC investigated the dramatic rise in short-selling activity in 38 companies during the days preceding the terrorist incidents. Unusual trading and subsequent disproportionate drops in stock prices of airlines, insurers, securities firms, and other companies during the week before the incidents included: AMR Corp., UAL Corp., U.S. Airways, Chubb Corp., MetLife Inc., and Morgan Stanley. Some of the affected companies were major tenants at the World Trade Center or in sectors that would be directly harmed in case of such an attack. The U.S. Secret Service contacted bond traders regarding large purchases of 5-year Treasury notes before the attacks. Investigators are examining whether terrorists, or people affiliated with terrorist organizations, bought 5-year notes.

While the FBI, SEC, and other organizations are still investigating possible short-selling, the head of the FBI's financial crimes unit stated that as of October 3, 2001, "there are no flags or indicators" that terrorists undertook such securities transactions. Difficulties in following such transactions may stem from the lack of cooperation from some foreign governments as well as terrorists' use of front companies and shell accounts.

Capitol Security

In October 2001, U.S. congressional leaders, in concert with U.S. Capitol Police, discussed a $600 million security proposal for fortifying the U.S. Capitol and the establishment of a Visitors' Center. With regard to security matters, the plan identified the need to restrict public access, increase the number of police officers, and extend perimeters around the 276-acre Capitol area. The 19-building complex houses 20,000 employees and hosts 1.8 million visitors annually. Immediately after the World Trade Center and Pentagon attacks, additional security measures around the Capitol were implemented, including: the ban of commercial traffic within a 40-block area of Capitol Hill, use of concrete barriers, and erection of protective fences as strategic locations.

Miscellaneous U.S. Government Activities

Various U.S. governmental departments are involved in investigative, diplomatic, and other roles arising in relation to the September 11, 2001, terrorist attacks and their aftermath. Also, many nations are contributing various resources, particularly intelligence, in support of U.S. anti-terrorism military efforts. A number of examples of such activities (some alluded to earlier) are set out below:

Department of the Treasury/Bureau of Alcohol, Tobacco and Firearms

- Adopted a Terrorist Financing Executive Order

- Froze approximately 30 al-Qaida accounts in the United States and almost 20 al-Qaida accounts overseas

- Put 27 names of individuals and organizations on the Terrorist Financing List

- Reviewed additional persons and entities for possible inclusion on the Terrorist Financing List

- Froze over $26 million in Taliban and al-Qaida assets (by the United States) and over $17 milion linked to terrorists (by other nations)

- Bank accounts connected to terrorist groups frozen by 105 countries

- Commenced investigation of 9,500 construction, mining, and other companies nationwide licensed to use explosives

- Announced the establishment of 2 multi-agency task forces to pursue financial networks of terrorists

Department of Defense

- Approximately 29,000 military personnel, 349 military aircraft, 1 Amphibious Ready Group, and 2 Carrier Battle Groups are currently deployed in theaters.

- Approximately 30,000 members of the Reserve have been called to active duty, and several thousand National Guard personnel are operating under state authority.

Department of Justice/Federal Bureau of Investigation/U.S. Customs Service

- Analyzed 241 serious/credible threats.

- Conducted over 600 interviews.

- Conducted 383 searches.

- Issued 4,407 subpoenas.

- Arrested/detained 1,047 persons, charging 182 with immigration violations.

- Approximately 30-plus countries offered support in criminal investigations.

- The FBI has more than 4,000 agents and 3,000 support staff working on the September 11, 2001, investigation.

- The U.S. Customs Service has more than 1,000 agents and intelligence analysts tracking leads and suspects. The U.S. Customs Service also has placed America's 301 ports of entry on high alert, assigned additional inspectors to our borders, and added barricades and surveillance cameras at selected border crossings.

Intelligence

- Over 100 countries have offered increased intelligence support.

- Over 250 arrests in at least 40 countries have been made of those individuals who are suspected members of the al-Qaida organization.

- Intensified counter-terrorist operations are underway with over 200 intelligence and security services worldwide.

U.S. Postal Service

- In late October 2001, President Bush pledged to spend $175 million for gloves and masks for use by U.S. Postal Service workers as a defense against exposure to anthrax and other pathogens.

VII Assistance to State Governments

Due to shortfalls in state taxes resulting from negative financial implications of the September 11, 2001, terrorist attacks, state governors have sought some types of financial and other assistance from the federal government. More specifically, the National Governors Association (NGA) requested the Bush administration and Congress to include emergency assistance for states in the upcoming stimulus package. For instance, the governors endeavored to ease eligibility rules for disaster-related unemployment insurance, rescind scheduled cuts in reemployment aid to displaced workers, and create sliding-scale subsidies for health insurance premiums for individuals who lost coverage when laid off. Also, the governors sought relief from some federal regulations and called for the suspension of state matching requirements on major federal highways.

Michigan Governor John Engler (Republican), the chairman of the NGA, noted that due to the September 11, 2001, terrorist incidents, many states have witnessed a double-digit decline in state revenues compared with the figure from the preceding year. Because of this decline, some states need to modify budget plans to deal with the serious decline in tax receipts. The State of Washington estimated losses totaling $1 billion. Florida predicted a downfall during 2001-2002 at about $3 billion. Other states projecting budgetary short-falls, due in part to smaller state taxes collected from businesses and tourists, include: Arizona, $1.6 billion; Connecticut, $302 million; Tennessee, $300 million; Nebraska, $220 million; Alabama, $168 million; and Iowa, $158 million.

In November 2001, the Employment Policy Foundation announced that according to Labor Department figures, 23 states barely have enough funds to cover 1 year of unemployment benefits. The foundation projected that should unemployment increase by 2%, 35 states' unemployment would require an injection of $20 billion in federal funds to stay afloat, including: $3 billion in New York, $2.3 billion in Texas, and $2 billion in Illinois.

Analogously, in late October 2001, the U.S. Conference of Mayors predicted that additional security measures instituted by municipalities in the wake of the World Trade Center and Pentagon incidents and the anthrax attacks may cost cities $1.5 billion in 2002. A November 2001 National League of Cities study found that the economic ramifications of the September 11 attacks—declining employment and tourism—would result in a 4% decrease in municipal revenues, amounting to $11.4 billion.

New York Governor George Pataki (Republican) requested $54 billion from the federal government for various measures, including:

- $20 billion for economic recovery and revitalization

- $19 billion for rebuilding and redevelopment efforts, including: $10.6 billion for the World Trade Center and hotel replacement; about $4 billion for transportation infrastructure, revenue loss, and operating costs; about $3 billion for Port Authority costs; and $1 billion for private-building cleaning, removal, and remediation

- $15 billion basic rescue and response, including: $5 billion for emergency construction costs and $3 billion in New York State requests for federal aid

- Creation of a federal World Trade Center recovery zone

In early November 2001, the Bush administration announced an assistance plan of $2.8 billion for New York to rebuild lower Manhattan and aid in job creation that includes: $2 billion for authorization of tax-free bonds to replace damaged buildings; $700 million in direct grants to assist businesses harmed by the attacks; and measures to modify federal welfare rules that would result in New York State saving $110 million.

VIII Foreign Aid and International Cooperation

Foreign Aid

The impact of the September 11, 2001, terrorist attacks led to an increase of another U.S. government expenditure: foreign aid. The Bush administration has rescheduled Pakistan's $379 million bilateral debt in recognition of its efforts in the military campaign against Usama bin Laden and the Taliban. Also, the Government of Pakistan requested that the United States reduce its tariffs on imports of Pakistani textiles.

On October 4, 2001, President Bush announced that the United States would contribute an additional $320 million in humanitarian assistance to the Afghan people. Prior to September 11, 2001, $174 million in humanitarian aid was allocated to the Afghan people. During the initial days of the U.S.

military operation in Afghanistan, U.S. troops successfully dropped over 275,000 meal rations for the Afghan people. This humanitarian operation was partially undermined by the Taliban regime that promised to poison the rations. Also, the meal rations have color packaging that is similar to U.S. cluster bombs, although this complexity was resolved with different packaging for the food. By November 20, 2001, the United States had also sent to Afghanistan basic medical supplies for 10,000 people for a period of several months.

In October 2001, President Bush established America's Fund for Afghan Children (Children's Fund) by which he asked American children to help Afghan children by individually contributing $1 (cash, check, or money order). President Bush noted that half of Afghan children suffer chronic malnutrition and 1 in 3 Afghan children is an orphan. Due to this request, schools, communities, and youth organizations organized money for the cause. As of November 1, 2001, the Children's Fund gathered more than $1 million.

In November 2001, the U.S. government was assessing whether to provide economic, security, and humanitarian aid to Uzbekistan, where about 1,000 U.S. forces are based. During the visit of Philippine President Gloria Macapagal Arroyo to the United States in November 2001, President Bush pledged $92.3 million in military aid to her country for use against insurgents and terrorist groups there. With support of the United States, the International Monetary Fund agreed to lend Turkey $10 billion. The approval was viewed by some as quid pro quo for Turkey's support for the U.S. war on terrorism.

In the coming months, it is expected that some countries that are assisting the United States—either openly or secretly—in the war against terrorism will seek various forms of economic, military, intelligence, and other aid to "compensate" them for their efforts. The costs of such rewards in terms of financial and other resources will likely place an additional drain on U.S. resources as well as possibly further entangle the United States with some fleeting and impermanent allies. Nevertheless, such deals might be necessary in order to continue the war on terrorism.

On November 17, 2001, First Lady Laura Bush delivered the Presidential Radio Address admonishing the Taliban's terrible treatment of children and women and underscoring U.S. resolve against such barbarity. Mrs. Bush remarked that the role of the United States was critical: "Fighting brutality against women and children is not the expression of a specific culture; it is the acceptance of our common humanity—a commitment shared by people of good will on every continent."

International Cooperation

At the Asia-Pacific Economic Cooperation Forum (APEC) Summit in Shanghai, China, in October, 2001, APEC leaders issued a statement on counter-terrorism in which they strongly condemned the September 11, 2001, attacks. Also, the APEC leaders pledged to improve counter-terrorism cooperation through:

- Appropriate financial measures to prevent the flow of funds to terrorists, including accelerating work on combating financial crimes through the APEC Finance Ministers' Working Group on Fighting Financial Crime and increasing involvement in related international standard-setting regimes.

- Adherence by all economies to relevant international requirements for the security of air and maritime transportation. Leaders call on transport ministers to actively take part in the discussions on enhancing airport, aircraft, and port security, achieve effective outcomes as early as possible, and assure full implementation and cooperation in this regard.

- Strengthening of energy security in the region through the mechanism of the APEC Energy Security Initiative, which examines measures to respond to temporary supply disruptions and long-term challenges facing the region's energy supply.

- Strengthening of APEC activities in the area of critical sector protection, including telecommunications, transportation, health, and energy.

- Enhancement of customs communications networks and expeditious development of a global integrated electronic customs network, which would allow customs authorities to better enforce laws while minimizing the impact on the flow of trade.

- Cooperation to develop electronic movement records systems that will enhance border security while ensuring that movement of legitimate travelers is not disrupted.

- Strengthening capacity building and economic and technical cooperation to enable member economies to put into place and enforce effective counter-terrorism measures.

- Cooperation to limit the economic fallout from the attacks and move to restore economic confidence in the region through policies and measures to increase economic growth as well as ensure stable environment for trade, investment, travel, and tourism.

Also, the Department of State was able to obtain various levels of international cooperation, including:

- Russia offered to share information and the use of its airspace for humanitarian flights.

- China offered to share information.

- India offered to share information and pledged support of U.S. actions.

- Japan offered diplomatic and military (logistical) support and assistance to Pakistan.

- Australia offered combat military forces and invoked Article IV of the ANZUS Treaty (the Pacific Security Agreement between Australia, New Zealand, and the United States), declaring the attack of September 11, 2001, as an attack on Australia.

- South Korea offered military, medical, and air and naval logistics support.

- United Arab Emirates and Saudi Arabia broke diplomatic relations with the Taliban.

- Pakistan agreed to cooperate fully with the request for assistance and support.

- The United States secured overflight and landing rights for 27 countries.

- The United States obtained 46 multilateral declarations of support.

- Nineteen nations of the North Atlantic Treaty Organization (NATO) invoked Article V of the NATO Treaty declaring an attack on one as an attack on all.

- The UN Security Council unanimously enacted a binding resolution requiring all member states to pursue terrorists and those who support them, including states providing financial support systems to the terrorists.

- The UN Security Council passed a resolution requiring all nations to deny safe haven to terrorists.

Conclusion

From time immemorial, terrorism, one of the most common expressions of man's inhumanity to man, takes on the form of random and systematic intimidation, coercion, repression, or destruction of human lives and property. Used intentionally by individuals, groups, and state actors to create a climate of extreme fear in order to obtain avowed realistic or imaginary political, social, economic, and strategic goals, terrorism has been a strategy utilized by both the strong and the weak in the struggle for power within and among nations.

The tyranny and fear instituted and the terror employed during the French Revolution have been duplicated often in modern times. The last century, particularly in the post-World War I period, will be recorded in history as unique in terms of extraordinary psychological terror and physical violence employed by state and sub-state actors, domestically and internationally. Epitomizing the state of anarchy of contemporary life and increasingly becoming a universal nightmare, terrorist operations have recently included suicide terrorists driving trucks packed with explosives targeted at civilian and military facilities worldwide.

As we entered the twenty-first century, the use of terrorism remains intact. Indeed, the appalling catastrophe of September 11, 2001, regarded as the most devastating terrorist attack in modern history, elevated Sun Tzu's "war in the shadows" to an unprecedented level. More specifically, the hijacking of four airliners by al-Qaida operatives on that infamous day was not a conventional attack. During this attack, the suicide pilots employed "airplane missile" weapons, causing significant human, economic, and political costs.

The dire consequences of the September 11 trauma were particularly felt by families, workers, businesses, and the economy, and by governmental, and non-governmental institutions. Thousands of innocent victims were killed or injured in the terrorist attacks. Several others have died following the distribution of anthrax-laced letters during autumn 2001. In light of these tragedies, the nation came to grips with the possible dangers of living in the post-September 11 era: potentially being victimized not only by catastrophic conventional acts of terrorism but also by unconventional ones such as biological, chemical, nuclear, and cyber attacks.

U.S. labor was also critically affected. Previously, safety issues at the workplace were often limited to those in high-risk jobs, such as police officers. Now, U.S. workers are beginning to come to terms with the possibility that a calculated terrorist attack could be initiated against them while at their office or traveling on business, as on an airplane.

Due to such anticipated risks, workers will seek greater protections while at work, such as requests for employers to provide better physical security at offices—metal detectors, security guards, and controlled access. Labor will be more cognizant of potential threats while traveling on mass transit systems, airplanes, roads, and bridges.

Given the presence of military reserves and the National Guard within employee ranks, the partial mobilization of armed forces, for service at home and abroad, likewise exemplified the impact of the September 11 attacks.

With reference to the consequences of the attacks on the U.S. economy—which was already in a non-technical recession at the time of the September 11, 2001, incidents—ample evidence exists that they were severe, at least in the short term. For example, the negative effects included: substantial declines in stock markets and the capitalization of companies in selected sectors (e.g., airlines and insurance); economic growth declined, unemployment rose, while consumer spending and confidence dropped; commodity prices, such as oil and gold, spiked prior to dipping; and reduced interest rates were spurred through active intervention by the Federal Reserve Board.

The Washington, D.C., area and Manhattan were particularly hard hit economically, as witnessed especially in the tourism, hospitality, financial, and real estate sectors. Throughout the United States, the September 11 attacks played havoc on segments of the economy, such as the tourism, hospitality, insurance, and airlines.

The impact of the incidents on the world economy was likewise negative. The harmful consequences were notably evident in Japan and Europe, which were already experiencing recessions before the terrorist events occurred. The neighbors of the United States—Mexico and Canada—likewise suffered during the economic downturn that followed the attacks, especially in the tourism, hospitality, and airline sectors.

Corporate America suffered severe initial damage to particular businesses, such as airlines, tourism, hospitality, and insurance. Other sectors that witnessed some slump—in certain regions—were real estate, energy, technology, media and entertainment, and private and public mail carrier firms. Additional industries—transportation, retail, financial services, automotive, health services, pharmaceuticals, and biotechnology—were impacted by the terrorist incidents in varying degrees.

Other noteworthy consequences of the September 11 incidents included: transactions were cancelled or delayed; companies experienced some difficulties with sourcing, inventory levels, and logistics; the role and costs of terrorism risk and the means to reduce such threats (e.g., data storage and recovery services) received greater attention by companies; augmented importance was placed on corporate security; and increased interaction by business with governmental authorities occurred.

At the same time, the September 11 attacks enabled companies, already poised to counter multiple terrorist threats, to better showcase their capabilities. Numerous goods and services that will be critical in the war on terrorism, both at home and abroad, include: defense; security equipment, technology, and services; diverse technology products and services; pharmaceuticals, biotechnology, and forensics; germ detection and remediation; transportation; and "survivalist" and miscellaneous merchandise.

Governmental responses to the September 11 incidents were manifold and extensive. Emergency funding of $20 billion was approved within days of the attacks. Legislation aimed at aiding specific sectors, such as airlines, was passed. Laws geared towards improving security in the transportation industry were implemented. Also, many steps were taken by President George W. Bush and his administration—new rules, mandates, and policies. These nascent measures primarily sought to: investigate and enforce potential terrorists, tighten access to U.S. borders, and fight the sources and mechanics of terrorist funding.

The extensive role of the Federal Bureau of Investigation and other law enforcement agencies in the investigation of the attacks warrants commendations. The designation and sanctions against individuals, organizations, and groups believed to be terrorists (or aiding terrorists) also helped in the war on terrorism.

Governmental steps towards improving capabilities and responsiveness of the U.S. health system in the face of biological terrorist threats were adopted. For example, the Department of Health and Human Services contracted to acquire additional antibiotics and vaccines believed to be effective against such pathogens as anthrax and smallpox. The government also undertook steps to ease some burdens for terrorist victims and their families.

The military has served important functions both at home and abroad. Domestically, National Guard troops were called upon to assist in airport security as well as to relieve over-staffed U.S. Capitol Police. Overseas, the military's role in Afghanistan, in association with coalition members and Northern Alliance efforts, resulted in the stunning defeat of the Taliban in most of the country and a weakening of al-Qaida's base in Afghanistan. U.S. intelligence services, including the Central Intelligence Agency, are believed to have played an important role in military operations. The United States has also conducted other anti-terrorism efforts in various countries that have not been disclosed in full for tactical and operational reasons.

The generosity demonstrated by the American public, industry, employers, unions, and organizations following the September 11 events has been very impressive. Various charitable funds were established in fall 2001 to aid the victims and their families. By mid-October 2001, charities raised $1.4 billion for the survivors and their families; by mid-November 2001, the Red Cross had raised slightly over $560 million.

Also, people volunteered in rescue, search, and recovery stages of the attacks. Individuals supplied free goods and services to police, firefighters, and rescue personnel.

While the foregoing governmental and non-governmental responses have been commendable, the war against terrorism is not over. It is premature to forecast whether the United States would follow its military action in Afghanistan with incursions into Sudan, Somalia, Yemen, Iraq, Iran, or other state sponsors of terrorism. Yet, one can presume that whatever happens next, the U.S. economy, companies, and workers will be affected in similar respects to the ramifications resulting from U.S. activities in Afghanistan.

Additionally, should another devastating terrorist attack along the magnitude of September 11 occur in the United States, it is probable that some of the same negative consequences witnessed in the wake of those attacks will revisit America with some disparate manifestations. Potential near-term threats may involve attacks by al-Qaida operatives at: the Winter 2002 Olympics in Salt Lake City, Utah; the Super Bowl in New Orleans, Louisiana, in February 2002; or American business targets in the United States and overseas.

In the long term, by the year 2025, it is anticipated that terrorism directed against America and the civilized world will continue and even escalate to higher levels of threats. A warning for such eventuality was issued by the United States Commission on National Security/21st Century. In a report released on March 15, 2001, the commission asserted, "Global trends in scientific, technological, economic, socio-political and military-security domains . . . will produce fundamental qualitative changes in the U.S. national security environment." Furthermore, the report concludes, "The United States will become increasingly vulnerable to hostile attack on the American homeland, and U.S. military superiority will not entirely protect us."

Indeed, there are both generic and specific factors that will affect the nature and intensity of future terrorist challenges. Generic components that will contribute to terrorism include: ethnic, racial, religious, and tribal intolerance and violence; escalation of propaganda and psychological warfare; extreme nationalism; regional conflicts that defy easy solutions; intensification of criminal activities such as narco-trafficking; population explosion, migration expansion, and unemployment; widening economic gap between industrialized and developing countries; environmental challenges; arms developments and proliferation of conventional and unconventional weapons; and increased growth of global mobility and sophisticated communication systems.

Specific factors and conditions that will encourage terrorism in the future include: the absence of a universal definition of terrorism; disagreement as to the root causes of terrorism; religionization of politics; exploitation of the media; double standard of morality; loss of resolve by governments to take effective action against terrorism; weak punishment of terrorists; violation of international law by, and promotion of, terrorism by some nations; complexity of modern societies; and high cost of security in democracies.

In light of these contributing variables to the further expansion of terrorist threats presently and in the future, the vulnerability of the U.S. business community is of particular concern. As the world's largest economy, the leading military power, and a major democracy, the United States, and U.S. businesses worldwide, have been prime targets of international terrorism for many years. The levels and types of victimization involving the facilities, personnel, and operations of U.S. corporations suggest that the direct, indirect, and intangible costs of terrorism have a negative impact on the worldwide economy.

Although American businesspeople are increasingly sensing the changing environment of risks, they are still uncertain about how to assess and respond to terrorism. The inexorable advancement of technology is adding to the concerns of business. New technologies present business with heightened risks of vulnerability and lethality as a result of greater availability of modern weaponry and communications devices at the disposal of terrorists.

Despite improvements by the United States in the wake of September 11, government authorities cannot offer any guarantee of protection against terrorists' threats and attacks in their conventional and unconventional forms. It is increasingly important that the business community understand the expected dangers. Therefore, companies should better prepare themselves to counter terrorist threats. How to reduce this vulnerability is a major problem that will require improving security systems of U.S. corporations domestically and internationally.

Even with the end of the Cold War, the evolving era of the New World Order, and the current military successes against the Taliban in Afghanistan and al-Qaida's network, terrorism remains as threatening as ever. Undoubtedly, conflicts emerging from ideological, religious, and national animosities will continue to make this challenge a global problem well into the twenty-first century. The vulnerability of modern society and its economic infrastructure, coupled with the opportunities for the utilization of sophisticated high-leverage conventional and unconventional weaponry, require nation-states both unilaterally and in concert, to develop credible responses and capabilities to minimize future threats.

Ensuring the safety and interests of its citizens at home and abroad will continue to be every government's paramount responsibility in the future. Understanding the methods of operation employed by terrorists, identifying the threats and specific targets, both present and future, and becoming fully aware of the damage and consequences which may result from acts of terror will assist the government, with the help of the business community, in responding effectively to the specter of terrorism nationally and globally.

Since terrorism, both on the conventional and the unconventional levels, projects a clear and present danger to the very survival of civilization itself, it would behoove us to recall the profound remarks offered by Sir Winston Churchill to the House of Commons on May 13, 1940: "Victory at all costs, victory in spite of all terror, victory however long and hard the road may be; for without victory there is no survival."

Bibliography

Chapter I – Terrorism and Business: Historical and Contemporary Perspectives

1. Tunde Adeniran and Yonah Alexander. Eds. *International Violence*. (New York: Praeger, 1983).
2. Dean C. Alexander. "Maritime Terrorism and Legal Responses." *Den. J. Int'l L. & Pol.*, Vol. 19, No. 3, 1991, 529-567.
3. Yonah Alexander. "A New Response to Terror." *M.E. Ins.*, Vol. 16, No. 2, April-May 2001, pp. 27-29, 77.
4. _____. "Chechnya's Suicide Bombings: The Worst is Yet to Come." *Central Asia-Caucasus Analyst*, July 19, 2000.
5. _____, Ed. *International Terrorism: National, Regional, and Global Perspectives*. (New York: Praeger Publishers, 1976).
6. _____, Ed. *International Terrorism: Political and Legal Documents*. (Dordrecht: Martinus Nijhoff, 1992).
7. _____, Ed. *Middle East Terrorism: Current Threats and Future Prospects*. (New York: G.K. Hall, 1994).
8. _____. *Middle East Terrorism: Selected Group Profiles*. (Washington, D.C.: JINSA, 1994).
9. _____. "Missing Mideast Peace Partner." *Wash. Times*, Aug. 8, 2000.
10. _____. "Peace and Religion Symbiosis." *Jer. Post*, Sept. 3, 2000.
11. _____. *Political Communication and Persuasion: An International Journal*, Vols. 1-8, (New York: Taylor & Francis), 1980-1991.
12. _____. *Terrorism: An Annotated Bibliography, 1970-1989*. (Ann Arbor, Michigan: UMI), 1986-1991.
13. _____. *Terrorism: An International Journal*, Vols. 1-14, (New York: Taylor & Francis), 1977-1991.
14. _____. *Terrorism: An International Resource File, 1970-1979 Index*. (Ann Arbor, Michigan: UMI, 1990).
15. _____. Ed. *Terrorism: An International Resource File, 1990 Index*. (Ann Arbor, Michigan: UMI, 1991).
16. _____. Ed., *TerrorismCentral.com*, 2001.

17. _____. "Terrorism in the Twenty-First Century: Threats and Responses." *DePaul Bus. L.J.*, Vol. 12, No. 1, 2000, pp. 59-96.

18. _____. Ed. *The 1986 Annual on Terrorism.* (Dordrecht, The Netherlands: Martinus Nijhoff, 1987).

19. _____. *The Role of Communication in the Middle East Conflict: Ideological and Religious Aspects.* (New York, Praeger Publishers, 1973).

20. Yonah Alexander and Edgar H. Brenner, Eds. *Legal Aspects of Terrorism in the United States.* 4 Vols. (Dobbs Ferry, New York: Oceana Publications, 2000).

21. _____. *Terrorism and the Law.* (Ardsley, New York: Transnational Publishers, 2001).

22. Yonah Alexander, Marjorie A. Browne, and Allan S. Nanes, Eds. *Control of Terrorism: International Documents.* (New York: Crane, Russak, 1979).

23. Yonah Alexander, David Carlton, and Paul Wilkinson, Eds. *Terrorism: Theory and Practice.* (Boulder, Colorado: Westview Press, 1979).

24. Yonah Alexander and James Denton, Eds. *Governmental Responses to Terrorism.* (Fairfax, Virginia: Hero Books, 1987).

25. Yonah Alexander and Charles K. Ebinger, Eds. *Political Terrorism and Energy: The Threat and Response.* (New York: Praeger Publishers, 1982).

26. Yonah Alexander and Seymour M. Finger, Eds. *Terrorism: Interdisciplinary Perspectives.* (New York: John Jay Press, 1977).

27. Yonah Alexander and Abraham Foxman, Eds. *The 1987 Annual on Terrorism.* (Dordrecht, The Netherlands: Martinus Nijhoff, 1989).

28. _____. *The 1988-1989 Annual on Terrorism.* (Dordrecht, The Netherlands: Martinus Nijhoff, 1990).

29. Yonah Alexander and Robert Friedlander, Eds. *Self-Determination: National, Regional, and Global Dimensions.* (Boulder, Colorado: Westview Press, 1980).

30. Yonah Alexander and John M. Gleason, Eds. *Behavioral and Quantitative Perspectives on Terrorism.* (New York: Pergamon Press, 1981).

31. Yonah Alexander and Milton Hoenig. "Nuclear Terrorism Moves Closer to Home." *LA Times*, July 10, 2000.

32. _____. *Super Terrorism: Biological, Chemical, Nuclear.* (Ardsley, New York: Transnational Publishers, 2001).

33. Yonah Alexander and Robert A. Kilmarx, Eds. *Business and the Middle East: Threats and Prospects.* (New York: Pergamon Press, 1982).

34. _____. *Political Terrorism and Business: The Threat and Response.* (New York: Praeger, 1979).

35. Yonah Alexander and Nicholas N. Kittrie, Eds. *Crescent and Star: Arab and Israeli Perspectives on the Middle East Conflict.* (New York: AMS Press, 1973).

36. Yonah Alexander and Richard Latter, Eds. *Terrorism and the Media: Dilemmas for Government, Journalists and the Public*. (Washington: Brassey's (U.S.), 1990).

37. Yonah Alexander and Donald Musch, Eds. *Terrorism: Documents of Local and International Control - U.S Perspectives*, Vols. 15-29. (Dobbs Ferry, New York: Oceana Publications, 1999-2001).

38. Yonah Alexander and Kenneth A. Myers, Eds. *Terrorism in Europe*. (New York: St. Martin's Press, 1982).

39. Yonah Alexander and Allan S. Nanes, Eds. *Legislative Responses to Terrorism*. (Dordrecht, The Netherlands: Martinus Nijhoff, 1986).

40. _____, *The United States and Iran: A Documentary History*. (Frederick, Maryland: University Publications of America, 1980).

41. Yonah Alexander and Alan O'Day, Eds. *Ireland's Terrorist Dilemma*. (Dordrecht, The Netherlands: Martinus Nijhoff, 1986).

42. _____, *Ireland's Terrorist Trauma: Interdisciplinary Perspectives*. (United Kingdom: Harvester Wheatsheaf/United States: Simon and Schuster and St. Martin's Press, 1989).

43. Yonah Alexander and Robert G. Picard, Eds. *In the Camera's Eye: New Coverage of Terrorist Events*. (Washington, D.C.: Brassey's (U.S.), 1991).

44. Yonah Alexander and Dennis A. Pluchinsky, Eds. *European Terrorism: Today and Tomorrow*. (Washington: Brassey's (U.S.), 1992).

45. _____. *Europe's Red Terrorists: The Fighting Communist Organizations*. (London, Frank Cass, 1992).

46. Yonah Alexander and Stephen Prior, Eds. *Terrorism and Medical Responses: U.S. Lessons and Policy Implications*. (Ardsley, New York: Transnational Publishers, 2001).

47. Yonah Alexander and David C. Rapoport, Eds. *The Morality of Terrorism: Religious and Secular Justifications*. (New York: Pergamon Press, 1982).

48. Yonah Alexander and Joshua Sinai, *Terrorism: The PLO Connection*. (New York: Crane Russak, 1989).

49. Yonah Alexander and Eugene Sochor, Eds. *Aerial Piracy and Aviation Security*. (Dordrecht, The Netherlands: Martinus Nijhoff, 1990).

50. Yonah Alexander and Michael S. Swetnam, Eds. *Cyber Terrorism and Information Warfare: Threats and Responses*. (Ardsley, New York: Transnational Publishers, 2001).

51. _____, "Freedom Fighters or Terrorist?" *Wash. Times*, June 9, 1999.

52. _____. *Information Warfare and Cyber Terrorism: Threats and Responses*, 4 Vols. (Dobbs Ferry, New York: Oceana Publications, 1999).

53. _____. *Usama bin Laden's al-Qaida: Profile of a Terrorist Network*. (Ardsley, New York: Transnational Publishers, 2001).

54. Yonah Alexander, Michael S. Swetnam, and Herbert M. Levine. *ETA: Profile of a Terrorist Group*. (Ardsley, New York: Transnational Publishers, 2001).

55. Yonah Alexander and Eli Tavin, Eds. *Terrorists or Freedom Fighters?* (Fairfax, Virginia: HERO Books, 1986).

56. *America's National Interests*. Report of the Commission on America's National Interests, July 2000.

57. Simon Apiku. "Wanted: Terrorists Living Abroad." *M.E. Times*, Apr. 25, 1999.

58. Mohamad Bazzi. "Bin Laden May Be Ready to Turn Over Terrorist Network to Aide." *Houston Chron.*, Feb. 22, 2000.

59. Ray S. Cline and Yonah Alexander. *State-Sponsored Terrorism*. (U.S. Senate Report: Subcommittee on Security and Terrorism, 1985).

60. ____. *Terrorism as State-Sponsored Covert Warfare*. (Fairfax, Virginia: HERO Books, 1986).

61. ____. *Terrorism: The Soviet Connection*. (New York: Crane Russak, 1984).

62. "Combating Terrorism: A Matter of Leverage: A Panel Report on Terrorism." Proceedings Report, *Center for Strategic and International Studies*, June 1996.

63. "Countering the Challenging Threat of International Terrorism." *National Commission on Terrorism*, 2000.

64. "Counter Terrorism Strategies for the 21st Century: Asian and Pacific Basin Perspectives." Proceeding Report (PIPS 99-8), *Potomac Institute for Policy Studies*, Arlington, Virginia, Aug. 26, 1999.

65. "Counter Terrorism Strategies for the 21st Century: Cyber Challenges." Proceedings Report, (PIPS 00-4) *Potomac Institute for Policy Studies*, Arlington, Virginia, Apr. 2000.

66. "Counter Terrorism Strategies for the 21st Century: European, Latin American, and U.S. Perspectives." Proceedings Report, (PIPS 00-2) *Potomac Institute for Policy Studies*, Arlington, Virginia, Feb. 2000.

67. "Counter Terrorism Strategies for the 21st Century: Latin American Perspectives." Proceedings Report, *International Law Institute*, Washington, DC, Aug. 12, 1999.

68. "Counter Terrorism Strategies for the 21st Century: Middle Eastern and Asian Perspectives." Proceedings Report, (PIPS 00-3) *Potomac Institute for Policy Studies*, Arlington, Virginia, Mar. 2000.

69. "Counter Terrorism Strategies for the 21st Century: Millennial Challenges." Proceedings Report, (PIPS 00-1) *Potomac Institute for Policy Studies*, Arlington, Virginia, Feb. 2000.

70. "Counter Terrorism Strategies for the 21st Century: Recent Developments in South Asia." Proceedings Report, (PIPS 00-8) *Potomac Institute for Policy Studies*, Arlington, Virginia, Oct. 2000.

71. "Counter Terrorism Strategies for the 21ˢᵗ Century: Selected Perspectives." Proceedings Report, (PIPS 00-7) *Potomac Institute for Policy Studies*, Arlington, Virginia, Oct. 2000.

72. "Counter Terrorism Strategies for the 21ˢᵗ Century: Some Legal Perspectives." Proceedings Report, (PIPS 00-05), *Potomac Institute for Policy Studies*, Arlington, Virginia, July 2000.

73. "Counter Terrorism Strategies for the 21ˢᵗ Century: US Perspectives." Proceedings Report, (PIPS 99-6), *Potomac Institute for Policy Studies*, Arlington, Virginia, July 28, 1999.

74. "FBI Agents Ill-Equipped To Predict Terror Acts." *Wash. Post*, Sept. 24, 2001.

75. "FBI Questioned Flight School Two Weeks Before Attacks, Student Now in Custody." *AP*, Sept. 19, 2001.

76. Peter Finn, "German Officials Link Hijackers to Al Qaeda Group." *Wash. Post*, Sept. 27, 2001.

77. Lawrence Z. Freedman and Yonah Alexander, Eds. *Perspectives on Terrorism.* (Wilmington, Delaware: Scholarly Resources, 1983).

78. Walter Laqueur and Yonah Alexander, Eds. *The Terrorism Reader: A Historical Anthology.* Rev. Ed. (New York: New American Library Penguin, 1987).

79. Joe Lauria, "A Wide Plot to Kill Americans Alleged in Embassy Bomb Trial." *Boston Globe*, Feb. 6, 2001.

80. Paul Leventhal and Yonah Alexander, Eds. *Nuclear Terrorism: Defining the Threat.* (Washington: Pergamon-Brassey's, 1986).

81. _____ . *Preventing Nuclear Terrorism: The Report and Papers of the International Task Force on Prevention of Nuclear Terrorism.* (Lexington, Massachusetts: Lexington Books, 1987).

82. *New World Coming: American Security in the 21ˢᵗ Century*, United States Commission on National Security/21ˢᵗ Century, Sept. 15, 1999.

83. Michael F. Noone and Yonah Alexander, Eds. *Cases and Materials on Terrorism: Three Nations' Response.* (The Hague: Kluwer Law International, 1997).

84. "Number of Missing in N.Y. Down to 5,960." *Wash. Post*, Sept. 28, 2001.

85. David Ottaway and Dan Morgan, "Muslim Charities Under Scrutiny." *Wash. Post*, Sept. 29, 2001.

86. Walter Pincus, "Bin Laden Seeks Instability In Mideast, Ex-Agent Says." *Wash. Post*, Sept. 30, 2001.

87. David C. Rapoport and Yonah Alexander, Eds. *The Morality of Terrorism: Religious and Secular Justifications.* Rev. Ed. (New York: Columbia University Press, 1989).

88. _____. *The Rationalization of Terrorism.* (Frederick, Maryland: University Publications of America, 1982).

89. *Report of the Policy Study Group on Terrorism.* New York State, Division of Criminal Justice Services, Nov. 1985.

90. *Strategic Assessment 1998: Engaging Power for Peace.* (Washington, D.C.: National Defense University, 1998).

91. "The Age of Super and Cyber Terrorism: Selected Papers," *Potomac Institute for Policy Studies*, Arlington, Virginia (PIPS 99-5), Sum. 1999.

92. "The Plot: A Web of Connections." *Wash. Post*, Sept. 30, 2001.

93. T.R. Reid and Allan Lengel, "Scotland Yard Says Hijackers May Have Trained in Britain." *Wash. Post*, Sept. 27, 2001.

94. Benjamin Weiser, "Ex-Aide to Bin Laden Describes Terror Campaign Aimed at U.S." *NY Times*, Feb. 7, 2001.

Chapter 2 - The Economic Costs to the United States: An Overview

1. "A Maker of Air-Conditioners Says it Will Cut 1,000 Jobs." *NY Times*, Oct. 17, 2001.

2. "A Stumble, Then a Rally Amid Bad News." *NY Times*, Nov. 4, 2001.

3. "An Old Economy Crunch." *The Economist*, Oct. 26, 2001.

4. "A Rally Spurred by Technology Buying." *NY Times*, Oct. 7, 2001.

5. "A Terrible Excuse." *Forbes*, Oct. 15, 2001.

6. Timothy Aeppel, "Goodyear to Lay Off Up to 1,400 Workers At Five U.S. Plants." *Wall St. J.*, Oct. 11, 2001.

7. Daniel Akst, "It's Time for Terror-Proof Markets." *NY Times*, Oct. 7, 2001.

8. Edmund Andrews, "Europe Holds the Line on Rates." *NY Times*, Oct. 26, 2001.

9. Edmund Andrews, "European Central Bank Cuts Key Interest Rate 0.5%." *NY Times*, Nov. 9, 2001.

10. Edmund Andrews, "More Signs Of Downturn For Europe." *NY Times*, Nov. 15, 2001.

11. "Asian Pacific Countries Count Economic Costs." *Bus. Day*, Oct. 10, 2001.

12. "Attack on America." *Dallas Morning News*, Oct. 18, 2001.

13. "Attacks' Economic Effects Reverberate Through Area." *Dallas Morning News*, Sept. 23, 2001.

14. "Attacks on US Hurt Africa." *Bus. Day*, Oct. 10, 2001.

15. "August Layoffs Nearly Doubled." *Wash. Post*, Sept. 27, 2001.

16. David Barboza, "Investors Try To Adjust To A New Set of Realities." *NY Times*, Sept. 24, 2001.

17. Robert Barro, "Why the War Against Terror Will Boost the Economy." *Bus. Wk.*, Nov. 5, 2001.
18. "Battered But Unbroken." *Fortune*, Oct. 1, 2001.
19. Gary S. Becker & Kevin M. Murphy, "Prosperity Will Rise Out of the Ashes." *Wall St J.*, Oct. 29, 2001.
20. Peter Behr and Renaw Merle, "Building Washington, One War At A Time." *Wash. Post*, Oct. 1, 2001.
21. Ken Belson, "Heavier Economic Clouds Are Gathering Over Japan." *NY Times*, Oct. 16, 2001.
22. Ken Belson, "Japan's Revised Forecast Sees Deepest Slump in 2 Decades." *NY Times*, Nov. 10, 2001.
23. Ken Belson, "Sony Loss of $107 Million Adds to Gloom in Japan." *NY Times*, Oct. 26, 2001.
24. Ken Belson, "3 Asian Exporting Countries Show More Signs of Trouble." *NY Times*, Nov. 7, 2001.
25. Ken Belson, "Unemployment in Japan Hits Postwar High of 5.3%." *NY Times*, Oct. 31, 2001.
26. Alex Berenson, "Feeling Vulnerable At Heart of Wall St." *NY Times*, Oct. 12, 2001.
27. John Berry & Daniela Deane, "Consumer Sentiment Improves Slightly." *Wash. Post*, Oct. 27, 2001.
28. John Berry, "Economy Shrinks for First Time Since 1993." *Wash Post.*, Nov. 1, 2001.
29. John Berry, "Falling Gas Costs Lead Decline in Consumer Prices." *Wash Post.*, Nov. 7, 2001.
30. John Berry, "Fed Decided Against Reducing Rates Two Days After Attacks." *Wash. Post*, Oct. 5, 2001.
31. John Berry, "Fed Officials Hint at Further Rate Cuts." *Wash. Post*, Oct. 17, 2001.
32. John Berry, "Fed Perceived Recession on Oct. 2." *Wash. Post*, Nov. 9, 2001.
33. John Berry, "Global Slump Checks Inflation." *Wash. Post*, Nov. 10, 2001.
34. John Berry, "New Sign of a Sharp Downturn." *Wash. Post*, Nov. 2, 2001.
35. John Berry & Frank Swoboda, "7.1% Jump in Retail Sales Sets a Record." *Wash. Post*, Nov. 15, 2001.
36. John Berry & Steven Pearlstein, "Terror Feeds Recession Fear." *Wash. Post*, Sept. 12, 2001.
37. John Berry, "Survey Indicates Rising Confidence." *Wash. Post*, Oct. 13, 2001.
38. John Berry, "U.S. Productivity Rises 2.7%." *Wash. Post*, Nov. 8, 2001.
39. "Big Economies Near a Standstill, O.E.C.D. Says." *AP*, Nov. 21, 2001.

40. "Blue Chips Up, but Cut in Economic Forecast Limits Gains." *AP*, Nov. 15, 2001.

41. Paul Blustein & John Berry, "Investors Gird for Market Reopening." *Wash. Post*, Sept. 15, 2001.

42. David Bogoslaw, "Gold Falls Again-Short of Its Crisis Expectations." *Wall St. J.*, Oct. 23, 2001.

43. Jason Booth, "Terror Attacks to Harm Asian Economies." *Wall St. J.*, Oct. 16, 2001.

44. "Brazil: Growth Forecast Lowered." *NY Times*, Sept. 29, 2001.

45. Michael Brick, "Despite Dismal Economic News, Shares Post Solid Gains." *NY Times*, Oct. 26, 2001.

46. Michael Brick & Floyd Norris, "Stocks Surge; Most Indexes Have Recouped September Loss." *NY Times*, Oct. 12, 2001.

47. Michael Brick, "Stocks End The Week On An Uptick." *NY Times*, Sept. 29, 2001.

48. DeNeen Brown, "Fallout From Terrorist Attacks Punishes Canadian Companies." *Wash. Post*, Oct. 20, 2001.

49. Ken Brown, "At Fred Alger, Close Ties Lured Back Alumni." *Wall St. J.*, Nov. 15, 2001.

50. Ken Brown & Mitchell Pacelle, "Some Telecom Shares Soar, While Bonds Stay Discounted." *Wall St. J.*, Oct. 29, 2001.

51. E.S. Browning, "Blue Chips Decline as Investors React With Surprising Calm to U.S. Attacks." *Wall St. J.*, Oct. 9, 2001.

52. E.S. Browning, "Markets Soar to Highest Closes Since Attacks." *Wall St. J.*, Oct. 4, 2001.

53. E.S. Browning, "Stocks Fend Off Anthrax News With Slim Drop." *Wall St. J.*, Oct 24, 2001.

54. E.S. Browning, "Stocks Finish Mostly Lower for Second Straight Session." *Wall St. J.*, Oct. 19, 2001.

55. E.S. Browning, "Stock Investors Show a 'Comfort' Level." *Wall St. J.*, Oct. 3, 2001.

56. E.S. Browning, "Stocks Resume Rise, as Hopes For Turnaround Outweigh News." *Wall St. J.*, Oct. 17, 2001.

57. E.S. Browning, "U.S. Stocks Recover Their Post-attack Declines." *Wall St. J.*, Oct. 12, 2001.

58. E.S. Browning, "U.S. Stocks Sag on Latest Anthrax Worries." *Wall St. J.*, Oct. 18, 2001.

59. Nanette Byrnes, "Rebuilding the City Underground." *Bus. Wk.*, Oct. 22, 2001.

60. "Claims Filed By Jobless Remain Near 9-Year High." *Bloomberg News*, Oct. 18, 2001.

61. Liz Clarke, "Redskins' Home Opener a Bust." *Wash. Post*, Sept. 30, 2001.
62. Jonathan Clements, "Companies' Cash Piles May Not Help You." *Wall St. J.*, Oct. 30, 2001.
63. Mark Clifford, "Trapped In the Tornado." *Bus. Wk.*, Oct. 8, 2001.
64. "Fed Cuts Rates, Fearing Attacks' Economic Impact." *NY Times*, Oct. 5, 2001.
65. "Commerce One to Cut 1,300 Jobs and Spin Off Some Units." *NY Times*, Oct. 16, 2001.
66. "Confidence of Consumers Is Up a Bit, Survey Shows." *NY Times*, Oct. 27, 2001.
67. Michelle Conlin, "Where Layoffs Are A Last Resort." *Bus. Wk.*, Oct. 8, 2001.
68. "Corporate America Braces For The Shakeout." *Bus. Wk.*, Oct. 15, 2001.
69. Peter Coy, "The Center Must Hold." *Bus. Wk.*, Oct. 22, 2001.
70. Susanne Craig, "SEC Examines Trading in Firms Before Sept. 11." *Wall. St. J.*, Oct. 3, 2001.
71. Albert Crenshaw, "A Holiday Surprise for Retailers?." *Wash. Post*, Nov. 11, 2001.
72. Albert Crenshaw, "Flight From Stock Funds Continues." *Wash. Post*, Sept. 22, 2001.
73. Sherri Day, "Equities Withstand Some Shaky News on the Economy." *NY Times* , Nov. 3, 2001.
74. Sherri Day, "More Than Earnings on Traders' Minds." *NY Times*, Oct. 21, 2001.
75. Sherri Day, "Stocks Tumble, Spurred by Dive in Consumer Confidence." *NY Times*, Oct. 21, 2001.
76. Sherri Day, "Technology Shares Fall, With Nasdaq Losing 4.4%." *NY Times*, Oct. 18, 2001.
77. Sherri Day, "Technology Shares Rebound, With the Nasdaq Up 22.79." *Wall St. J.*, Nov. 1, 2001.
78. Daniela Deane, "Building Of Homes Slow Down." *Wash. Post*, Nov. 20, 2001.
79. "Discounters Give Lift to Retail Sales." *NY Times*, Nov. 9, 2001.
80. Robert Dodge, "Fed Chief: Economy is Continuing." *Dallas Morning News* , Oct. 21, 2001.
81. "Domestic Stocks." *Wall St. J.*, Nov. 8, 2001.
82. "Dow Breaks Through Pre-Attack Level." *NY Times*, Nov. 11, 2001.
83. "Dow Closes Higher, But Rally Is Stunted." *Wash. Post*, Nov. 9, 2001.
84. "Dow Falls; Nasdaq Ekes Out a Gain." *Wash. Post*, Oct. 19, 2001.
85. "Dow Regains Pre-Sept. 11 Level." *Wash. Post*, Nov. 10, 2001.
86. William Drozdiak, "Central Banks In Europe Trim Rates." *Wash. Post*, Nov. 9, 2001.

87. "Economic Data Point Down." *Wash. Post*, Oct. 26, 2001.
88. "Economic Impact of the September 11 World Trade Center Attack." *Fiscal Policy Institute*, Sept. 28, 2001.
89. "Economy Is Still Teetering Near Recession, Data Show." *NY Times*, Sept. 29, 2001.
90. Dina El Boghdady & Carol Vinzant, "Some Are Hit Hard; For Others, It's Time to Spend." *Wash. Post*, Oct. 28, 2001.
91. Dina El Boghdady, "MicroStrategy, Net2000 Slash Jobs." *Wash. Post*, Sept. 29, 2001.
92. Stuart Elliott, "Advertising." *NY Times*, Oct. 16, 2001.
93. Pete Engardio, "A New World." *Bus. Wk.*, Oct. 8, 2001.
94. Jack Ewing, "Why Germany's Economy is Stalling Out." *Bus. Wk.*, Nov. 19, 2001.
95. Anthony Faiola, "Argentine Economy Dives, Setting Off Investor Panic." *Wash. Post*, Oct. 6, 2001.
96. Anthony Faiola & Paul Blustein, "Argentine Rates Surge as Fears of Debt Default Grow." *Wash. Post*, Nov. 3, 2001.
97. "Fed Cuts Rates, Fearing Attacks' Economic Impact." *NY Times*, Oct. 5, 2001.
98. Manny Fernandez & Spencer S. Hsu, "Security Tightened For Tree Lighting." *Wash. Post*, Nov. 17, 2001.
99. Sandra Fleishman, "As Rate Slide continues, Mortgages Hit New Lows." *Wash. Post*, Nov. 9, 2001.
100. Sandra Fleishman, "When Refinancing, It's Hurry Up and Wait." *Wash. Post*, Nov. 10, 2001.
101. "Forget About A Turnaround Now." *Bus. Wk.*, Oct. 15, 2001.
102. "French Quarter Struggling To Braek An Uneasy Silence." *Dallas Morning News*, Sept. 23, 2001.
103. Jonathan Fuerbringer, "Stocks, Fall, Them Rise as Fears of Terrorism as Crash's Cause Abate." *NY Times*, Nov. 13, 2001.
104. Jonathan Fuerbringer, "U.S. Acts On Shortage Of Treasuries." *NY Times*, Sept. 24, 2001.
105. Stephen S. Fuller, "What Now? - Washington's Wartime Economy." *Wash. Bus. Forward*, Nov. 2001.
106. Chris Gaither, "Intel Meets Forecasts and Expects Slightly Better Earnings." *NY Times*, Oct. 17, 2001.
107. Charles Gasparino, "Bear Stearns Will Announce Big Staff Cuts." *Wall St. J.*, Oct. 18, 2001.
108. Charles Gasparino, "Goldman Sachs Sets Plan to Cut Up to 400 Jobs." *Wall St. J.*, Oct. 10, 2001.
109. Charles Gasparion, "Merrill Lynch Prepares for Retrenchment, May Cut Up to 10,000 Jobs World-Wide." *Wall St. J.*, Oct. 17, 2001.

110. Justin Gillis & Robert O'Harrow Jr., "A $90 Billion Hole in N.Y." *Wash. Post*, Oct. 13, 2001.

111. "Greenspan Rejects Idea of Inflation Targets." *Bloomberg*, Oct. 11, 2001.

112. "Greenspan Says Too Early to Assess Economic Effects of Terrorism." *AP*, Oct. 17, 2001.

113. Eric Gunn, "Laid Off And Joining A Crowd." *Wash. Post*, Oct. 18, 2001.

114. Kristin Downey Grimsley, "Unemployed Flock to National Airport." *Wash. Post*, Sept. 26, 2001.

115. Danny Hakim, "Booming Car Sales, but at a Price." *NY Times*, Oct 24, 2001.

116. Constance L. Hays, "Slow Lane to Kmart's Recovery." *NY Times*, Nov. 8, 2001.

117. Dana Hedgpeth & Neil Irwin, "Running on Empty." *Wash. Post*, Sept. 26, 2001.

118. Raymond Hennessey, "IPO Market, After Hiatus, Makes Speculative Return." *Wall St. J.*, Oct. 8, 2001.

119. Patrice Hill, "Feds Probe Reports of Profiting From Terrorism." *Wash. Times*, Sept. 19, 2001.

120. Jon E. Hilsenrath, "Consumer Confidence Edges Up; Other Indicators Spur Pessimism." *Wall St. J.*, Oct. 29, 2001.

121. Mara Der Hovanesian, "The Worst May Not Be Over." *Bus. Wk.*, Oct. 8, 2001.

122. "How Far Down?" *The Economist*, Oct. 26, 2001.

123. "Investors Seem to Ignore Discouraging News." *NY Times*, Oct. 28, 2001.

124. "Investors Without A Compass." *Bus. Wk.*, Oct. 8, 2001.

125. Greg Ip, "Home Sales Dropped 11.7% in September." *Wall St. J.*, Oct. 26, 2001.

126. Greg Ip, "Productivity Grew a Brisk 2.7% In Quarter as Output Declined." *Wall St. J.*, Nov. 8, 2001.

127. Neil Irwin & Carol Vinzant, "Stocks Return to Pre-Attack Level." *Wash. Post*, Oct. 12, 2001.

128. Neil Irwin, "Layoffs Were Rising Even Before Attack." *Wash. Post* , Nov 12, 2001.

129. Neil Irwin, "Longtime Analyst Is Bullish on D.C. Region." *Wash. Post*, Oct. 15, 2001.

130. Neil Irwin & Peter Behr, "Running for Cover." *Wash. Post*, Oct. 8, 2001.

131. "Jobless Claims Drop for Third Consecutive Week." *Bloomberg*, Nov. 15, 2001.

132. Sabrina Jones, "Maryland Economy Slips but Shows Signs of Strength." *Wash. Post*, Nov. 9, 2001.

133. Craig Karmin & Pamela Druckerman, "Fingers Crossed, Emerging-Market Investors Hope a Default by Argentina Won't Sting." *Wall St. J.*, Nov. 2, 2001.

134. Jonathan Karp, "Markets Reflect Brazil's Effort to Detach From Neighbor." *Wall St. J.*, Nov. 13, 2001.

135. Sara Kehaulani Goo, "County Feels Impact of Decline in Travel Industry." *Wash. Post*, Oct. 11, 2001.

136. Sara Kehaulani Goo, "National's Reopening Won't Stem All Losses." *Wash. Post*, Oct. 3, 2001.

137. Sara Kehaulani Goo, "Panel to Advise Duncan on Montgomery County Economy." *Wash. Post*, Oct. 12, 2001.

138. Elizabeth Kelleher, "Those Who Did, Shopped Discount." *NY Times*, Nov. 11, 2001.

139. Kate Kelly, "Intrepid Public Shows Appetite For Small IPOs." *Wall St. J.*, Nov. 16, 2001.

140. Kate Kelly, "IPO Business Picks Up in Postattack Rally." *Wall St. J.*, Nov. 12, 2001.

141. Kate Kelly, "Stocks Rally Amid Positive News on War." *Wall St. J.*, Nov. 15, 2001.

142. Kate Kelly, "Stocks Rally 196.58 Points On War News." *Wall St. J.*, Nov. 14, 2001.

143. Kate Kelly, "Stocks Tumble After Jet Crash, Then Recover Most of Losses." *Wall St. J.*, Nov. 13, 2001.

144. Alec Klein, "Seattle Forecast: Gloomy." *Wash. Post*, Oct. 10, 2001.

145. Jerry Knight & Carol Vinzant, "Dow Falls, Rallies To Close Off 144." *Wash. Post*, Oct. 20, 2001.

146. Jerry Knight & Carol Vinzant, "Stocks Slide As Wall St. Rethinks Prospects." *Wash. Post*, Oct. 30, 2001.

147. Jerry Knight & Krissah Williams, "Nasdaq Soars 6% On Cisco Comment." *Wash. Post*, Oct. 4, 2001.

148. Jerry Knight & Krissah Williams, "Stock Indexes Close In On Pre-Attack Levels." *Wash. Post*, Oct. 5, 2001.

149. Clifford Kraus, "Economic Pain Spreads From U.S. Across Latin America." *NY Times*, Oct. 14, 2001.

150. Paul Krugman, "Fear Itself." *NY Times*, Sept. 30, 2001.

151. Joanne Legomsky, "Forecasters Try To Assess The Terror Factor." *NY Times*, Sept. 30, 2001.

152. Robert Lenzer & Victoria Murphy, "The Big R." *Forbes*, Oct. 15, 2001.

153. David Leonhardt, "The Rust Belt With a Drawl." *NY Times*, Nov. 13, 2001.

154. Steve Lohr, "I.B.M. Seems Confident as It Reports Sound Profits." *NY Times*, Oct. 17, 2001.

155. Suzanne McGee & Susanne Craig, "Investors Turn Out for Principal Financial's IPO." *Wall St. J.*, Oct. 23, 2001.

156. Peter A. McKay, "Stocks Decline, Then Surge, Despite Data; Bonds Rise, Too." *Wall St. J.*, Oct. 26, 2001.

157. Peter A. McKay, "Stock Prices Take a Breather, As Bonds Rise." *Wall St. J.*, Nov. 8, 2001.

158. "Market Indicators." *NY Times*, Sept. 18, 2001.

159. "Market Indicators." *NY Times*, Sept. 22, 2001.

160. "Market Indicators." *NY Times*, Nov. 2, 2001.

161. "Market Indicators." *NY Times*, Nov. 6, 2001.

162. "Market Indicators." *NY Times*, Nov. 9, 2001.

163. "Market Indicators." *NY Times*, Nov. 13, 2001.

164. "Market Indicators." *NY Times*, Nov. 14, 2001.

165. "Market Indicators." *NY Times*, Nov. 16, 2001.

166. "Market Indicators." *NY Times*, Nov. 17, 2001.

167. "Market Reactions." *NY Times*, Sept. 18, 2001.

168. "Market Watch." *Wash. Post*, Sept. 20, 2001.

169. "Market Watch." *Wash. Post*, Oct. 26, 2001.

170. "Market Watch." *Wash. Post*, Oct. 29, 2001.

171. "Market Watch." *Wash. Post*, Nov. 6, 2001.

172. "Market Watch." *Wash. Post*, Nov. 7, 2001.

173. "Market Watch." *Wash. Post*, Nov. 10, 2001.

174. "Market Watch." *Wash. Post* , Nov. 13, 2001.

175. "Market Watch." *Wash. Post*, Nov. 16, 2001.

176. Micheline Maynard, "Some Rental Car Companies Lobby for U.S. to Back Loans." *NY Times*, Oct. 5, 2001.

177. Renae Merle, "Jack London's Calling." *Wash. Post*, Nov. 12, 2001.

178. Dana Milbank & Glenn Kessler, "Bush 'Deeply Concerned' Abound Possible Recession." *Wash. Post*, Nov. 1, 2001.

179. Eugene L. Meyer, "National Harbor Hotel Plan Stalls." *Wash. Post*, Nov. 17, 2001.

180. Rich Miller, "Greenspan & Co. Have More Cutting To Do." *Bus. Wk.*, Nov. 19, 2001.

181. "More Americans See Recession." *cnnmoney.com*, Oct. 26, 2001.

182. "Nasdaq Up On Mostly Down Day." *Wash. Post*, Nov. 8, 2001.

183. Yuki Noguchi, "Net2000 Cuts Jobs, Closes Some Offices." *Wash. Post.*, Oct 23, 2001.

184. Floyd Norris & Jonathan Fuerbringer, "Stocks Tumble Abroad; Exchanges in New York Never Opened for the Day." *NY Times*, Sept 12, 2001.

185. "New Unemployment Claims Drop Sharply." *NY Times*, Nov. 9, 2001.

186. Floyd Norris, "Recession Is Scary, But Is There an Alternative to Stocks?" *NY Times*, Sept. 24, 2001.

187. Bruce Nussbaum, "A Shock To The Equity Culture." *Bus. Wk.*, Oct. 8, 2001.

188. Jeff D. Opdyke, "Economic Fears Push Industrials Down 3%." *Wall St. J.*, Oct. 30, 2001.

189. Jeff D. Opdyke, "Microsoft News Sends Industrials Up 188.76 Points, Economy Aside." *Wall St. J.*, Nov. 2, 2001.

190. Jeff D. Opdyke, "Worries Pull Stocks Down Another Day." *Wall St. J.*, Oct. 31, 2001.

191. Robert O'Brien, "Sink or Swim? Investors Ponder the Lows." *Wall St. J.*, Oct. 1, 2001.

192. Steven Pearlstein, "Attacks' Toll Elusive As Money Shifts From Sector to Sector." *Wash. Post*, Oct. 28, 2001.

193. Steven Pearlstein, "Confidence, Already Damaged by U.S. Slump, Further Dented by Attacks and War Concerns." *Wash. Post*, Sept. 26, 2001.

194. Steven Pearlstein, "Deep Into 'Recession'" *Wash. Post*, Nov. 3, 2001.

195. Steven Pearlstein, "Impasse on Stimulus Could Deepen Downturn." *Wash. Post*, Nov. 8, 2001.

196. Steven Pearlstein, "In Surprise, Treasury Holds Auction of 10-Year Notes." *Wash. Post*, Oct. 5, 2001.

197. Steven Pearlstein, "Slump Stirs Specter of Worldwide Recession." *Wash. Post.*, Nov. 4, 2001.

198. Steven Pearlstein, "Risk Factors Taking A Toll On Economy." *Wash. Post*, Oct. 5, 2001.

199. Steven Pearlstein, "Workforce Down 199,000 Before Attacks Unemployment Rate Expected to Surge." *Wash. Post*, Oct. 6, 2001.

200. Robert Pierre, "A Region Stays Revved Up." *Wash. Post*, Oct. 23, 2001.

201. Eduardo Porter et al, "Unions Refocus to Give Support To Workers After Layoffs, Attacks." *Wall St. J.*, Oct. 12, 2001.

202. "President Says Terrorists Tried to Disrupt World Economy." *White House, Office of the Press Secretary*, Oct. 20, 2001.

203. "Press Release." *Federal Reserve Board*, Sept. 17, 2001.

204. "Press Release." *Federal Reserve Board*, Oct. 2, 2001.

205. "Reuters Trims Its Sales Forecast and Will Cut 500 Jobs." *NY Times*, Oct. 17, 2001.

206. Matt Richtel, "Promised Land No Longer." *NY Times*, Nov. 10, 2001.

207. Jennifer Rich, "Feeling the American Aftershock." *NY Times*, Sept. 18, 2001.

208. Christopher Rhoads, "German Data Show Economy Appears on Cusp On a Recession." *Wall St. J.*, Nov. 20, 2001.

209. Christopher Rhoads, "Recession Fears Mount in Europe, But Consensus Forecasts Growth." *Wall St. J.*, Oct. 15, 2001.
210. Simon Romero, "Lucent Reports $8.8 Billion Loss and a Dim Outlook." *NY Times*, Oct. 24, 2001.
211. Rene Sanchez, "Illegal Immigrants Feel Attacks' Economic Fallout." *Wash. Post*, Oct. 19, 2001.
212. Greg Schneider & Carol Vinzant, "Stocks Fall for 4th Straight Day." *Wash. Post*, Sept. 21, 2001.
213. Michael Schuman, "Asia's Slump Could Prove More Persistent Than 1997 Crisis." *Wall St. J.*, Oct. 24, 2001.
214. Nelson Schwartz, "What Now For Investors?" *Fortune*, Oct. 1, 2001.
215. Henny Sender, "New York to Sell Debt to Finance Recovery Effort." *Wall St. J.*, Oct. 1, 2001.
216. Michael R. Sesit, "Dollar Has Rebounded Since Sept. 11, Aided by Maneuvers of Central Banks." *Wall St. J.*, Oct. 23, 2001.
217. Michael R. Sesit, "If Argentina's Woes Worsen, Effects May Spread Through Markets With Links to Latin America." *Wall St. J.*, Oct. 29, 2001.
218. "Shares Are Mixed Despite an Early Boost From Europe." *NY Times*, Nov. 9, 2001.
219. "Shares Close Moderately Lower, Reversing Early Gains." *NY Times*, Oct. 24, 2001.
220. "Shares Lose Momentum And Give Up Sharp Gains." *NY Times*, Nov. 8, 2001.
221. "Shares Prices Advances on a Record Surge in Retail Sales." *NY Times*, Nov. 15, 2001.
222. Amy Shipley, "D. C. - Baltimore Makes Cut." *Wash. Post*, Oct. 27, 2001.
223. Amy Shipley, "Olympic Bid Still Viable." *Wash. Post*, Sept. 28, 2001.
224. Jon E. Hilsenrath, "Shopper Satisfaction Takes Another Hit." *Wall St. J.*, Nov. 19, 2001.
225. Ruth Simon, "Many Consumers Can Cut Cost of Credit." *Wall St. J.*, Oct. 25, 2001.
226. G. Thomas Sims, "Euro-Zone Growth Shows Increase in Third Quarter." *Wall St. J.*, Nov. 16, 2001.
227. Randall Smith & Marcus Walker, "CSFB Will Report a Loss, As Wall Street Profits Fall." *Wall St. J.*, Oct. 10, 2001.
228. Deborah Solomon, "AT&T Is Planning More Job Cuts Amid Continuing Telecom Woes." *Wall St. J.*, Oct. 23, 2001.
229. "Spending Edges Up, But Factory Index Drops." *AP*, Oct. 1, 2001.
230. "Statement of the Managing Director on the Situation of the World Economy and the Fund Response." *International Monetary Fund* , Oct. 5, 2001.

231. Richard Stevenson, "Central Banks Inject Billions In Move to Stem Risks of Panic." *NY Times*, Sept. 13, 2001.
232. Richard Stevenson, "Fed Chief Urges a Considered Recovery Plan." *NY Times*, Oct. 2, 2001.
233. Richard Stevenson, "Fed Cuts Rates By Half-Point In an Attempt To Aid Stocks."*NY Times*, Sept. 18, 2001.
234. Richard Stevenson, "Rate Reduction Expected, but How Big?" *NY Times*, Nov. 6, 2001.
235. Richard Stevenson & Stephen Labaton, "The Financial World Is Left Reeling by Attack." *NY Times*, Sept. 12, 2001.
236. "Stock Indexes Extend Gains." *AP*, Nov. 14, 2001.
237. "Stocks Rise On Hopes of New Rate Cut." *Wash. Post*, Nov. 6, 2001.
238. "Stocks Steady After Scare." *Wash. Post*, Nov 13, 2001.
239. "Summary of Commentary on Current Economic Conditions by Federal Reserve District." *Federal Reserve Board*, Oct. 24, 2001.
240. "Taking the Consumers' Pulse." *NY Times*, Oct. 7, 2001.
241. "Taking the Consumers' Pulse." *NY Times*, Oct. 28, 2001.
242. "Technology News Lifts Stock Indexes." *Wash. Post*, Nov. 2, 2001.
243. "Technology Shares Lead Gains After Fed Cuts Rates." *NY Times*, Nov. 7, 2001.
244. "Terror Makes Itself Felt on Wall Street." *NY Times*, Sept. 23, 2001.
245. "Terrorist Attacks Also Bad News for Mexico's Struggling Economy." *AP*, Sept. 26, 2001.
246. "Terror's Aftermath: Layoffs." *Bus. Wk.*, Oct. 8, 2001.
247. "The Fallout in Europe." *Bus. Wk.*, Oct. 8, 2001.
248. "The September 11 Tragedy and the Response of the Financial Industry, Remarks by Chairman Alan Greenspan." *Federal Reserve Board*, Oct. 23, 2001.
249. "Thinking the Unthinkable." *Bus. Wk.*, Nov. 19, 2001.
250. "This Is Going To Leave A Huge Scar On All of Us." *Fortune*, Oct. 1, 2001.
251. Craig Timberg & Daniel LeDuc, "Md., Va. Warn Tax Revenue Shrinking." *Wash. Post*, Oct. 16, 2001.
252. "Tough Times: How Long?" *Bus. Wk.*, Oct. 15, 2001.
253. "Trade Deficit Posts Decline That Is Largest on Record." *NY Times*, Nov. 21, 2001.
254. "Trading on Wall St. Comes to Standstill." *Wash. Post*, Sept. 12, 2001.
255. Louis Uchitelle, "Dazed Companies Sit on Their Wallets." *NY Times*, Sept. 23, 2001.
256. Louis Uchitelle, "Fed Reduces Short-Term Rates to Lowest Level Since 1961." *NY Times*, Nov. 7, 2001.

257. Louis Uchitelle, "The Heartland Hunkers Down." *NY Times*, Nov. 6, 2001.
258. "Unemployment Claims Post a Sharp Increase." *Bloomberg News*, Oct. 11, 2001.
259. "Unisys to Cut 3,000 Jobs as Profit Falls." *NY Times*, Oct. 16, 2001.
260. "United Technologies to Cut 5,000 Jobs in Two Divisions." *NY Times*, Oct. 17, 2001.
261. "U.S. Figures Show Rate of Productivity Gained in Third Quarter." *NY Times*, Nov. 8. 2001.
262. "U.S. Vehicle Sales in October." *NY Times*, Nov. 3, 2001.
263. "Wall Street Summary." *USA Today*, Nov. 3, 2001.
264. Mary Williams Walsh, "A Mainstay of U.S. Job Creation Is Hit Hard by Sept. 11."*NY Times*, Nov. 3, 2001.
265. Mary Williams Walsh, "Urban Pain, From Sea to Sea." *NY Times*, Sept. 30, 2001.
266. "Washington Tries To Spell Relief." *Bus. Wk.*, Oct. 8, 2001.
267. "Weekly Stocks at a Glance." *Wash. Post*, Nov. 11, 2001.
268. Barbara Whitaker, "In the Great Job Desert, Some Hidden Oases." *NY Times*, Nov. 4, 2001.
269. Karen DeYoung and Dan Eggen, "$100 Million in Terrorists' Assets Frozen, U.S. Says." *Wash. Post*, Oct. 3, 2001.
270. Gregory Zuckerman & Jathon Sapsford, "Some Companies Weather Squeeze on Credit." *Wall St. J.*, Oct. 29, 2001.
271. Gregory Zuckerman & Michael Schroeder, "Goodbye to the 30-Year Treasury Bond." *Wall St. J.*, Nov. 1, 2001.

Chapter 3 – Terrorism and Corporate America: Impact on Selected Sectors

1. "A Ruinous Day For Insurers." *Bus. Wk.*, Sept. 24, 2001.
2. Reed Abelson, "In a Chorus of Caution, Some Still Chant Boldness." *NY Times*, Oct. 7, 2001.
3. Reed Abelson & Jonathan D. Glater, "Businesses Finding That Good Security Is No Longer Optional." *NY Times*, Oct. 17, 2001.
4. "ABI World Bankruptcy Headlines." *American Bankruptcy Institute*, Oct. 15, 2001.
5. Spencer Abraham, Statement, *45th General Conference of the International Atomic Energy Agency*, Sept. 17, 2001.
6. "Airports Council International—North American Calls On Congress To Focus Attention on Airports." *Airports Council International*, Sept. 25, 2001.

7. Keith Alexander, "Discount Campaigns Increase As Airlines Try To Spur Travel." *Wash. Post*, Oct. 3, 2001.
8. Keith Alexander & Frank Swoboda, "Delta To Cut 13,000 Jobs, Reduce Flight Schedule by 15%." *Wash. Post*, Sept. 27, 2001.
9. *American Bus Association*, www.buses.org.
10. *American Society for Industrial Security*, www.asisonline.org.
11. "Association Works to Allay Economic Impact of Terrorist Attacks." *National Restaurant Association*, Oct. 4, 2001.
12. Riva D. Atlas, "Bill to Alter Bankruptcy Seems to Stall." *NY Times*, Oct. 19, 2001.
13. Riva D. Atlas, "Lending Slows, Forcing Delays Of Some Deals." *NY Times*, Oct. 9, 2001.
14. Bhushan Bahree, "OPEC Warns of Price Collapse Next Year." *Wall St. J.*, Oct. 30, 2001.
15. Jeff Bailey, "Small-Business Owners Pare Spending, Fearing Sales Will Dwindle After Attacks." *Wall St. J.*, Oct. 3, 2001.
16. Chris Baker, "Networks Lose $500 Million." *Wash. Times*, Sept. 19, 2001.
17. James Bandler, "Kodak Net Plummets 77% on Weak Sales." *Wall St. J.*, Oct. 25, 2001.
18. Neela Banerjee, "Fears, Again, of Oil Supplies at Risk." *NY Times*, Oct. 14, 2001.
19. Neela Banerjee, "Oil Companies Are Increasing Their Already Tight Security." *NY Times*, Oct. 10, 2001.
20. David Barboza, "When Golden Arches Are Too Red, White and Blue." *NY Times*, Oct. 14, 2001.
21. Felicity Barringer, "Many at Wall St. Journal Set to Return to Manhattan." *NY Times*, Oct. 17, 2001.
22. Felicity Barringer, "New Tactic Of Terrorists Is to Attack The Media." *NY Times*, Oct. 15, 2001.
23. Peter Behr, "Bethlehem Steel Files for Bankruptcy." *Wash. Post*, Oct. 16, 2001.
24. Peter Behr, "Nuclear Plants' Vulnerability Raised Attack Concerns." *Wash. Post*, Oct. 21, 2001.
25. "Belly Up." *The Economist*, Oct. 26, 2001.
26. Alex Berenson, "900 Workers In Software To Lose Jobs." *NY Times*, Oct. 12, 2001.
27. Alex Berenson, "Uncertainly, Market Reopens Today." *NY Times*, Sept. 17, 2001.
28. "Big Increase in Real Estate Insurance Premiums On the Way, Professionals." *International Council of Shopping Centers*, Oct. 12, 2001.
29. Paul Blustein, "U.S. Seeks to Lower Duties for Pakistan." *Wash. Post*, Oct. 30, 2001.

30. "Bombardier to Cut 3,800 Jobs." *Dallas Morning News*, Oct. 23, 2001.
31. Lisa Bransten, "Entrepreneurs Find Investors Are Venturing Less Capital." *Wall St. J.*, Oct. 29, 2001.
32. Rick Brooks, "Corporate Mailrooms Are First Line of Defense Against Bioterrorism." *Wall St. J.* , Oct. 15, 2001.
33. DeNeen L. Brown, "Fallout From Terrorist Attacks Punishes Canadian Companies." *Wash. Post*, Oct. 20, 2001.
34. E.S. Browning, "Rebound in Tech Stocks Prompts Skepticism About Rally." *Wall St. J.*, Oct. 15, 2001.
35. Rebecca Buckman, "Microsoft Net Slips as Investments Are Hit." *Wall St. J.*, Oct. 19, 2001.
36. Robert Burgess, "Insurers Dispute Trade Center Claim." *Wash. Post*, Oct. 9, 2001.
37. Susan Carey & Martha Brannigan, "Flights Attendants Say They Lack Training for New Role in Security." *Wall St. J.*, Oct. 8, 2001.
38. Susan Carey, "Maverick Alaska Air Bucks Industry Slide By Posting Profit, Planning More Flights." *Wall St. J.*, Oct. 19, 2001.
39. Susan Carey & Motoko Rich, "I'll Be Here for Christmas." *Wall St. J.*, Oct. 23, 2001.
40. "Cendant, Hotel Owner, Lowers Projection On Income." *NY Times*, Sept. 29, 2001.
41. Anne Marie Chaker, "Tax Issues Loom For Recipients of Sept. 11 Aid." *Wall St. J.* , Oct. 24, 2001.
42. "Chapter 11 Is Becoming A More Popular Read." *Wall St. J.*, Oct. 8, 2001.
43. Terence Chea, "Security Demands May Boost Area Firms." *Wash. Post*, Oct. 20, 2001.
44. Michelle Conlin, "Where Layoffs Are A Last Resort." *Bus. Wk.*, Oct. 8, 2001.
45. Carrie Coolidge, "Risky Business." *Forbes*, Oct. 15, 2001.
46. James C. Cooper & Kathleen Madigan, "Corporate America's Double Blow: Sagging Demand, Rising Costs." *Bus. Wk.*, Nov. 5, 2001.
47. "Corporate America Braces For The Shakeout." *Bus. Wk.*, Oct. 15, 2001.
48. Amy Cortese, "Venture Capital, Withering And Dying." *NY Times*, Oct. 21, 2001.
49. Susanne Craig, "Morgan Stanley May Abandon New Complex in Manhattan." *Wall St. J.*, Oct. 5, 2001.
50. Susanne Craig, "Some Missing Funds Turn Up in First Equity Probe." *Wall St. J.*, Oct. 29, 2001.
51. Albert Crenshaw, "A Jolt of Morality." *Wash. Post*, Sept. 30, 2001.
52. Albert Crenshaw, "Businesses Face an Insurance Crunch." *Wash. Post*, Oct. 11, 2001.

53. "Damage Report From Ground Zero." *Fortune*, Oct. 1, 2001.
54. Christian Davenport & Manuel Roig-Franzia, "Truckers Subject to Growing Scrutiny." *Wash. Post*, Oct.13, 2001.
55. Daniela Deane, "Puttin' Off the Ritz." *Wash. Post*, Oct. 5, 2001.
56. "Defense Stocks Await Spending Surge." *www.moneycentral/msn.com*, Oct. 2, 2001.
57. "Despite Tough Market, Give Venture-Backed Companies Squeak Out Successful IPOs in Q3." *National Venture Capital Association*, Oct. 2, 2001.
58. Robert Dodge, "Security to Drive Coming Economy." *Dallas Morning News*, Oct. 14, 2001.
59. Charles Dubow, "Six Stocks That Step On the Gas." *Forbes.com*, Oct. 24, 2001.
60. Charles Dubow, "The Cost of Oil." *Forbes.com*, Oct. 22, 2001.
61. "Economic Support Urgently Needed for the U.S. Motorcoach Industry to Remain Solvent." *American Bus Association*, undated.
62. "EDS Cut Severance Pay For Laid Off Employees Before Axing Workers." *Wall St. J.*, Oct. 23, 2001.
63. Kurt Eichenwald, "Bin Laden Family Liquidates Holdings With Carlyle Group." *NY Times*, Oct. 26, 2001.
64. Stuart Elliott, "Advertising." *NY Times*, Oct. 16, 2001.
65. Stuart Elliott, "Advertising." *NY Times*, Oct. 23, 2001.
66. Steven Erlanger, "The World Gets Its Guard Up." *NY Times*, Oct. 21, 2001.
67. Sandra I. Erwin, "New Smart Weapons Are High On Air Force Chief's Agenda." *Nat'l. Def.*, undated.
68. Kristi Essick, "Venture Funds Renew Focus in Security, Mull Opportunities in a Climate of Fear." *Wall St. J.*, Oct. 9, 2001.
69. "ExxonMobil and Its Employees Donate Up to $20 Million for Disaster Relief." *Bus. Wire*, Sept. 14, 2001.
70. Geraldine Fabrikant, "Americans, Seeking Escape, Look to Hollywood for Relief." *NY Times*, Sept. 17, 2001.
71. Geraldine Fabrikant, "Editors Rush to Revise Long-Made Plans." *NY Times*, Sept. 17, 2001.
72. Gerladine Fabrikant & Seth Schiesel, "Suddenly, the Magic Is in Short Supply." *NY Times*, Sept. 23, 2001.
73. Barnaby J. Feder, "Trying to Plan for the Unthinkable Disaster." *NY Times*, Sept. 17, 2001.
74. "Firms Reviewing Mail-Handling Methods." *Dallas Morning News*, Oct. 15, 2001.
75. Stephane Fitch et al., "They Will Rise Again." *Forbes*, Oct. 15, 2001.

76. Michael Freedman & Daniel Kruger, "Collateral Damage." *Forbes*, Oct. 15, 2001.
77. Milt Freudenheim, "Companies, Even Rivals, Help." *NY Times*, Sept. 17, 2001.
78. Chris Gaither, "Internet Access Service on Verge of Closing." *NY Times*, Oct. 12, 2001.
79. "GAMA Stresses To Congress The Industry's Need For Resumption of All Operations." *General Aviation Manufacturers Association*, Sept. 25, 2001.
80. "Germany: Airline Cuts More Flights." *NY Times*, Sept. 29, 2001.
81. Milo Geyelin, "Lawyers Wonder, Who is Liable for Sept. 11?" *Wall St. J.*, Oct. 18, 2001.
82. Justin Gillis, "Life At the Makeshift Office." *Wash. Post*, Oct. 2, 2001.
83. Pallavi Gogoi, "Suddenly, Everyone's Looking for Life Insurance." *Bus. Wk.*, Nov. 5, 2001.
84. Peter Grant & Charles Gasparing, "Lehman Will Move Its Base out of Wall Street." *Wall St. J.*, Oct. 9, 2001.
85. Kirstin Downey Grimsley, "Many Firms Lack Plans For Disaster." *Wash. Post*, Oct. 3, 2001.
86. Kristin Downey Grimsley, "Tourists Gamble Closer To Home." *Wash. Post*, Sept. 30, 2001.
87. Danny Hakim, "Bracing for Reaction When Trades Resume." *NY Times*, Sept. 17, 2001.
88. Tom Hamburger & Christopher Oster, "Insurance Industry Backs U.S. Terrorism Fund." *Wall St. J.*, Oct. 9, 2001.
89. Martha McNeil Hamilton, "Airports Seek Federal Bailout As Traffic Falls, Expenses Rise." *Wash. Post*, Oct. 2, 2001.
90. Martha McNeil Hamilton & Frank Swoboda, "US Airways Plans Sharp But in BWI Jet Service." *Wash. Post*, Oct. 9, 2001.
91. Saul Hansell, "Ads Down, Yahoo Expects A Hard Quarter." *NY Times*, Oct. 11, 2001.
92. Saul Hansell, "Bank of New York Estimates Its Loss Will Be $125 Million." *NY Times*, Sept. 29, 2001.
93. Saul Hansell, "EBay Continues to Flourish Despite Faltering Economy." *NY Times*, Oct. 19, 2001.
94. Saul Hansell & Riva Atlas, "Wall St. Lifeline Shakes Off Dust, and Critics." *NY Times*, Oct. 6, 2001.
95. Amy Harmon, "New Economy." *NY Times*, Sept. 17, 2001.
96. Gardiner Harris et al., "Drug Makers Offer Grim or No Prognosis on Earnings." *Wall St. J.*, Oct. 24, 2001.

97. Crayton Harrison, "Worst-Case Scenarios Now Worse: Companies Demanding Help Preparing For Disaster." *Dallas Morning News*, Oct. 23, 2001.

98. Dana Hedgpeth, "Big-City Hotels Suffer a Relapse." *Wash. Post*, Oct. 26, 2001.

99. Dana Hedgpeth, "D.C. Tourism Fears a New Blow." *Wash. Post*, Oct. 18, 2001.

100. Dana Hedgpeth, "Demand Drops, But Convention Center Still Rises." *Wash. Post*, Oct. 1, 2001.

101. Dana Hedgpeth, "Marriott Readies A Layoff Option." *Wash. Post*, Sept. 28, 2001.

102. David Henry, "Putting On A Grim New Face." *Bus. Wk.*, Oct. 15, 2001.

103. Jon E. Hilsenrath & Rebecca Buckman, "Travelers Bypass the Bright Lights." *Wall St. J.*, Oct. 26, 2001.

104. Jon Hilsenrath, "Terror's Toll on the Economy." *Wall St. J.*, Oct. 9, 2001.

105. Laura M. Holson, "Pushing Limits, Finding None." *NY Times*, Nov. 1, 2001.

106. Laura M. Holson, "Sudden Sense of Insecurity at Many Companies." *NY Times*, Sept. 16, 2001.

107. Hollister H. Hovey, "Aggregate Firms Expected to Post Gains, Benefiting From Public-Works Spending." *Wall St. J.*, Oct. 16, 2001.

108. "How Much Heavier Can The Baggage Get?" *Bus. Wk.*, Sept. 24, 2001.

109. Spencer S. Hsu, "Agency Responses To Mail Scares Vary." *Wash. Post*, Oct. 27, 2001.

110. "ICSC Joins Call For Government Terror Insurance Guarantees." *International Council of Shopping Centers*, Oct. 10, 2001.

111. "Industry Recovery and Action Plans." *American Hotel & Lodging Association*, undated.

112. *International Association of Amusement Parks and Attractions*, www.iaapa.org

113. "Internet Security Alliance Commends Creation of Office of Cyber Security." *Electronic Industries Alliance*, Oct. 1, 2001.

114. Greg Ip, "As Security Worries Intensify, Companies See Efficiencies Erode." *Wall St. J.*, Oct. 24, 2001.

115. Greg Ip & Jacob M. Schlesinger, "Even Temporary Disruption in Delivery Of Mail Could Be Another Economic Blow." *Wall St. J.*, Oct. 23, 2001.

116. "It's Rough All Over." *Bus. Wk.*, Oct. 8, 2001.

117. "Jersey City: 'Wall Street West'" *Bus. Wk.*, Oct. 29, 2001.

118. David Cay Johnston & William K. Rashbaum, "Firm Reported To Be Missing $105 Million Since Attacks." *Wall St. J.*, Oct. 27, 2001.

119. Amy Joyce, "Atlantic Coast Finds Profit in Slump." *Wash. Post*, Oct. 10, 2001.

120. Amy Joyce & Nicole Wong, "Touring the Home Front." *Wash. Post*, Oct. 11, 2001.

121. Leslie Kaufman, "Retail Sales for September Show Allure of Discounters." *NY Times*, Oct. 12, 2001.

122. Elizabeth Kelleher, "Stents and Scalpels, As a Defensive Bet." *NY Times*, Oct. 28, 2001.

123. Kate Kelly & Dean Starkman, "Nasdaq Mover? The Market May Forsake Financial District for Midtown Manhattan." *Wall St. J.*, Oct. 23, 2001.

124. Harold Kennedy, "Unmanned Aircraft Attract New Interest From Pentagon." *Nat'l. Def.*, undated.

125. Kathleen Kerwin, "So Much For Detroit's Cash Cushion." *Bus. Wk.*, Nov. 5, 2001.

126. Don Kirk, "South Korea: Airline Assistance." *NY Times*, Oct. 27, 2001.

127. Alec Klein, "AOL Time Warner Cuts Its Earnings Forecast." *Wash. Post*, Sept. 25, 2001.

128. Nicholas Kulish et al, "U.S. Postal Service to Seek Federal Aid To Deal With Anthrax-Related Expenses." *Wall St. J.*, Oct. 29, 2001.

129. Howard Kurtz, "Anthrax Has Newsrooms On the Alert." *Wash. Post*, Oct. 13, 2001.

130. Stephen Labaton, "Insurer Sues to Limit Its Payout for World Trade Center." *NY Times*, Oct. 23, 2001.

131. Stephen Labaton & Jonathan Glater, "Twin Towers At the Center of Legal Brawl." *NY Times*, Nov. 3, 2001.

132. Stephen Labaton & Joseph B. Treaster, "Government Role at Issue In Proposal to Help Industry." *NY Times*, Oct. 12, 2001.

133. Lyndsey Layton, "Metro Moves to Improve Rail, Bus Security." *Wash. Post* , Sept. 21, 2001.

134. "Leaders and Laggards in the Quarter." *NY Times*, Sept. 29, 2001.

135. "Lechters Going Out of Business." *Wash. Post* , Oct. 13, 2001.

136. "Lehman Buys N.Y. Building." *Wash. Post*, Oct. 9, 2001.

137. "Lenders Offer Relief to Borrowers, Support for Funds Following September 11th Tragedies." *American Financial Services Association*, Oct. 1, 2001.

138. Steve Liesman, "Accountants, in a Reversal, Say Costs From the Attack Aren't 'Extraordinary.'" *Wall St. J.*, Oct. 1, 2001.

139. Connie Ling, "Asian Insurance Firms Stand to Benefit From Limited Exposure to Sept. 11 Attacks." *Wall St. J.*, Oct. 16, 2001.

140. Steve Lohr, "In the Computer Sector, a 'Blanket of Hesitation'" *NY Times*, Sept. 24, 2001.

141. David Lonhardt, "Airlines Try To Smooth Fear Out of Waiting." *NY Times*, Oct. 11, 2001.

142. J. Lynn Lunsford, "Boeing Raises Estimated Deliveries for '01, Foresees Sharper Production Drop in '02." *Wall St. J.*, Oct. 18, 2001.

143. Scott McCartney & Melanie Trottman, "Bailout Lifts Continental to Profit And Halves America West's Loss." *Wall St. J.*, Nov. 1, 2001.

144. Gary McWilliams, "PC Makers Face Possibility of Additional Layoffs." *Wall St. J.*, Oct. 4, 2001.

145. Daniel Machalaba, "Amtrak's Acela Traffic Rises 35% As Airline Disruptions Add Riders." *Wall St. J.*, Oct. 23, 2001.

146. Daniel Machalaba, "Union Pacific Seeks to Boost Revenue in Unlikely Places." *Wall St. J.*, Oct. 16, 2001.

147. Paul Magnusson et al, "The Squeeze on the States Just Got Worse." *Bus. Wk.*, Oct. 15, 2001.

148. Michael Mandel, "Capital Spending: Further Cuts?" *Bus. Wk.* , Oct. 22, 2001.

149. Donna De Marco, "A Suddenly Inhospital Industry." *Wash. Times*, Sept. 19, 2001.

150. Suzanne Marta, "Dallas-Area Hotels Endure Lonely Nights After Attacks." *Dallas Morning News*, Oct. 10, 2001.

151. Joseph Martha & Sunil Subbakrishna, "When Just-in-Time Becomes Just-in-Case." *Wall St. J.*, Oct. 23, 2001.

152. Terry Maxon, "Delta to Cut 13,000 Positions." *Dallas Morning News*, Oct. 23, 2001.

153. Caroline E. Mayer, "Anthrax Scare Forces Postal Changes." *Wash. Post*, Oct. 17, 2001.

154. Paul Meller, "Europe Agrees to Belgian Rescue of Sabena." *NY Times*, Oct. 18, 2001.

155. Paul Meller, "European Commission Approves Aid for Airlines." *NY Times*, Oct. 11, 2001.

156. Paul Meller, "Sabena of Belgium Gets Loan and Asks For Court Protection." *NY Times*, Oct. 4, 2001.

157. "Mergers Snapshot/Slowdown." *Wall St. J.*, Oct. 17, 2001.

158. "Message From AphA's President and CEO." *American Pharmaceuticals Association*, Oct. 2001.

159. Daniel Michaels & Zach Coleman, "Airlines With Closest Ties to U.S. Face a Painful Future." *Wall St. J.*, Oct. 1, 2001.

160. Bruce Mohl, "So Far, Energy Conservation Lacking in War on Terrorism." *Boston Globe*, Sept. 23, 2001.

161. Gretchen Morgenson, "Companies' Big Debts Now Carry Big Risks." *NY Times*, Oct. 7, 2001.

162. Gretchen Morgenson, "Stock Market Shrugs Off Airstrikes." *NY Times*, Oct. 9, 2001.

163. Gretchen Morgenson, "The Risk of Not Weighing Risk." *NY Times*, Oct. 28, 2001.

164. Timothy Mullaney, "Dashed Hopes For Dot-Coms." *Bus. Wk.*, Oct. 15, 2001.

165. Mike Musgrove, "For PC Industry, a Bad Year Gets Worse." *Wash. Post*, Oct. 3, 2001.

166. Mike Musgrove, "Polaroid Files for Chapter 11 Bankruptcy." *Wash. Post*, Oct. 13, 2001.

167. "NAM Endorses President Bush's Economic Stimulus Plan." *National Association of Manufacturers*, Press Release, Oct. 5, 2001.

168. "NASD Companies Donate $1 Million to Aid Victims of September 11 Attacks." *NASD*, undated.

169. "NBSU Chairman Testifies on Economic Recovery In Front of House Committee on Small Business." *National Small Business United*, Oct. 10, 2001.

170. "New Survey Finds A Majority of Americans Will Keep Travel Plans After Terrorist Attacks." *Travel Industry Association of America*, Oct. 2, 2001.

171. "No Silver Lining For Tech Sales." *Bus. Wk.*, Oct. 22, 2001.

172. Yuki Noguchi & Cynthia Webb, "Region's High-Tech Sector Suffers A Steep, Cruel Fall." *Wash. Post*, Oct. 8, 2001.

173. Yuki Noguchi, "Preparing for the Worst." *Wash. Post*, Oct. 30, 2001.

174. Floyd Norris, "After Terror, Insiders Switched From Selling to Buying." *NY Times*, Oct. 19, 2001.

175. Floyd Norris & Edmund L. Andrews, "An Inquiry On Stock Gains Yields Little." *NY Times*, Sept. 17, 2001.

176. Floyd Norris, "No Special Accounting Breaks for Recent Corporate Setbacks." *NY Times*, Oct. 2, 2001.

177. "Now Make the Traveler Want to Travel." *NY Times*, Sept. 30, 2001.

178. "Now, Profits Are in Free Fall." *Bus. Wk.*, Nov. 5, 2001.

179. Donald Ogilvie, "ABA Statement on Executive Order to Block Terrorist Assets." *American Bankers Association*, Sept. 24, 2001.

180. Elizabeth Olson, "More Swissair Problems." *NY Times*, Oct. 18, 2001.

181. Elizabeth Olson, "Swissair to Resume Some Flights Today Thanks to a Bailout." *NY Times*, Oct. 4, 2001.

182. Christopher Oster, "Insurance Rates Rocket Across Industries, But Unlike Airlines, Help May Not Come." *Wall St. J.*, Oct. 8, 2001.

183. Christopher Oster & Tom Hamburger, "Property Insurers Seek to Exclude Future Coverage Against Terrorism." *Wall St. J.*, Oct. 10, 2001.

184. Mitchell Pacelle, "Waiving or Drowning: Banks Face Loan Bind." *Wall St. J.*, Oct. 16, 2001.

185. Steven Pearlstein, "Collateral Damage." *Wash. Post*, Sept. 16, 2001.

186. Steven Pearlstein, "Confusing Contrasts in The Financial Picture." *Wash. Post*, Oct. 28, 2001.

187. Martin Peers & Joe Flint, "Media Executives Diverge on Ad Outlook." *Wall St. J.*, Oct. 3, 2001.

188. Don Phillips, "Amtrak: The Boost That Began Sept. 11 May Not Be Temporary." *Wash. Post*, Sept. 23, 2001.

189. Andrew Pollack, "Drug Makers Wrestle With World's New Rules." *NY Times*, Oct. 21, 2001.

190. Stephen Power & Rick Brooks, "Post Office Shifts Mail Off Passenger Jets." *Wall St. J.*, Oct. 16, 2001.

191. Sue Anne Pressley & Pamela Ferdinand, "Layoffs, Dwindling Tourism a Blow to Struggling States." *Wash. Post*, Sept. 27, 2001.

192. Sue Anne Pressley, "The Crowds That Aren't." *Wash. Post*, Oct. 10, 2001.

193. "Questions and Answers about Life Insurers' Response to the Tragic Events of September 11." *American Council of Life Insurers*.

194. Tome Ramstack, "Chemicals Firms Use Stricter Security." *Wash. Times*, Oct. 16, 2001.

195. "Red Cross Estimates $300 Million Required To Meet Needs Following September 11th." *Red Cross*, www.redcross.org

196. Stanley Reed, "Why OPEC Can't Handle The Price Slide." *Bus. Wk.*, Oct. 8 , 2001.

197. Motoko Rich, "Attacks Seen Worsening Real-Estate Slump." *Wall St. J.*, Oct. 17, 2001.

198. Motoko Rich, "Firms, Employees Look to Home Offices Again." *Wall St. J.*, Oct. 3, 2001.

199. Motoko Rich and Ray Smith, "New York Real-Estate Markets Pick Up Again Following Attacks." *Wall St. J.*, Oct. 3, 2001.

200. Motoko Rich, "Small Firms Near Trade Center Struggle to Find Homes." *Wall St. J.*, Oct. 16, 2001.

201. Simon Romero, "Attacks Expose Telephone's Soft Underbelly." *NY Times*, Oct. 15, 2001.

202. Simon Romero, "Lucent Reports $8.8 Billion Loss and a Dim Outlook." *NY Times*, Oct. 24, 2001.

203. Jathon Sapsford et al., "Attacks Derailed Keefe-BNP Talks." *Wall St. J.*, Oct. 10, 2001.

204. Seth Schiesel & Felicity Barringer, "News Media Risk Big Losses To Cover War." *NY Times*, Oct. 22, 2001.

205. Richard B. Schmitt, "Homeless, A Wall Street Law Firm Improvises." *Wall St. J.*, Oct. 10, 2001.

206. Nelson Schwartz, "What Now For Investors?" *Fortune*, Oct. 1, 2001.

207. *Security Management Online.* www.securitymanagement.com/library/ Counter_terror.html
208. Joe Sharkey, "Thousands of Jobs At Stake As Terminal Shops Struggle." *NY Times*, Sept. 29, 2001.
209. Amy Shipley, "D.C.-Baltimore Makes Cut." *Wash. Post*, Oct. 27, 2001.
210. Stuart Silverstein, "Filling Empty Rooms." *LA Times*, Oct. 22, 2001.
211. Bernard Simon, "Air Canada Puts Best Face On a Big Loss." *NY Times*, Nov. 3, 2001.
212. Bernard Simon, "Shake-Up in the Shipping Industry." *NY Times*, Oct. 10, 2001.
213. Ray A. Smith, "Arbitrator Is Urged for Towers-Area Renters." *Wall St. J.*, Oct. 29, 2001.
214. Ray A. Smith, "Despite Slow Sales, Shopping-Mall Firms Rise on Traffic Rebound." *Wall St. J.*, Oct. 17, 2001.
215. Ray A. Smith, "'Telecom Hotels' Find Interest Once More." *Wall St. J.*, Oct. 10, 2001.
216. Andrew Ross Sorkin & Jonathan D. Glater, "Merger Deals Are Stalled Amid Doubt." *NY Times*, Sept. 17, 2001.
217. Andrew Ross Sorkin, "NBC Is Paying $1.98 Billion For Telemundo." *NY Times*, Oct. 23, 2001.
218. Jackie Spinner, "Bills Differ on Aid to Insurance Industry." *Wash. Post*, Nov. 2, 2001.
219. Jackie Spinner, "Displaced Pentagon Staffers Set Up Shop in Crystal City." *Wash. Post* , Sept. 19, 2001.
220. Jackie Spinner, "Insurance Industry Can Pay Claims." *Wash. Post*, Sept. 26, 2001.
221. Jackie Spinner, "Insurers May Drop Coverage of Terrorism." *Wash. Post*, Sept. 27, 2001.
222. Jackie Spinner, "Insurers Seek Help With Terror Coverage." *Wash. Post*, Oct. 11, 2001.
223. Jackie Spinner, "Life Insurers Want Study of Future Terrorism's Cost." *Wash. Post*, Oct. 19, 2001.
224. Jackie Spinner, "White House Offers Insurance Plan." *Wash. Post*, Oct. 16, 2001.
225. Anne Marie Squeo & Daniel Michaels, "Boeing Seeks To Expand Its Range In U.S. Missiles Market." *Wall St. J.*, Oct. 3, 2001.
226. John Stanton, "No-Frills Agency Accelerates Fielding of Anti-Terror Tools." *Nat'l Def.*, undated.
227. Dean Starkman, "Brookfield Can't Escape Ground Zero." *Wall St. J.*, Oct. 19, 2001.
228. Dean Starkman, "Foot Traffic in Malls Is Rebounding Close To Pre-Attack Levels." *Wall St. J.*, Oct. 3, 2001.

229. Dean Starkman, "Office Vacancies Rise, Spurred by Layoffs." *Wall St. J.*, Nov. 1, 2001.

230. Dean Starkman & Peter Grant, "Brookfield and Silverstein Hold Talks On Future of World Trade Center Site." *Wall St. J.*, Oct. 16, 2001.

231. "State Governments Encouraging Biotechnology Growth." *Biotechnology Industry Organization*, Oct. 1, 2001.

232. Frank Swoboda & Martha McNeil Hamilton, "For Strong Airlines, an Edge on Aid." *Wash. Post*, Oct. 6, 2001.

233. Frank Swoboda & Martha McNeil Hamilton, "United Chairman's Alarm Is Assailed." *Wash. Post*, Oct. 18, 2001.

234. Chad Terhune, "Local Public-Health Leaders Want More Funding to Fight Bioterrorism." *Wall St. J.*, Oct. 23, 2001.

235. "The $30 Billion Explosion." *Fortune*, Oct. 1, 2001.

236. "Top 25 International Reinsurer Groups." *Reinsurance Association of America*, undated.

237. "Top U.S. Reinsurance Companies." *Reinsurance Association of America*, undated.

238. "Tourists Line Up at Empire State Building." *Wash. Post*, Sept. 30, 2001.

239. "Travel America Now Act Supported By Industry Leaders." *Travel Industry Association of America*, Oct. 12, 2001.

240. *Travel Industry Association of America.* www.tia.org/home.org

241. Joseph B. Treaster & Jennifer Lee, "Big Insurance Brokers Need Help After Trade Center Blast." NY Times, Sept. 18, 2001.

242. Joseph B. Treaster, "Life Insurers Seek Study Of Terror Aid." *NY Times*, Oct. 18, 2001.

243. Jacqueline Trescott, "Smithsonian Attendance Plummeted Since Attacks." *Wash. Post*, Sept. 28, 2001.

244. Melanie Trottman & Susan Carey, "Southwest, Alaska Saw Profits in Quarter." *Wall St. J.*, Oct. 19, 2001.

245. Shawn Tully, "Rebuilding Wall Street." *Fortune*, Oct. 1, 2001.

246. "Two Major Cruise Lines Announce Big Cutbacks." *Dallas Morning News*, Sept. 27, 2001.

247. Louis Uchitelle, "Dazed Companies Sit on Their Wallets." *NY Times*, Sept. 23, 2001.

248. "U.S. Chamber Pledges Continued Support for Victims, President and Economic Recovery." Press Release, *U.S. Chamber of Commerce*, Sept. 26, 2001.

249. Lisa Vickery & Gordon Fairclough, "Convention Organizers Scramble to Salvage Events." *Wall St. J.*, Oct. 11, 2001.

250. Sharon Waxman, "Strike Two: Emmy Awards Called Off Again." *Wash. Post*, Oct. 8, 2001.

251. Neil Weinberg, "Rubbing Elbows." *Forbes*, Oct. 15, 2001.
252. Erin White & Ann Zimmerman, "As Sales Slow, Bargains Pile Up." *Wash. Post*, Oct. 8, 2001.
253. Gregory L. White, "GM Has Loss, and Profit Before Charges Falls 54%." *Wall St. J.*, Oct. 19, 2001.
254. Debbi Wilgoren, "New Places to Live Downtown." *Wash. Post*, Oct. 13, 2001.
255. Ron Winslow, "U.S. Hospitals May Need $10 Billion To Be Prepared for Bioterror Attack." *Wall St. J.*, Oct. 29, 2001.
256. Nicole C. Wong, "Postal Delays Worrying Small Retailers." *Wash. Post*, Oct. 20, 2001.
257. Ann Wozencraft & Joseph B. Treaster, "Lebenthal to Be Acquired by the MONY Group." *NY Times*, Oct. 9, 2001.
258. Emily Yellin, "Back in the Air Again, and Feeling a Special Rush." *NY Times*, Oct. 15, 2001.
259. Shawn Young, "Bell South Net Dives 99% on Qwest Stake; 3,000 Workers, 2.7% of Staff, to Be Cut." *Wall St. J.*, Oct. 19, 2001.
260. Shawn Young, "SBC Plans Layoffs as Net Tumbles 31%." *Wall St. J.*, Oct. 23, 2001.
261. Ann Zimmerman, "Malls' Challenge: Protect Shoppers, Soothe Nerves." *Wall St. J.*, Oct. 18, 2001.
262. Ann Zimmerman, "Retailers Face Rough Holidays After a Dismal Month." *Wall St. J.*, Oct. 12, 2001.
263. Ann Zimmerman, "Wal-Mart Continues Plans to Expand At Aggressive Pace." *Wall St. J.*, Oct. 3, 2001.
264. Laurence Zuckerman, "Do All Airlines Deserve A Taxpayer Rescue?" *NY Times*, Oct. 21, 2001.
265. Lawrence Zuckerman, "New Airline Board Is Given Wide Authority to Support the Industry." *NY Times*, Oct. 6, 2001.
266. www.aa.com
267. www.abc.com
268. www.aeromexico.com
269. www.aha.org
270. www.aircanada.com
271. www.airfrance.com
272. www.alaska-air.com
273. www.amd.com
274. www.americanexpress.com
275. www.americanwest.com
276. www.ansett.com
277. www.atlanticcoast.com

278. www.bethsteel.com
279. www.bofa.com
280. www.britishairways.com
281. www.brookfieldproperties.com
282. www.canada3000.com
283. www.cbs.com
284. www.cendant.com
285. www.cgsh.com
286. www.chevrontexaco.com
287. www.choicehotels.com
288. www.citigroup.com
289. www.comdisco.com
290. www.conning.com
291. www.conoco.com
292. www.crengland.com
293. www.crossair.com
294. www.daimlerchrysler.com
295. www.daysinn.com
296. www.dell.com
297. www.delta.com
298. www.disney.com
299. www.doubletreerockville.com
300. www.eastman.com
301. www.empireblue.com
302. www.enron.com
303. www.exxonmobil.com
304. www.fedex.com
305. www.flyasiana.com
306. www.gap.com
307. www.gartner.com
308. www.ge.com
309. www.generalgrowth.com
310. www.gigaweb.com
311. www.gs.com
312. www.gm.com
313. www.idc.com
314. www.iii.org
315. www.jal.co.jp/e/
316. www.kbw.com
317. www.koreanair.com
318. www.lebenthal.com

319. www.lehman.com
320. www.lloyds.com
321. www.lufthansa.com
322. www.marriott.com
323. www.miga.org
324. www.morganstanley.com
325. www.naccho.org
326. www.nasdr.com/special_exec.htm
327. www.nbc.com
328. www.neimanmarcus.com
329. www.nybot.com
330. www.opec.org
331. www.opic.gov
332. www.panynj.gov
333. www.philipmorris.com
334. www.phillips66.com
335. www.polaroid.gov
336. www.sabena.com
337. www.sas.se
338. www.sears.com
339. www.slc2002.org
340. www.southwest.com
341. www.statefarm.com
342. www.str-online.com
343. www.sunguard.com
344. www.superbowl.com
345. www.swissair.com
346. www.swissre.com
347. www.target.com
348. www.ual.com
349. www.ubs.com
350. www.unumprovident.com
351. www.varig.com.br/
352. www.virginatlantic.com
353. www.walgreens.com
354. www.walmart.com

Chapter 4 – War on Terrorism: The Role of Industry

1. Tom Abate, "Bioterrorism Defense Being Developed: Bay Area Companies Collaborate With Federal Agencies." *SF Chron.*, Sept. 25, 2001.
2. Timothy Aeppel, "Now Is the Time to Sell 'U.S.-Made'" *Wall St. J.*, Oct. 22, 2001.
3. Mark Anderson, "Chaos Has Awakened Giant." moneycentral.msn.com, Oct. 1, 2001.
4. Keith Alexander, "Shuttles From National Lose Business to Train." *Wash. Post*, Oct. 3, 2001.
5. Julia Angwin, "Demand for Cipro Brings Sales—and Scrutiny—to Online Supplier." Wall St. J., Oct. 22, 2001.
6. Julia Angwin, "Getting Web Anthrax Data: a Review of Four Sites." *Wall St. J.*, Oct. 25, 2001.
7. Julia Angwin, "Medical Board in North Carolina Acts to Curb Online Cipro Sales." *Wall St. J.*, Oct. 29, 2001.
8. "Anthrax Infects Only by Big Dose, Can Be Treated With Antibiotics." *Wall St. J.*, Oct. 9, 2001.
9. *Bayer Lauds Cipro Alternative*, cnnmoney, Oct. 22, 2001, http://money.cnn.com/2001/10/22/companies/bayer/
10. Luisa Beltran, "Will Anthrax Fears Spur E-Mail Growth?" Oct. 25, 2001, http://money.cnn.com/2001/10/25/news/anthrax_mail/
11. Dennis Berman, "Disaster Gives New Life to Wireless Telecom Firms." *Wall St. J.*, Oct. 3, 2001.
12. Amy Borrus, "When Right and Left See Eye-to-Eye." *Bus. Wk.*, Nov. 5, 2001.
13. John Breeden, "UPSes Keep Networks Running When the Power Goes Out." Wash. Post, Oct. 28, 2001.
14. Rick Brooks & Ann Davis, "Postal Service Policies on Protective Gear Against Anthrax Are Confusing Workers." *Wall St. J.*, Oct. 24, 2001.
15. David Brown, "Maker of Anthrax Vaccine to Reopen After Renovating Mich. Plant." Wash. Post, Nov. 1, 2001.
16. William M. Bulkeley, et al., "Amid Anthrax, Businesses Sour On U.S. Mail." *Wall* St. J., Oct. 25, 2001.
17. Andrew Caffrey & Russell Gold, "The High Cost of Public Safety." *Wall St. J.*, Oct. 25, 2001.
18. Jill Carroll, "U.S. Takes Bids to Make Smallpox Vaccine." *Wall St. J.*, Oct. 26, 2001.
19. Jill Carroll & Ron Winslow, "Bayer to Slash Price U.S. Pays for Anthrax Drug." Wall St. J., Oct. 25, 2001.
20. Barbara Carton, "Apocalypse Now: Stocking Up to Survive the Worst." Wall St. J., Oct. 10, 2001.

21. "Cepheid and ETG to Develop Biological Agent Detection Systems for Military and Other Applications." Press Release, Cepheid, Aug. 13, 2001. www.cepheid.com/pages/press/010813.html
22. "Cepheid's Products – DNA Analysis When & Where You Need It." *Cepheid*, www.cepheid.com/pages/products.html
23. John Chartier, "Fighting Bioterror." *money.cnn.com*, Oct. 25, 2001.
24. Terence Chea, "A Genetic Blueprint for Justice." *Wash. Post*, Oct. 8, 2001.
25. Terence Chea, "A Growth Spurt For Biotechnology." *Wash. Post*, Oct. 19, 2001.
26. Terence Chea, "In the Right Place At the Wrong Time." *Wash. Post*, Oct. 22, 2001.
27. Terence Chea & Justin Gillis, "Drug Firms Scramble on Scare." *Wash. Post*, Oct. 18, 2001.
28. "DOD at a Glance." www.defenselink.mil/pubs/almanac/almanac/at_a_glance.html
29. Don Clark, "Security Experts Are on Alert Over Wireless Hacking Technique." Wall St. J., Oct. 15, 2001.
30. Ariana Eunjung Cha, "Alert System Sought For Internet Attacks." *Wash. Post*, Oct. 25, 2001.
31. Marilyn Chase, "DCD and States Draw Up Plans Top Stop Smallpox." *Wall St. J.*, Oct. 26, 2001.
32. Lara Petusky Coger, "A Security Virtuoso's Big Test." *NY Times*, Sept. 30, 2001.
33. Daniel Costello, "The Other Way To Fly." *Wall St. J.*, Oct. 5, 2001.
34. Grainger David, "You Just Hired Him." *Fortune*, Oct. 29, 2001.
35. "Decontamination Solutions." *Modec, Inc.* www.deconsolutions.com
36. Claudia H. Deutsch, "An Economy Keeping Its Guard Up." *NY Times*, Oct. 26, 2001.
37. "EFT" (Envirofoam Technologies, Inc.), www.envirofoam.com/aboutus.htm
38. "Egis II Explosives Detection Systems." *Thermo Electron Corporation.* www.thermo.com/eThermo/CDA/Products/Prod.../1,1075,14817-167-X-1-13795,00.htm
39. Juliet Eilperin & Helen Dewar, "Congress Returns, Warily." *Wash. Post*, Oct. 23, 2001.
40. Dina El Boghdady, "Safeguarding Data Gains New Urgency." *Wash. Post*, Oct. 29, 2001.
41. Jonathan Fahey, "We See You." *Forbes*, Oct. 15, 2001.
42. "F.B.I. List of Problems Released." *NY Times*, Oct. 2, 2001.
43. "Features of the R.A.P.I.D." *R.A.P.I.D.*, www.idahotech.com/rapid/features.htm

44. Gary Fields & Sarah Lueck, "Officials Say More Anthrax-Laced Letters May Surface." *Wall St. J.*, Oct. 29, 2001.

45. David Freedman, "The De-Hijacking Swtich." *Business 2.0*, Nov. 2001.

46. "From Smart to Brilliant Weapons." *Bus. Wk.*, Oct. 8, 2001.

47. Vanessa Fuhrmans, "Bayer May Ask Rivals to Help Make Cipro." *Wall St. J.*, Oct. 18, 2001.

48. Justin Gillis, "Backup Systems Passed Trying Test." *Wash. Post*, Sept. 27, 2001.

49. Justin Gillis & Ceci Connolly, "Emphasis on Cipro Worries Officials." *Wash. Post*, Oct. 19, 2001.

50. William Glanz, "Fear of Flying Boosts Train Ridership." *Wash. Times*, Sept. 19, 2001.

51. Victor Godinez, "Protection Services Firms See a Surge in Demand." *dallasnews.com*, Oct. 23, 2001.

52. Abigail Goldman & Mitchell Landsberg, "Consumers Focus on Security, Home Comfort." *latimes.com*, Oct. 14, 2001.

53. Guy Gugliotta, "Tech Companies See Market for Detection." *Wash. Post*, Sept. 28, 2001.

54. "Greyhound Faces Bumps in Its Road to Steady Growth." *Wall St. J.*, Oct. 5, 2001.

55. Amy Harmon, "Remote Rendezvous." *NY Times*, Sept. 24, 2001.

56. Scott Hensley, "Antibiotic Purchases Jump in New York." *Wall St. J.*, Oct. 9, 2001.

57. Scott Hensley & Rachel Zimmerman, "Drug Firms Offer to Aid Bioterror Fight." *Wall. St. J.*, Oct. 25, 2001.

58. Hollister H. Hovey, "Aggregate Firms Expected to Post Gains, Benefiting From Public-Works Spending." *Wall St. J.*, Oct. 16, 2001.

59. "Threats Pose Risk to Allergy Sufferers." *Wall St. J.*, Oct. 16, 2001.

60. Laura Johannes et al, "Companies Hire Private Firms For Anthrax Test." *Wall St. J.*, Oct. 22, 2001.

61. Mary Jordan & Kevin Sullivan, "With Security Tight, Border Officials Focus on Fake Ids." *Wash. Post*, Oct. 30, 2001.

62. Paul Kaihla, "Weapons of the Secret War." *Business 2.0*, Nov. 2001.

63. Rich Karlgaard, "The Enemy Beneath." *Forbes*, Oct. 15, 2001.

64. Marty Katz, "Hand-Held Satellite Telephones Resurface in Wake of Tragedy." *NY Times*, Sept. 24, 2001.

65. Tomas Kellner, "Total Recall." *Forbes*, Oct. 15, 2001.

66. Jerry Knight, "Sorting Out Winners in War on Terrorism." *Wash. Post*, Oct. 20, 2001.

67. Daniel LeDuc, "Va., Md. Warn of Internet Cipro Sales." *Wash. Post*, Oct. 27, 2001.

68. "Lockheed Martin Team Wins Joint Strike Fighter Competition, Pledges Full Commitment to This Cornerstone of Future Defense Capability." Press Release, *Lockheed Martin Aeronautics*, Oct. 26, 2001.

69. Steve Lohr, "In the Computer Sector, a 'Blanket of Hesitation'" *NY Times*, Sept. 24, 2001.

70. Steve Lohr, "Giving Away Computers, Dispensing Peace of Mind." *NY Times*, Sept. 24, 2001.

71. Daniel Lyons and William Barrett, "Toughening Up." *Forbes*, Oct. 15, 2001.

72. Laurie McGinley, "Maker of New Smallpox Vaccine Is Sharply Accelerating Output." *Wall St. J.*, Oct. 1, 2001.

73. Paul Magnusson, "Yes, They Certainly Will." *Bus. Wk.*, Nov. 5, 2001.

74. Stephen Manes, "Redundancy Saves." *Forbes*, Oct. 15, 2001.

75. Kevin Maney, "The Internet Could Save Us From Bioterrorism." *usatoday.com*, Oct. 25, 2001.

76. Gene G. Marcial, "A Brisk Trade in Cars." *Bus. Wk.*, Oct. 22, 2001.

77. Gene G. Marcial, "Avant: Set To Make An Anthrax Vaccine." *Bus. Wk.*, Nov. 5, 2001.

78. Gene G. Marcial, "Sniffing Out Bombs." *Bus. Wk.*, Nov. 5, 2001.

79. Suzanne Marta, "Carrollton Company Helps with Both Guns and Butter." *dallasnews.com*, Oct. 23, 2001.

80. Barbara Martinez & Gardiner Harris, "Anxious Patients Plead With Doctors for Antibiotics." *Wall St. J.*, Oct. 15, 2001.

81. Anna Wilde Mathews, "Coordinating Disaster Relief Over the Web." *Wall St. J.*, Oct 23, 2001.

82. Micheline Maynard, "Corporate Planes: Perks or Necessities?" *NY Times*, Sept. 23, 2001.

83. Micheline Maynard, "With Aircraft Idle, Income Reads Zero." *NY Times*, Oct. 28, 2001.

84. Michael Menduno, "Spotting The Bad Guys." *Business 2.0*, Nov. 2001

85. Renae Merle, "CACI Profit Up 51%; Federal Work Grows." *Wash. Post*, Oct. 19, 2001.

86. Mike Musgrove, "Fear, Mother of Invention." *Wash. Post*, Oct. 25, 2001.

87. "One Hundred Companies Listed According To Net Value of Prime Contract Awards and Category of Procurement, Department of Defense Top Defense Contractors, Fiscal Year 2000." defenselink.mil. www.defenselink.mil/pubs/almanac/almanac/money/top100fy2000.html

88. Michael Menduno, "Spotting The Bad Guys." *Business 2.0*, Nov. 2001.

89. "ORIGEN Products May Enhance Nation's Ability to Rapidly Detect Biological Agents." *Igen International, Inc.*, Oct. 12, 2001. www.corporate-ir.ne

90. "Overview." *Nanogen.* www.corporateir.net./ireye/ir_site.zhtml?ticker =NGEN&script=2100

91. "No Place to Hide." *Bus. Wk.*, Nov. 5, 2001.

92. Yuki Noguchi, "For Many Without Guns, Attack Was a Call to Arm." *Wash. Post*, Oct. 2, 2001.

93. Yuki Noguchi, "Cellular Firms Seek 911 Delay." *Wash. Post*, Sept. 27, 2001.

94. Don Oldenburg, "Stocking Up in Hopes of Breathing Easier." *Wash. Post*, Oct. 10, 2001.

95. David Orenstein, "How A Bomb Sniffer Works." *Business 2.0*, Nov. 2001.

96. Peter Pae, "Defense Buildup Is Expected to Be Gradual and Targeted." *latimes.com*, Oct. 9, 2001.

97. Andy Pasztor, "Aviation Sector Seems Cool to Idea of Remotely Flying Hijacked Jets." *Wall St. J.*, Oct. 19, 2001.

98. Andy Pasztor, "Qualcomm Set to Unveil System That Broadcasts Live From Jetliners." *Wall St. J.*, Oct. 29, 2001.

99. Andy Pasztor & Anne Marie Squeo, "B-2 Bomber Emerges as Focus of Budget Battles." *Wall St. J.*, Oct. 24, 2001.

100. Andy Pasztor, "C-17 Transport Plane, Long Controversial, Becomes an Unlikely Star of Campaign." *Wall St. J.*, Oct. 9, 2001.

101. Andy Pasztor & Daniel Michaels, "Airbus Beats U.S. Rival to Offer Standard For Cockpit Door That Resists Hijackers." *Wall St. J.*, Oct. 17, 2001.

102. Andrea Petersen & Joseph Pereira, "Citizens Prepare Homes, Kids, Medicine Chests in Fear of New Attacks." *Wall St. J.*, Oct. 9, 2001.

103. Melody Petersen, "With Anthrax Fears, Bayer is to Lift Antibiotic Output." *NY Times*, Oct. 10, 2001.

104. Don Phillips, "Airport Security Company Faulted." *Wash. Post*, Oct. 12, 2001.

105. Don Phillips, "Baggage Screening Firm Settles With U.S." *Wash. Post*, Oct. 20, 2001.

106. Don Phillips, "FAA May Start Using Scanner That Looks Inside the Body." *Wash. Post*, Oct. 26, 2001.

107. Andrew Pollack, "A Rush to Biotech, Based on a Scare." *NY Times*, Oct. 14, 2001.

108. Andrew Pollack, "Identifying the Dead, 2,000 Miles Away." *NY Times*, Sept. 30, 2001.

109. Stephen Powell and Greg Hitt, "Airline-Secuirty Industry Fights for Its Life." *Wall St. J.*, Oct. 31, 2001.

110. John Pomfret, "Chinese Working Overtime to Sew U.S. Flags." *Wash. Post*, Sept. 20, 2001.

111. Stephen Power, "Argenbright Faces Charges on Vetting of Airport Workers." *Wall St. J.*, Oct. 12, 2001.
112. "Product CBMS." *Bruker Daltonics.* www.brukerdaltonics.com/products/nigas.htm
113. "Product NIGAS." *Bruker Daltonics.* www.brukerdaltonics.com/products/nigas.htm
114. "Product Description." *Cyrano Sciences Inc.* http://cyranosciences.com/products/
115. "Profile – AVANT Immunotherapeutics." http://biz.yahoo.com/p/a/avan.html
116. Thomas E. Ricks, "U.S. Arms Unmanned Aircraft." *Wash. Post*, Oct. 18, 2001.
117. Teresa Riordan, "Patents." *NY Times*, Oct. 25, 2001.
118. Monica Roman, "Healthy Risk." *Bus. Wk.*, Oct. 22, 2001.
119. Lois Romano, "At Tulsa Gun Show, Searching for Safety." *Wash. Post*, Oct. 22, 2001.
120. Simon Romero, "New Economy." *NY Times*, Oct. 22, 2001.
121. Jan M. Rosen, "Playing the Potential In Internet Security." *NY Times*, Oct. 14, 2001.
122. Michael E. Ruane, "Irradiation Explored As Answer to Anthrax." *Wash. Post*, Oct. 23, 2001.
123. Ron Scherer, "Show Business Gets in the Act of Cheering Troops." *Chr. Sc. Mon.*, Oct. 22, 2001.
124. Greg Schneider, "Air Force Chief Opposes Purchase of More B-2s." *Wash. Post*, Oct. 24, 2001.
125. Greg Schneider, "Lockheed Martin Beats Boeing for Fighter Contract." *Wash. Post*, Oct. 27, 2001.
126. Greg Schneider, "Pentagon Backs Northrop Bid for Shipbuilder." *Wash. Post*, Oct. 24, 2001.
127. Greg Schneider & Robert O'Harrow Jr., "Pentagon Makes Rush Order For Anti-Terror Technology." *Wash. Post*, Oct. 26, 2001.
128. Michael Schrage, "Don't Go There." *Fortune*, Oct. 29, 2001.
129. John Simons, "Greed Meets Terror." *Fortune*, Oct. 29, 2001.
130. Elliot Spagat, "Delays at the Baggage Scanner." *Wall St. J.*, Oct. 29, 2001.
131. Anne Marie Squeo, "Air Force Purchases Solipsys Software To Help In Detection of Wayward Planes." *Wall St. J.*, Oct. 1, 2001.
132. Anne Marie Squeo, "Northrop Offer for Newport Wins Support of Pentagon Over General Dynamics Bid." *Wall St. J.*, Oct. 24, 2001.
133. Anne Marie Squeo, "Stock Prices Gyrate on Defense Firms' Good, Bad News." *Wall St. J.*, Oct. 18, 2001.

134. Anne Marie Squeo & J. Lynn Lunsford, "Arsenal for a New Kind of War." *Wall St. J.*, Oct. 5, 2001.

135. Valerie Strauss, "New Weapon Wielded In Cleanup of Anthrax." *Wash. Post*, Oct. 29, 2001.

136. "SureBeam Selected To Provide Electron Mail Beta Systems For Eliminating Anthrax Threat in U.S. Mail." Press Release, *SureBeam Corp.*, Oct. 29, 2001.

137. Eve Tahminciouglu, "Tense Employers Step Up Background Checks." *NY Times*, Oct. 3, 2001.

138. "The Silicon Brigade Signs Up." *Bus. Wk.*, Oct. 8, 2001.

139. Robert Tomsho, "BioPort Altered Vaccine Filters." *Wall St. J.*, Oct. 25, 2001.

140. "Translating Genomics and Proteomics into Drugs and Diagnostics." www.igen.com/mainframe.htm

141. Shankar Vedantam, "HHS's Varying Costs for Cipro Criticized." *Wash. Post*, Oct. 26, 2001.

142. Shankar Vedantam & Terrence Chea, "Drug Firm Plays Defense in Anthrax Scare." *Wash. Post*, Oct. 20, 2001.

143. Matthew L. Wald & Matt Richtel, "Passenger-Screening Companies Lobby for Expanded Role." *Wash. Post*, Oct. 11, 2001.

144. Edward Walsh & Ellen Nakashima, "USPS Can't Vouch For Safety of Mail." *Wash. Post*, Oct. 25, 2001.

145. Thomas E. Weber, "Anthrax-Laced Letters Boost E-Mail's Allure, But Paper Isn't Dead." *Wall. St. J.*, Oct. 29, 2001.

146. Arlene Weintraub & Alex Salkever, "Killer Tests For Deadly Germs." *Bus. Wk.*, Nov. 5, 2001.

147. Mimi Whitefield & Beatrice Garcia, "High Security: Globalization and Technology Have Opened Up New Possibilities For Business—and Their Enemies." *Miami Herald*, Sept. 17, 2001.

148. Lorraine Woellert, "National IDs Won't Work." *Bus. Wk.*, Nov. 5, 2001.

149. Scott Woolley, "Spotting Evil." *Forbes*, Oct. 15, 2001.

150. Rachel Zimmerman & Ron Winslow, "Emergency Rooms Watch for Symptoms of Biological Attacks." *Wall St. J.*, Oct. 10, 2001.

151. www.acambis.com

152. www.activcard.com

153. www.alerttech.com

154. www.amtrak.com

155. www.apotex.com

156. www.as-e.com

157. www.asinc.com

158. www.avantimmune.com/main.htm

159. www.barringer.com
160. www.bidjetcharter.com
161. www.biodefense.net
162. www.bioreliance.com
163. www.boeing.com
164. www.ca.com
165. www.checkpoint.com
166. www.cigitallabs.com
167. www.clearcross.com
168. www.creative.com
169. www.cubic.com
170. www.cyberguardcorp.com
171. www.cyterracorp.com
172. www.dallasnews.com/attack_on_america
173. www.defenselink.mil/pubs/almanac/almanac/forces
174. www.dynport.com/dynport/
175. www.earthcam.com
176. www.echomail.com
177. www.eds.com
178. www.emc.com
179. www.essentech.com
180. www.evive.com
181. www.flexjet.com
182. www.generaldynamics.com
183. www.genesoft.com
184. www.geomet.com
185. www.globeaviation.com
186. www.greyhound.com
187. www.guardsmark.com
188. www.hadron.com
189. www.handspring.com
190. www.ibm.com
191. www.identix.com
192. www.infosat.com
193. www.infragard.net
194. www.iridiantech.com
195. www.iristech.com
196. www.iss.net
197. www.itsw.com
198. www.johnsonandjohnson.com
199. www.l-3com.com

200. www.litton.com
201. www.meridianmeds.com
202. www.micronel.com
203. www.netjets.com
204. www.newworldaviation.com
205. www.nai.com
206. www.northgrum.com
207. www.nwijet.com
208. www.oracle.com
209. www.palm.com
210. www.pitt.edu/HOME/GHNet.html
211. www.pyramidvision.com
212. www.qualcomm.com
213. www.raytheon.com
214. www.rsasecurity.com
215. www.saic.com
216. www.solipsys.com
217. www.specialtybags.com
218. www.symantec.com
219. www.symbol.com
220. www.taser.com
221. www.teradata.com
222. www.tetracore.com
223. www.trw.com
224. www.tulsagunshow.com
225. www.utc.com
226. www.veritas.com
227. www.viisage.com
228. www.visionics.com
229. www.wackenhut.com

Chapter 5 – Terrorism and the Impact on U. S. Labor

1. "Airline Pilot Association, Pilots Reaching Out." Press Release, *AIPA*, Sept. 27, 2001. www.alpa.org/Pilots_Reaching_Out.htm.
2. *AFL-CIO web site*, http://aflcio.org/sept-11/news.htm.
3. "AFT Members Among Victims of Terrorist Attacks." *American Federation of Teachers*, Oct. 3, 2001, www.aft.org/news/aft_victims.html.
4. *Amalgamated Transit Union web site*, http://www.atu.org.
5. Riva Atlas & Geraldine Fabrikant, "After Havoc, Reviving a Legacy." *NY Times*, Sept. 29, 2001.

6. Julie Appleby, "Bioterrorism Changes How Health Care Works." *USA Today*, Oct. 31, 2001.
7. Peter Behr, "Bond Firm To Aid Kin Of Terror Victims." *Wash. Post*, Oct. 11, 2001.
8. Justin Blum, "Irradiated Mail's Delivery Delayed." *Wash. Post*, Nov. 17, 2001.
9. Justin Blum & Manny Fernandez, "Area Postal Workers Undergo Anthrax Screenings." *Wash. Post*, Oct. 22, 2001.
10. Sandra G. Boodman, "EMDR, In the Eye of the Storm." *Wash. Post*, Oct. 30, 2001.
11. Rick Brooks, "U.S. Postal Service To Test Facilities, Give Workers Gloves." *Wall St. J.*, Oct. 26, 2001.
12. Lynnley Browning, "Do You Speak Uzbek? Translators Are in Demand." *NY Times*, Oct. 21, 2001.
13. John Byrne, "How Much Loss Can a Firm Take?" *Bus. Wk.*, Oct. 8, 2001.
14. "Call to Active Duty Can Bring Financial Challenges." *Wash. Post*, Oct 11, 2001.
15. Anne Marie Chaker & David Bank, "For Regular Charities, There's Little Relief After Terror Attacks." *Wall St. J.*, Oct. 8, 2001.
16. Michelle Colin et al., "When The Office Is The War Zone." *Bus. Wk.*, Nov. 19, 2001.
17. "CWA Mourns Members Lost in Terrorist Attacks." *Communications Workers of America*, www.cwa-union.org/about/9-11-01_story.asp
18. Karen Dee Davis, "U.S. Arsenal: Levels of Mobilization." *dallasnews.com*, Oct. 23, 2001.
19. Abby Ellin, "Traumatized Workers Look for Healing On the Job." *NY Times*, Sept. 30, 2001.
20. Juliet Eilperin, "Debating the Limites of Liability." *Wash. Post*, Nov. 17, 2001.
21. Gary Fields et al., "Ashcroft Warns of New Attacks After Threat." *Wall St. J.*, Oct. 30, 2001.
22. "Flight Attendants Testify Before Congress on Aircraft Security Issue." *Association of Flight Attendants*, Sept. 25, 2001. ww.alpa.org/Pilots_Reaching_Out.htm.
23. "Flight Attendants Calls for Strong New Airline Safety & Security Reforms." *Association of Flight Attendants*, Sept 18, 2001. www.afanet.org/pr092501congress.htm.
24. Jonathan Glater, "Defiantly, The Street Retakes The Street." *NY Times*, Sept. 23, 2001.
25. Michael Greenspon & Neil Irwin, "Anthrax Attacks, Who's Liable?" *Wash. Post*, Nov. 14, 2001.

26. Kirstin Downey Grimsley, "Increasingly Unsafe and Sorry." *Wash. Post*, Nov. 1, 2001.
27. Constance L. Hays, "A Company Faces a Calamity's Personal Side." *NY Times*, Sept. 30, 2001.
28. Constance Hays, "Trying to Reweave Threads of Tattered Offices." *NY Times*, Sept. 29, 2001.
29. "Hiring Prospects Are Flat, Survey Shows." *Wash. Post*, Nov. 19, 2001.
30. Jim Hopkins, "Executives at Small Firm Don Another Hat: Therapist to Workers." *USA Today*, Oct. 31, 2001.
31. "News and Information." *Hotel Employees and Restaurant Employees International Union*, www.hereunion.org/newsinfo.
32. Anne Hull, "New York's Firefighters Grieve for Lost Brothers." *Wash. Post*, Sept. 14, 2001.
33. Lawrence Ingrassia, "The Human Toll." *Wall St. J.*, Oct. 11, 2001.
34. Carol Hymowitz, "Firms That Get Stingy With Layoff Packages May Pay a High Price." *Wall St. J.*, Oct. 30, 2001.
35. Neil Irwin & Amy Joyce, "In Pursuit of Idealism." *Wash. Post*, Oct. 22, 2001.
36. Carrie Johnson, "Flight Attendants Increasingly Demanding Greater Safeguards." *Wash. Post*, Oct. 5, 2001.
37. Carrie Johnson, "The Firms They Left Behind." *Wash. Post*, Sept. 19, 2001.
38. Maggie Jackson, "Contingency Plans to Fill Reservists' Shoes." *NY Times*, Oct. 10, 2001.
39. Carrie Johnson, "Requests for Skilled-Worker Visas Fell Short of Limit." *Wash. Post*, Nov. 6, 2001.
40. Steve Jones et al, "America the Beautiful, In Three-Part Harmony." *USA Today*, Oct. 22, 2001.
41. Ralph King, "If Looks Could Kill." *Bus. 2.0*, Dec. 2001.
42. Barbara Kantrowitz and Keith Naughton, "Generation 9-11." *Newswk.*, Nov. 12, 2001.
43. Tom Lauricella, "Struggling for a Normal Day at the Office." *Wall St. J.*, Oct. 17, 2001.
44. Shirley Leung & Patricia Callahan, "Security Executives Have Been Tough To Recruit Lately." *Wall St. J.*, Oct. 26, 2001.
45. David Maraniss, "Sept. 11, 2001." *Wash. Post*, Sept. 16, 2001.
46. Barbara Martinez, "Anthrax Victim's Son Sues Kaiser Facility His Father Consulted." *Wall. St. J.*, Nov. 14, 2001.
47. Carol Morello & Justin Blum, "Spores Shut 2 More Area Post Offices." *Wash. Post*, Oct. 31, 2001.
48. Ellen Nakashima, "Potter Defends USPS Response to Anthrax Fears." *Wash. Post*, Oct. 31, 2001.

49. Ellen Nakashima & Sylvia Moreno, "Latest Mailroom Finds Fuel Workers' Worries." Wash. Post, Oct. 30, 2001.
50. "Organizations Seeking Donations to Help Victims." *Wash. Post*, Sept. 26, 2001.
51. "Paying Reservists." *Bus. Wk.*, Nov. 26, 2001.
52. Michael Powell & Ceci Connolly, "Experts Warn Bioterrorism Could Expand." *Wash. Post*, Nov. 1, 2001.
53. Michael Powell and Ceci Connolly, "N.Y. Worker's Anthrax Deepens Mystery." *Wash. Post*, Oct. 31, 2001.
54. "International Association of Fire Fighters." *AFL-CIO*, www.iaff.org.
55. Maria Puente et al, "Stories and Faces Personalize Victims." *USA Today*, Sept. 13, 2001.
56. "Reserve, National Guard Units Called Up – Oct. 17." *Defense Link*, Oct. 17, 2001.
57. Dale Russakoff & Adriana Eunjung Cha, "Sketches of the Missing: Hard-Working, Early Risers." *Wash. Post*, Sept. 14, 2001.
58. Jacqueline L. Salmon, "Aid Groups Face Unusual Quandries." *Wash. Post*, Sept. 30, 2001.
59. Jacqueline L. Salmon, "Red Cross Distributing $100 Million." *Wash. Post*, Sept. 26, 2001.
60. Jacqueline L. Salmon & Ann O'Hanlon, "For Pentagon Families, Grief and Paperwork." *Wash. Post*, Nov. 18, 2001.
61. Susan Schmidt & Rick Weiss, "Hill Mail Still Untested 2 Weeks After Daschle Letter." *Wash. Post*, Oct. 31, 2001.
62. Sue Shellenbarger, "Readers Face Dilemma Over How Far to Alter Post-Attack Workplace." *Wall St. J.*, Oct. 31, 2001.
63. Michelle Singletary, "Call to Active Duty Can Bring Financial Challenges." *Wash. Post*, Oct. 11, 2001.
64. Sana Siwolop, "A Legal Tightrope for Employers After Attacks." *NY Times*, Oct. 24, 2001.
65. Leef Smith & Avram Goldstein, "Jittery Patients Pack Hospitals." *Wash. Post*, Oct. 26, 2001.
66. "Teamsters Condemn Terrorist Attack, Call on Members to Donate Blood, Resources." *Teamsters*, Sept. 13, 2001, www.teamster.org/disaster/sept11.htm.
67. "The Victims." *Wash. Post*, Sept. 14, 2001.
68. "The Victims." *Wash. Post*, Sept. 27, 2001.
69. "This is Going to Leave a Huge Scar on All of Us." *Fortune*, Oct. 1, 2001.
70. "Too Big A Helping Hand?" *Bus. Wk.*, Oct. 29, 2001.
71. Abigail Trafford, "Terror Attacks the Mentally Ill." *Wash. Post*, Oct. 23, 2001.

72. Shawn Tully, "Rebuilding Wall Street." *Fortune*, Oct. 1, 2001.
73. Steve Twomey & Avram Goldstein, "2 Others at Sorting Facility Hospitalized With Disease." *Wash. Post*, Oct. 23, 2001.
74. "U.S. Office of Personnel Management: Post-Disaster Guidance and Other Information." *OPM*, www.opm.gov/guidance/index.htm.
75. "UAW Contributes $250,000 to Relief Efforts, Urges Additional Fundraising by UAW 63." Press Release, *UAW*, Sept. 18, 2001.
76. Lawrence Van Gelder, "Regrouping, or Not, at the Office." *NY Times* , Oct. 28, 2001.
77. Nicole C. Wong, "Wanted: Temps to Push the Envelopes." *Wash. Post*, Nov. 17, 2001.
78. Anna Wilde Mathews, "Black Spots Got a 'No', But Who Can Object To Red, White and Blue?" *Wall St. J.*, Oct. 25, 2001.
79. www.americanexpress.com
80. www.aon.com
81. www.bah.com
82. www.cantor.com
83. www.carr.com
84. www.dowjones.com
85. www.fiduciary-trust.com
86. www.fredalger.com
87. www.garban-intercapital.com
88. www.genzyme.com
89. www.kbw.com
90. www.lehman.com
91. www.metrocall.com
92. www.morganstanley.com
93. www.sidley.com
94. www.sun.com
95. www.tjmaxx.com

Chapter 6 - Terrorism and U.S. Government Responses

1. Chris Adams, "INS Is Retooling To Cast Agency As Two Bureaus." *Wall St. J.*, Nov. 15, 2001.
2. "America's Fund for Afghan Children." *Office of the Press Secretary, White House*, undated, www.whitehouse.gov/afac
3. "Amtrak Safety Drives $1.8 Billion Package." *AP*, Oct. 18, 2001.
4. "APEC Leaders Statement on Counter-Terrorism." *Office of the Press Secretary, White House*, Oct. 21, 2001.

5. "At O'Hare, President Says 'Get On Board." *Office of the Press Secretary, White House*, Sept. 27, 2001, www.whitehouse.gov/news/releases/2001/09/print/20010927.
6. "Battered But Unbroken." *Fortune*, Oct. 1, 2001.
7. Paul Beckett, "U.S. Customs Takes Major Role in Efforts To Sever Terrorists From Their Funding." *Wall St. J.*, Oct. 26, 2001.
8. Paul Blustein, "Aid to Turkey Raising Issue of Motive." *Wash. Post*, Nov. 23, 2001.
9. Richard Boucher, "Designation of 22 Foreign Terrorist Organizations Under Executive Order 13224." *Office of the Spokesman, U.S. Dept. of State*, Nov. 2, 2001.
10. Amy Borrus, "Keep America's Gates Open. Just Watch Them Better." *Bus. Wk.*, Nov. 12, 2001.
11. David Boyer, "Bush Lobbies To Limit Emergency Spending." *Wash. Times*, Nov. 9, 2001.
12. David Boyer, "O'Neill Sees Backing From GOP, Democrats." *Wash. Times*, Nov. 21, 2001.
13. David Boyer, "Senate Deadlocks On Stimulus Bill." *Wash. Times*, Nov. 14, 2001.
14. David Broder, "Governors Appeal For Emergency Assistance." *Wash. Post*, Oct. 5, 2001.
15. "Businesses Scramble to Push for Tax Breaks." *Wall St. J.*, Oct. 10, 2001.
16. Susan Carey, "Airlines Install Reinforcing Bars To Secure Cockpits." *Wall St. J.*, Oct. 3, 2001.
17. Ira Carnahan, "Who Gets The $20 Billion." *Forbes*, Oct. 15, 2001.
18. "Citizen Preparedness in War on Terrorism Executive Order." *Office of the Press Secretary, White House*, Nov. 9, 2001.
19. Ceci Connolly, "U.S. Officials Reorganize Strategy on Bioterrorism." *Wash. Post*, Nov. 8, 2001.
20. Ceci Connolly & Steven Gray, "Thompson Seeks $1.2 Billion To Expand Stockpile of Drugs." *Wash. Post*, Oct. 18, 2001.
21. Joseph Curl, "President Approves Trials By Military." *Wash. Times*, Nov. 14, 2001.
22. Kathleen Day, "Money-Laundering Bill Passes." *Wash. Post*, Oct. 8, 2001.
23. Kathleen Day, "O'Neill Seeks Freedom to Trace Money to Sources." *Wash. Post*, Oct. 4, 2001.
24. Thomas Edsall & Juliet Eilperin, "Bush Pursues Two Tracks on Stimulus Bill." *Wash. Post*, Oct. 17, 2001.
25. Juliet Eilperin, "House Approves Economic Stimulus Package." *Wash. Post*, Oct. 25, 2001.

26. Juliet Eilperin & Caroline Mayer, "Federal Air-Security Bill Clears Congress." *Wash. Post*, Nov. 17, 2001.

27. "Enhancing Aviation Safety & Security." *Office of the Press Secretary*, *White House*, Sept. 27, 2001.

28. "Executive Order on Terrorist Financing." *Office of the Press Secretary*, *White House*, Sept. 24, 2001, www.whitehouse.gov/news/releases/2001/09/2010924-1.html.

29. "Fact Sheet on Increasing Immigration Safeguards and Improving Vital Information Sharing." *Office of the Press Secretary*, *White House*, Oct. 29, 2001.

30. "Fact Sheet: Organization and Operation of the Homeland Security Council." *Office of the Press Secretary*, *White House*, Oct. 29, 2001.

31. "Fact Sheet: Secretary of State Designates Foreign Terrorist Organizations." *Office of the Spokesman*, U.S. Dept. of State, Oct. 5, 2001.

32. "Fact Sheet, The List of Most Wanted Terrorists." *Office of the Press Secretary*, *The White House*, Oct. 10, 2001.

33. "FBI Director Robert S. Mueller, III, Press Conference." *FBI National Press Office*, Oct. 16, 2001.

34. "Federal Recovery Actions." *Office of the Press Secretary*, *White House*, undated.

35. Bruce Fein and Yonah Alexander, "Wars Not Won By Queensberry Rules." *Wash. Times*, Nov. 20, 2001.

36. "Financial Actions." *Office of the Press Secretary*, *White House*, undated.

37. Pamela Ferdinand, "Mayors in Bind of Rising Costs Of Security, Declining Revenue." *Wash. Post*, Nov. 23, 2001.

38. William Glaberson, "Claims to Federal Fund For Victims Trickle In." *NY Times*, Oct. 23, 2001.

39. Bradley Graham, "Military Favors a Homeland Command." *Wash. Post*, Nov. 12, 2001.

40. Kirstin Downey Grimsley, "State Funds For Jobless Run Low in Slowdown." *Wash. Post*, Nov. 16, 2001.

41. Ralph Hallow, "States Tremble From Terror Spending." *Wash. Times*, Nov. 12, 2001.

42. Thomas Hargrove, "Children's Fund Nets $1 Million." *Wash. Times*, Nov. 1, 2001.

43. Greg Hitt & Martha Brannigan, "Air-Security Bill Poses Tough Challenges." *Wall St. J.*, Nov. 19, 2001.

44. Greg Hitt & Martha Brannigan, "Bush Backs Pact to Federalize Air Security." *Wall St. J.*, Nov. 16, 2001.

45. Greg Hitt & Jim Vandehei, "New York Starts to Meet Resistance on Requests For Assistance Money from White House, Congress." *Wall St. J.*, Oct. 12, 2001.

46. Greg Hitt, "Senate Unanimously Approves Airport, Airline Security Measure." *Wall St. J.*, Oct. 12, 2001.
47. James Hookway, "Philippine Leader To Request Increase In U.S. Military Aid." *Wall St. J.*, Nov. 14, 2001.
48. Spencer Hsu, "D.C. Ill-Prepared For Terrorism, Lawmaker Says." *Wash. Post*, Nov. 15, 2001.
49. "Humanitarian Actions." *White House*, undated.
50. Al Hunt, "Anti-Terrorism Spending Trumps Tax Cuts." *Wall St. J.*, Nov. 15, 2001.
51. "If You Receive a Suspicious Letter or Package What Should You Do?" Bomb Data Center, Weapons of Mass Destruction Operations Unit, *FBI General Information Bulletin 2000-3*.
52. "Investigation Actions." *White House*, undated.
53. Kevin Johnson, "Justice Seeks To Question 5,000 Possible Witnesses." *USA Today*, Nov. 14, 2001.
54. Leslie Kaufman, "Pakistanis Urge U.S. to Suspend Textile Tariffs." *NY Times*, Nov. 8, 2001.
55. Kathy Kiely, "Negotiators Feel Pressure to Resolve Bill Dispute." *USA Today*, Nov. 13, 2001.
56. Glenn Kessler, "Bush Tax Plan Could Cost $120 Billion '02." *Wash. Post*, Oct. 11, 2001.
57. Glenn Kessler, "OMB Chief Signals New Spending Goals." *Wash. Post*, Oct. 17, 2001.
58. Glenn Kessler, "Quick Action Urged on Economic Stimulus." *Wash. Post*, Oct. 31, 2001.
59. Glenn Kessler, "Riding to the Economy's Rescue." *Wash. Post*, Sept. 25, 2001.
60. Glenn Kessler, "Senators Begin Debating Democratic Stimulus Plan." *Wash. Post*, Nov. 14, 2001.
61. Glenn Kessler, "Senate GOP Blocks Democrats' Version of Stimulus Plan." *Wash. Post*, Nov. 15, 2001.
62. Donald Lambro, "GOP Willing To Meet On Bill." *Wash. Times*, Nov. 16, 2001.
63. Scott McCartney & John McKinnon, "U.S. Loan Package Doesn't Shut Out Weak Airlines." *Wall St. J.*, Oct. 4, 2001.
64. Daniel LeDuc, "Md. to Seek $250 Million In Anti-Terrorism Funds." *Wash. Post*, Nov. 2, 2001.
65. Tim Lemke, "U.S. To Grant Virginia $10 Million Stimulus." *Wash. Times*, Nov. 2, 2001.
66. Laurie McGinley, "Bush Seeks More Funds to Boost Stockpiles of Anthrax Antibiotics." *Wall St. J.*, Oct. 15, 2001.

67. John McKinnon & Shailagh Murray, "White House Pressures Congress on Budget." *Wall St. J.*, Oct. 17, 2001.

68. John McKinnon & Shailagh Murray, "Bush Calls for $75 Billion Economic Boost." Wall St. J., Oct. 4, 2001.

69. John McKinnon & Damian Milverton, "White House Signals It Intends to Block Huge Tax-Cut Bill Voted by House Panel." *Wall St. J.*, Oct. 16, 2001.

70. Daniel Machalaba, "Amtrak Asks U.S. For $15 Million To Improve Security." *Wall St. J.*, Oct. 3, 2001.

71. Brooke Masters, "Any Terror Trials May Be in Va." *Wash. Post*, Nov. 21, 2001.

72. Tony Mauro, "Historic High Court Ruling Is Troublesome Model for Modern Terror Trials." *Am. Lawyer Media* , Nov. 19, 2001.

73. Jim McGee, "An Intelligence Giant in the Making." *Wash. Post*, Nov. 4, 2001.

74. James Michaels, "Liquidity – With Strings." *Forbes*, Oct. 15, 2001.

75. "Military Actions." *White House*, undated.

76. Dana Milbank, "In War, It's Power to the President." *Wash. Post*, Nov. 20, 2001.

77. "Most Wanted Terrorists." *FBI.* www.fbi.gov/mostwant/terrorists/fugitives.htm.

78. Dan Morgan, "Expenses Covered by Emergency Fund Rising Rapidly." *Wash. Post*, Oct. 2, 2001.

79. Dan Morgan, "$40 Billion 'Ample' For Months." *Wash. Post*, Oct. 18, 2001.

80. Dan Morgan, "House Committee Rejects Increase in Emergency Funding." *Wash. Post*, Nov. 15, 2001.

81. Dan Morgan, "House Panel Allocates $1.67 Billion For Pentagon Counterterrorism Bid." *Wash. Post*, Nov. 9, 2001.

82. Steve Mufson, "U.S. to Aid Philippines' Terrorism War." *Wash. Post*, Nov. 21, 2001.

83. Shailagh Murray, "Stimulus Package Produces Friction In House, Senate." *Wall St. J.*, Oct. 15, 2001.

84. "NAM Endorses President Bush's Economic Stimulus Plan." *National Association of Manufacturers*, Oct. 5, 2001.

85. John McKinnon, "Most of Emergency $40 Billion Aid Remains Unspent." *Wall St. J.*, Nov. 16, 2001.

86. Dana Milbank, "Congress Balks at Giving President Emergency Powers." *Wash. Post*, Oct. 23, 2001.

87. "National Security; Prevention of Acts of Violence and Terrorism." Bureau of Prisons, Department of Justice, *Fed. Reg.*, Vol, 66, No. 211, Oct. 31, 2001.

88. "New Counter-Terrorism and CyberSpace Security Positions Announced." *Office of the Press Secretary, White House*, Oct. 9, 2001.
89. "Office of Homeland Security." *White House*, undated.
90. "Operation Enduring Freedom Overview." *Office of the Press Secretary, White House*, Oct. 1, 2001.
91. Christopher Oster & Michael Schroeder, "Carriers Plan Lower-Cost Terror-Insurance Pool." *Wall St.*, Nov. 8, 2001.
92. "Patterns of Global Terrorism – 2000." *Office of the Coordinator for Counterterrorism, U.S. Dept. of State*, Apr. 2001.
93. Ben Pershing, "Final Approps Markup in Danger." *Roll Call*, Nov. 12, 2001.
94. Don Phillips & Ellen Nakashima, "FBI to Check More Airport Workers." *Wash. Post*, Oct. 18, 2001.
95. Michael Phillips, "Critics Frantically Try To Weaken Bills Aimed at Money Laundering." *Wall St. J.*, Oct. 17, 2001.
96. Michael Phillips & Jess Bravin, "Terrorism and Money-Laundering Bills Make Business Lobbyists Walk Fine Line." *Wall St. J.*, Oct. 16, 2001.
97. Michael Phillips, "White House Seeks Powers to Prevent Money Laundering." *Wall St. J.*, Oct. 4, 2001.
98. Eric Pianin, "Homeland Security Team's Key Members Announced." Wash. Post, Nov. 21, 2001.
99. Eric Pianin & Ellen Nakashima, "U.S. Seeks to Boost Security, Soothe Public." *Wash. Post*, Oct. 18, 2001.
100. Walter Pincus, "Senate Clears Bill Raising Intelligence Spending 7 Pct." *Wash. Post*, Nov. 9, 2001.
101. Will Pinkston, "States Convene Special Session." *Wall St. J.*, Oct. 24, 2001.
102. "Poverty and Terror." *Wash. Post*, Oct. 5, 2001.
103. Colin L. Powell, "Campaign Against Terrorism." Statement before House International Relations Committee, *U.S. Dept. of State*, Oct. 24, 2001.
104. Colin L. Powell, "Redesignation of Foreign Terrorist Organizations." *U.S. Dept. of State*, Oct. 5, 2001.
105. Stephen Power, "Airport-Security Oversight Agency Faces Tough Deadline on Luggage." *Wall St. J.*, Nov. 20, 2001.
106. "President Announces Crackdown on Terrorist Financial Network." *Office of the Press Secretary, White House*, Nov. 7, 2001.
107. "President Authorizes Emergency Response Fund Transfer." *Office of the Press Secretary, White House*, Oct. 22, 2001.
108. "President Authorizes Transfers from Emergency Response Fund." *Office of the Press Secretary, White House*, Nov. 5, 2001.

109. "President Issues Military Order." *Office of the Press Secretary, White House,* Nov. 13, 2001.

110. "President Bush Releases $5.1 Billion in Emergency Funds." *Office of Management and Budget, White House,* Sept. 21. 2001.

111. "President Commands House for Passing Airline Security Bill." *Office of the Press Secretary, White House,* Nov. 1, 2001.

112. "President Commends House for Passing Anti-Terrorism Bill." *Office of the Press Secretary, White House,* Oct. 12, 2001.

113. "President Directs Humanitarian Aid to Afghanistan." *Office of the Press Secretary, White House,* Oct. 4, 2001.

114. "President Establishes "America's Fund for Afghan Children." *Office of the Press Secretary,* White House, Undated.

115. "President Establishes Office of Homeland Security." *Office of the Press Secretary, White House,* Oct. 8, 2001.

116. "President Freezes Terrorists' Assets." *Office of the Press Secretary, White House,* Sept. 24, 2001.

117. "President's Letter to the Speaker on Airline Stabilization Funds." *Office of the Press Secretary, White House,* Sept. 25, 2001.

118. "President Orders Federal Aid for Virginia." *Office of the Press Secretary, White House,* Sept. 13, 2001.

119. "President Signs Anti-Terrorism Bill." *Office of the Press Secretary, White House,* Oct. 26, 2001.

120. "President Signs Aviation Security Legislation." *Office of the Press Secretary, White House,* Nov. 19, 2001.

121. "President Unveils 'Most Wanted' Terrorists." *Office of the Press Secretary, White House,* Oct. 10, 2001.

122. "President Works on Economic Recovery During NY Trip." *Office of the Press Secretary, White House,* Oct. 3, 2001.

123. "Press Release." *FBI National Press Office,* Oct. 11, 2001.

124. "Press Release." *FBI National Press Office,* Sept. 11, 2001.

125. "Press Release." *FBI National Press Office,* Sept. 14, 2001.

126. "Press Release." *FBI National Press Office,* Sept. 27, 2001.

127. "Procedures for Compensation of Air Carriers." *Office of the Secretary, Dept. of Treasury.*

128. Anita Raghavan et al, "Banks and Regulators Drew Together to Calm Markets After Attack." *Wall St. J.,* Oct. 18, 2001.

129. Robert Reich, "Subsidies Aren't a Wartime Necessity." *Wall St. J.,* Oct. 16, 2001.

130. "Remarks by the President at Photo Opportunity with House and Senate Leadership." *Office of the Press Secretary, The White House,* Sept. 19, 2001.

131. David Rogers, "Pentagon Is Set to Get Half of Aid Package." *Wall St. J.,* Oct. 11, 2001.

132. "Roll Call for GOP-Backed Aviation Security Bill." *usatoday.com*, Nov. 2, 2001.

133. "Roll Call on Senate-Passed Bill Air Security Bill." *usatoday.com*, Nov. 2, 2001.

134. Bill Sammon, "Bush Federalizes Force At Airports Nationwide." *Wash. Times*, Nov. 20, 2001.

135. Susan Schmidt, "Only One Barrel of Congress Mail Tainted." *Wash. Post*, Nov. 18, 2001.

136. "SEC Request Relating to Information Pertaining to the Terrorist Attacks." *Securities and Exchange Commission*, Oct. 18, 2001.

137. Howard Schneider, "Saudis See Obstacles in Freezing Accounts." Wash. Post, Oct. 25, 2001.

138. Michael Schroeder, "Delay of Terrorism-Insurance Bill Causes Concern." *Wall St. J.*, Nov. 19, 2001.

139. Jerry Seper, "FBI Issues Warning of Threat to Coastal Bridges." *Wash. Times*, Nov. 2, 2001.

140. "September 11: Here Come The Trial Lawyers." *Bus. Wk.*, Nov. 12, 2001.

141. Mary Beth Sheridan, "15 Hijackers Obtained Visas in Saudi Arabia." *Wash. Post*, Oct. 31, 2001.

142. Jackie Spinner, "Insurance Aid Plan Takes Shape." *Wash. Post*, Nov. 8, 2001.

143. Jackie Spinner, "Terror-Insurance Market in Limbo." *Wash. Post*, Nov. 21, 2001.

144. Richard Stevenson, "White House Balks At Further Bailouts." *NY Times*, Oct. 17, 2001.

145. "Stimulate The Economy, Sure. The Question Is How." *Bus. Wk.*, Oct. 15, 2001.

146. Frank Swoboda & Martha McNeil Hamilton, "For Strong Airlines, an Edge on Aid." *Wash. Post*, Oct. 6, 2001.

147. Chad Terhune et al., "CDC Is Stretched Thin as It Takes a Lead Role Fighting Bioterrorism." *Wall St.*, Nov. 14, 2001.

148. "The Back to Work Relief Package." *Office of the Press Secretary, White House*, Oct. 4, 2001.

149. Cheryl Thompson. "Audit Finds INS Mismanaged $31 Million Automation Project." *Wash. Post*, Nov. 12, 2001.

150. "Transportation Secretary Mineta Proposes Stronger Hazardous Materials Legislation To Improve Security and Safety." *Dept. of Transportation*, Oct. 10, 2001.

151. "Treasury Establishes Financial Institutions Hotline Relating to Terrorist Activity." *Department of Treasury*, Oct. 11, 2001.

152. "Untitled." *Office of the Press Secretary, White House*, undated.

153. "U.S., Africa Strengthen Counter-Terrorism and Economic Ties." *Office of the Press Secretary, White House*, Oct. 29, 2001.

154. "U.S. Draws Up List of Over 5,000 Men It Wants Interviewed in Terrorism Probe." *Wall St. J.*, Nov. 14, 2001.

155. "U.S. Ponders Aid Package For Uzbekistan." *AP*, Nov. 17, 2001.

156. Jim VandeHei & Milo Geyelin, "Bush Seeks to Limit Liability of Companies Sued as Result of Attacks." *Wall St. J.*, Oct. 25, 2001.

157. Joby Warrick & Steve Fainabu, "Bioterrorism Preparations Lacking at Lowest Levels." *Wash. Post*, Oct. 22, 2001.

158. "Washington Tries To Spell Relief." *Bus. Wk.*, Oct. 8, 2001.

159. William Welch, "Stimulus Package Stalled Over Tax Breaks, Spending." *USA Today*, Nov. 13, 2001.

160. Bob Woodward, "Secret CIA Units Playing A Central Combat Role." *Wash. Post*, Nov. 18, 2001.

161. www.whitehouse.gov/afac

162. www.whitehouse.gov/response/financialresponse.html.

163. www.whitehouse.gov/response/investigativeresponse.html.

Index

Abbott Laboratories, 32
ABC, 79, 129
Abercrombie & Fitch, 82
ABN Amro, 41-42, 74
Abu Nidal Organization, 6, 175
Abu Sayyaf Group, 175
Acambis, 113
Achille Lauro, 142
Ackerman, Alan, 53
ActivCard, 99
ADT Security Services, 99
Advanced Biosystems, 114
Advanced Micro Devices, 22, 78
Aer Lingus, 61
Aeromexico, 60
Afghanistan, xiv-xvi, xix, 15, 17, 19, 24, 27, 32, 33, 77, 80, 92, 146-147, 153, 186-187, 194, 196
A.G. Edwards, 24
Agere Systems, 48
AIM Group, 98
Air and Space Museum, 66
Air Canada, 42, 60
Air Force, 59, 87, 90, 115, 143
Air France, 61
Air India, 9
Air Line Pilots Association, 125, 127
Airline Transportation and Systems Stabilization Act, xx, 153, 160, 168
Air National Guard, 59, 115
Air New Zealand, 61

Airport and Seaport Terrorism Prevention Act, 165
Airports Council International, 62
Air Transport Association, 167
Air Transportation Board, 160
Alabama, 22, 185
Aladdin Gaming, 58
Alaska Air, 58
Al Barakaat, 181
Alcatel, 41
Alert Technologies, 106
Algeria, 75
Alitalia, 61
Al-Jihad (Egyptian Islamic Jihad), 175
Allianz, 68
All Nippon Airways, 61
Al-Qaida, xii-xviii, 6, 14-15, 102, 145-146, 153, 175-176, 178, 180-181, 183-184, 191, 194, 196
Al Taqwa, 181
Al-Zawahiri, Ayman, xiv, xvi, 175, 179
Ambrose, Paul, 126
American Airlines, xi, 12, 22, 27, 30, 34, 48, 58, 60, 67-68, 125, 141, 161
American-Arab Anti-Discrimination Committee, 140
American Association of Airport Executives, 62
American Association of Port Authorities, 81

About the Authors

Dean C. Alexander is a lawyer and writer based in the Washington, D.C., area. He served in executive, legal, and business development roles with companies in the United States, United Kingdom, Israel, Mexico, and Chile. He taught international business law at several universities. He has published 6 books and numerous articles on international business, investment, law, and terrorism.

Professor Yonah Alexander is founder and Co-Director of the Inter-University Center for Legal Studies at the International Law Institute (Washington, D.C.). He has advised U.S. and international companies on corporate security, terrorism, and political risk issues. Dr. Alexander founded and edited *Terrorism: An International Journal* and *Political Communication and Persuasion: An International Journal*. He has published over 80 books on the subjects of terrorism, international affairs, and business. Dr. Alexander has appeared on television and has been interviewed on radio programs in over 40 countries.